D1553181

WITHDRAWN

Pathways to Success in School
Culturally Responsive Teaching
ಐ❀ಜಿ

Pathways to Success in School
Culturally Responsive Teaching
ಬಿ❀ಛ

Edited by

Etta R. Hollins
Wright State University, Dayton
Eileen I. Oliver
California State University, San Marcos

LEA LAWRENCE ERLBAUM ASSOCIATES, PUBLISHERS
1999 Mahwah, New Jersey   London

Copyright © 1999 by Etta R. Hollins and Eileen I. Oliver.
Published by Lawrence Erlbaum Associates,
Publishers. All rights reserved. No part of this book may
be reproduced in any form, by photostat, microfilm, re-
trieval system, or any other means, without prior written
permission of the publisher, Etta R. Hollins, and Eileen
I. Oliver.

Lawrence Erlbaum Associates, Inc., Publishers
10 Industrial Avenue
Mahwah, NJ 07430

Cover design by Kathryn Houghtaling Lacey

Library of Congress Cataloging-in-Publication Data

Pathways to success in school : culturally responsive
teaching / edited by Etta R. Hollins, Eileen I. Oliver.
    p. cm.
Includes bibliographical references and indexes.
ISBN 0-8058-2806-0 (pbk. : alk. paper).
    1. Multicultural education—United States.   2. Teach-
ing—United States.   3. Minorities—Education—United
States. I. Hollins, Etta R., 1942- . II. Oliver Eileen Iscoff.

LC1099.3.P488   1998
370.117'0973—dc21   98-34839
                                        CIP

Books published by Lawrence Erlbaum Associates are printed
on acid-free paper, and their bindings are chosen for strength
and durability.

Printed in the United States of America
10 9 8 7 6 5 4 3 2 1

LC
1099.3
P488
1999

*Dedicated to the collective efforts and energies of those who
deliberate, collaborate, and actively participate
in transforming school practices for a culturally
diverse society—and to all who benefit*

Contents

Preface

Finding James Baldwin and writing him down at an Episcopal church camp during the Watts riots in 1965 (I was fifteen) probably determined the direction of my intellectual life more than did any other single factor. I wrote and rewrote verbatim his elegantly framed paragraphs, full of sentences that were at once somehow Henry Jamesian and King Jamesian, yet clothed in the cadences and figures of the spirituals ...
— Henry Louis Gates, Jr. (1990, p. 58)

In *Culturally Responsive Teaching* (1991), Villegas explains the difference between mainstream children, for whom school is an extension of the home and community, and children from parallel cultures, whose classrooms often clash with their home environments. For these children there is "discontinuity" in language and in the application of prior knowledge and, therefore, they are denied equitable access to learning. This theory of *cultural mismatch* posits that academic achievement is affected by the relation between school practices and values and those found in students' home culture (Hollins, 1996).

The purpose of this book is to help preservice and inservice teachers think about human diversity in ways that facilitate planning and engaging in productive teaching and learning in classrooms. This includes developing a metacognitive perspective and participating in learning experiences that are likely to expand one's own understanding of difference and human diversity.

To better serve an increasingly diverse population, it is imperative that teachers improve their competence in selecting and developing culturally responsive curricula and instructional approaches that better facilitate learning for all students. Teachers must be able to strategically select or develop instructional approaches that build on their students' learning propensities, cognitive schemata, experiential backgrounds, and perceptions in order to provide equitable access to learning.

This text is designed to assist preservice and inservice teachers in identifying pathways to productive teaching and learning for students from culturally and experientially diverse backgrounds. Each teacher practices within a unique context; however, there are common aspects to most teaching experiences. The authors in this text address both common and unique aspects of particular contexts in terms of learning to identify important factors that lead to pathways of success for students from diverse backgrounds. The authors in *Pathways to Success in School* present ways of understanding one's own thinking (*metacognition*) and ways of thinking about teaching and learning situations and identifying productive strategies. Each teacher must learn about the context in which he or she will practice, understand key aspects of the students' cultural and experiential background and learning preferences, and explore ways to bring these factors together in framing and selecting meaningful curriculum content and learning experiences.

Teachers must attend to diversity within and across cultural groups. The classroom is a place for all students to learn about other cultural heritages and to share their cultural heritage with other students. Teachers should validate cultural knowledge acquired outside of the classroom rather than dismiss it as inconsistent with value perspectives of the predominant group. This book is intended to assist teachers in understanding their own thinking and in identifying ways to draw from their students' experiential backgrounds and learning propensities to develop meaningful classroom learning experiences.

HOW THIS BOOK IS ORGANIZED

This book is organized into three interrelated parts: Part I— Becoming an Expert Navigator, Part II—Using Culture as a Compass, and Part III—Drawing on the Landscape. In Part I, the authors describe two approaches to becoming a competent practitioner. The first is intuitive, based on an awareness of the culture shared by the teacher and his or her students and the ability of the teacher to draw from the culture to develop a comfortable and supportive learning context and meaningful curriculum content and pedagogy. The second approach to becoming a competent practitioner involves deliberate and systematic inquiry and reflection using specific tools to enhance professional growth.

In Part II, the authors present approaches to developing and using culturally responsive pedagogy. Perspectives presented include those of preservice teachers reflecting on their elementary and secondary experiences in learning mathematics compared to those at the college level and those of two inservice elementary teachers, one using a culturally based approach and the other using an experiential approach. Part II also presents research conducted by an ethnographer demonstrating how to identify ways to make linkages between school learning and the home culture, and principles for implementing culturally responsive pedagogy.

In Part III, the authors address curriculum content and design. The factors influencing curriculum content and design include teachers' biases, cultural perspectives, historical traditions, educational and social purposes, and the perceived structure of academic disciplines. The authors present ways to design curriculum that embrace multiculturalism and integrate curriculum content across disciplines. The final chapter in Part III presents an approach for helping teachers overcome their own biases and prejudices.

PEDAGOGICAL FEATURES

Specific features are included to facilitate use of this book as a textbook. The *overview* for each part provides a summary of the main issues addressed and the relationship among ideas presented by different authors. *Focus questions* at the beginning of each chapter assist the reader in identifying complex issues to be examined. The chapters in each part are intended to generate discussion, critical thinking, and further investigation, rather than final solutions to complex issues. The *suggested learning experiences* have been selected as examples of ways to expand the reader's understanding of specific issues, practices, and questions addressed in each part. The *references* included at the end of each chapter may also be used to expand the reader's knowledge in specific areas.

INTENDED USES OF THIS BOOK

This book is primarily designed for preservice and inservice teacher education. It may be used in courses focused on instructional methodology, multicultural education, and multicultural foundations of education. The authors address substantive and complex issues concerning school practices in a culturally diverse society and providing productive learning experiences for all children.

This book can be used by practitioners to facilitate collaboration, deliberation, and decision making for learners from diverse cultural and experiential backgrounds, and in culturally diverse classroom settings. This book provides insights into such complex issues as developing professional competence for teaching in a culturally diverse society, identifying strategies that generate positive learning outcomes for traditionally underserved populations, reframing the curriculum for a culturally diverse society, and learning to minimize the influence of personal biases and prejudices on teaching practices.

In summary, this book provides important insights into the need for transforming school practices for a culturally diverse society and enhances the reader's ability to identify meaningful approaches to professional development.

ACKNOWLEDGMENTS

This book is the outgrowth of the collaborative efforts of many people, especially the contributors and those they relied on as primary sources to inform their thinking.

We are grateful to the contributors for their insights, thoughtfulness, and the deliberateness with which they developed the ideas presented in each chapter. We also appreciated their patience during the many delays in getting this volume completed.

We are grateful to Naomi Silverman for her direction, guidance, and patience in the development of this volume.

We are particularly appreciative of our family members who showed interest, patience, and understanding during our work on this volume.

—Etta R. Hollins
—Eileen I. Oliver

REFERENCES

Gates, H. L., Jr. 1990. "The master's pieces: On canon formation and the Afro-American tradition. In C. Moran & E. F. Penfield (Eds.), *Conversations: Contemporary Critical Theory and the Teaching of Literature* (pp. 55–75). Urbana, IL: National Council of Teachers of English.

Hollins, E. R. (1996). *Culture in school learning.* Mahwah, NJ: Lawrence Erlbaum Associates.

Villegas, A. M. (1991). *Culturally responsive teaching.* Princeton, NJ: Educational Testing Service.

BECOMING AN EXPERT NAVIGATOR: DEVELOPING TEACHING COMPETENCE

OVERVIEW

The authors in Part I describe two approaches to developing professional competence for teaching in a culturally diverse society. In the first chapter, K. Hollins describes her intuitive approach to learning to teach children in an inner-city elementary school. She chronicles her experiences from her first day through the following few weeks, a period in which she attempted to plan and deliver instruction based on preservice teacher preparation that was inadequate for the particular context in which she found herself. She explains the loss of her self-confidence, the support she received from a university faculty member familiar with the context of inner-city schools, and how she got beyond the facade of belligerence displayed by the children to gain their cooperation and their families' support. The author used her knowledge of the children's cultural backgrounds to build a bond with them, to create a comfortable and supportive classroom context, and to develop meaningful curriculum content and learning experiences. This very powerful narrative provides unique insights into the complexity of inner-city teaching and a real-life example of learning how to provide meaningful and productive learning experiences for the children in these settings.

In chapter 2, E. Hollins describes a deliberate and systematic approach to developing competence for teaching in a culturally diverse society by employing inquiry and reflection. Inquiry and reflection involve observa-

1

tion, investigation, documentation, and study. This is a process of studying one's own practice and the practices of colleagues, and engaging in collaboration and deliberation with those colleagues. In this approach, E. Hollins discusses the components of reflective thought and behavior, collaborative approaches to reflective practice, and tools that can be used to facilitate reflective practice.

Chapter 1

Learning to Build Bridges Over Troubled Waters

Karla D. Hollins
California Public Schools

FOCUS QUESTIONS

1. In this chapter, the author describes a very stressful initial experience as a beginning teacher. What do you think caused her to persist when others were intimidated to the point of leaving in violation of their contracts?
2. What can you glean from this author's account of her first year in an inner-city school that might help you get off to a smooth beginning, establish positive relationships in the classroom, and design meaningful instruction for this population of children?
3. What are the relations among ethnic-cultural identity, classroom instruction, and academic success?
4. How does a teacher decide which aspects of a particular culture should be used to enhance classroom instruction for children from a specific cultural group?
5. This author describes how she transformed her classroom for African American children and the successes that resulted. How would a teacher accommodate the way African American children learn in a culturally diverse classroom?

INTRODUCTION

Editorial note: In this chapter the author describes her first year as a beginning teacher in an inner-city classroom. She describes the conditions she faced, some of what she felt at the time, and strategies she employed to transform the classroom for meaningful learning for African American children. The author concludes with some thoughts about the demands of the profession and what it takes to persist.

Felicia called me early one morning. She told me that she had a friend who needed advice about managing her fifth-grade class. Earlier that week another girlfriend called about the same thing. In fact I have spoken with numerous teachers with similar concerns—chaos in the classroom, children out of control, lessons that were planned according to university instruction that did not work for the children in their classes. What went wrong?

What do we all have in common? We are all young, African American, beginning teachers employed in the inner city, and the majority of the children in our classes are African American. All of us have been trained at a reputable university with a nationally accredited teacher preparation program, yet we have not been prepared for the realities of teaching in an inner-city school district. All of us are asking the same question: "How do we educate this population of children successfully?"

THE FIRST DAY

When I walked into my classroom on the first day I was shocked at what I saw. In front of me were a group of third graders who were totally out of control. As a matter of fact, the children did not acknowledge my presence at first. Instead, they continued to throw books and paper at each other. After raising my voice several times, I finally got their attention. Their attention, however, only lasted about 5 minutes at a time. By the end of the day my voice was gone, I had been cursed at and threatened with bodily harm, and absolutely no teaching had occurred. All my intricately planned lessons, prepared meticulously with the guidance of my university professors, had failed miserably.

Later, I was told by a veteran teacher at the school that several teachers were so intimidated by the children in my new class that they had left the school district in violation of their contracts. The last teacher had placed Bibles and crosses in the classroom, claiming the children were possessed by demonic spirits. I was also informed that the majority of the children in the class could not read.

FLOUNDERING WITH THE POWER GAME

For the next several days I assumed the role of authoritative rule enforcer. This meant punishing the children for every infraction without exception. This was not effective. The children became more daring. They showed no signs of fear that they would be punished for violating the rules. Even more troubling was the fact that every time I spoke with parents about the behavior of their children I was treated as the enemy. The parents responded as though I personally singled out their particular child and fabricated stories to make him or her look bad.

STRUGGLING WITH THE LOSS OF SELF-CONFIDENCE

I began to question my competence as a teacher. Was I really in the right field? Was teaching too undefined for me? Did I really have the ability to problem solve in situations like this one? Why wasn't what I learned at the university working? What elements were missing?

After another very long and unproductive day, I contacted one of my professors for advice. She told me to remember that I am the adult and that I am smarter than any child in that classroom, and that they are just children, not adults.

I did some deep soul-searching that night and decided that I was going to have to be more honest with the students and with myself. Maybe the problem was more than just the children. Maybe it was also me.

LOOKING BEYOND THE FACADE

The next day I came armed with a video camera and a tape recorder. The children were out of control as usual. Instead of saying anything to them I just watched them for a while. I began to notice things about them that I had not noticed before—the way they were dressed, their complexions, their hair, the deep sad expression on many of their faces. Most of all I saw myself as a child and for some reason that scared me. It made me realize just how important these children were to my future and that they were victims like me.

That day I told the children that this job was my bread and butter and no one was going to take that away from me. They seemed to understand this. As planned, I videotaped and recorded their behavior throughout the day.

RALLYING SUPPORT FROM PARENTS

The first big change came on back-to-school night. The parents had heard about the videotape and each wanted to see their child in action. I started the meeting by introducing myself. Then I told the parents that I wanted them to watch a video of a very successful inner-city classroom in Missouri. Totally engaged, the parents and their children watched the video. Next, I put on the videotape of their children in the classroom. The children began to look at each other as the parents viewed the video in total silence. The embarrassed looks on the parents' faces grew stronger as the video continued to play.

Once the video ended, our discussion began. The parents decided that the children who did not want to learn should be isolated from the others. The parents agreed to do a sort of patrol. They would visit the classroom unannounced and assist with its management. Every day, two or three parents would observe the class. They identified children who needed isolation and reported to other parents their observations about their children's behaviors in the classroom.

THE FIRST DEVELOPMENTAL ASSESSMENT

Now I was finally able to focus on assessment and diagnosis. I decided to put everything I learned from my university courses aside and focus on the needs of each individual child. The needs that were found to be prevalent within the group would be taught to the whole class.

I decided to start with self-identity. I told the students that my people originally came from Africa. I showed them where Africa was on the map; then I drew a picture of Africa and wrote next to it, "I am African American." When I asked the children what nationality they were, nobody in the group would admit that their heritage began in Africa, although the majority of the children were African American. Instead, most of them said they were Native American or Mexican. Trying to get them to see that they were not Native Americans or Mexicans made them almost hostile toward me. I decided to leave that one alone for the time being.

Each child was given a coloring book and crayons and told to color freely for 15 minutes. Every child in the class created blond-headed, blue-eyed White people in their coloring books. I thought to myself, "Oh my goodness! What on earth has happened here?" Instead of trying to correct the situation verbally, however, I sat down at the table with one group and began coloring in one of the unused coloring books. I colored in Black people. I made them so beautiful that all the children stopped to watch me color. One child said that no one ever told him he could color in Black people if he wanted to. I seized the opportunity to explain to these children that the pictures are merely lines on a piece of paper and that when they color within these lines they can make them appear as they wish. There is no right or wrong way to color.

TRANSFORMING THE CLASSROOM

Every day I read aloud stories and folktales written by and for African Americans. The children loved story time. I also taught them the Black national anthem, "Lift Every Voice and Sing." We sang it every morning.

Sometimes I wore African clothes to school. We talked about the fine grain of cotton found in Africa and how expensive it is. I showed them jewelry from Africa and I brought in pictures of beautiful cities that are in Africa. Soon the children began to wear African clothes, draw African people, and feel proud of themselves and their heritage. The children started writing letters to me and calling me at home. Sometimes they referred to me as Mama.

Because most of the children were from a strong religious heritage and regularly attended church, I brought that piece of their culture into the classroom. Every child was to be addressed as Brother or Sister. I stressed that we were a family inside and outside of the classroom.

I always tried to compliment the children on everything they did successfully or when they put forth their best effort. Most of the time I spoke to them in a soft voice and treated them very gently. There were still a lot of problems, but the children were changing not just academically, but also emotionally.

Because the children's reading levels were very low (some had not advanced beyond recognition of the alphabet), I decided we would read most of the day, everyday. The children read orally in groups and independently. Passages were assigned for each child or group to practice and then read out loud to the class. The chairs were set up in rows like church pews and we clapped for each person or group, praising Brother John or Sister Betty for a fine performance. Everything they learned successfully had to be performed—multiplication tables, spelling words, vocabulary words, and so on. The children loved to perform and show off their skills for their peers. They never seemed to tire of the repetition in these performances as each child took his or her turn. This amazed me. Their skills continued to improve, as did their self-confidence. Every day I told them they were the best class and every day they tried to live up to that expectation.

THE PROBLEM WITH SUCCESS

One child, a male student who was in special education, improved so much that when he was re-tested he scored in the gifted range. Although this student no longer qualified for remedial special education, he was not removed. The student study team decided that the bond with the special education teacher was so strong that it had to be broken slowly. I find this decision incredible because the student would ask me on a regular basis when he was going to get out of special education and be in the classroom all day. As the year drew toward a close, this student became increasingly angry. He began to make physical threats to me and other teachers for lying to him about the rewards for doing good work. He promised serious retaliation against us when he grew up. He insisted that he had done what he was supposed to do and nothing had changed. I spoke with my principal about the student on numerous occasions. Each time I was reassured that the student was going to be placed in his age-appropriate grade. When the following year began, however, this was not the case.

Another student who was female, but not in special education, also scored in the gifted range. I was told by a teacher who had worked at the school for many years that no student had scored in the gifted range in 5 years.

EXPLAINING WHAT HAPPENED AND WHY IT WORKED

I am still not sure what actually improved the children's skills. At the time it seemed as though every day was a guessing game. I never had complete sets of books or teacher's manuals. There was nothing fancy about my lessons. They were basic and to the point. Those finely tuned and detailed lessons I learned to prepare in college never worked with this group of children. Whenever someone asks me exactly what I did and why it improved their reading and writing I never have a clear answer. Perhaps it was something I learned about the children and myself that led me to a pathway of success.

MY RESPONSE TO THE PROFESSION

One thing I am beginning to see is that teaching requires one to sacrifice personal and family time for the profession. A typical day leaves me with about 2 hours to spend with my own family. Suddenly my whole world becomes what the children need instead of what my family needs. Teaching is extremely time consuming, highly demanding, and low paying.

Limited budgets in inner-city school districts force teachers to use personal resources to do the job successfully. Many young teachers have yet to pay for the 5 years of university education required for teaching in my state. So many young people who want to become teachers simply cannot afford it.

Because there is little or no external recognition for those teachers who are successful in the classroom, one must become committed to the children. The children in my classroom showed their appreciation every day through notes to me, their hard work, and the big hugs they gave me when they saw me in the shopping mall or the grocery store. The parents also expressed their appreciation regularly. There are some who always want more or have their own complaints. Most parents want the best for their children and will work with the teacher to accomplish it. Of course, every new teacher would like to know that administrators and the community at large recognize and appreciate their hard work. As beginning teachers, we are aware that we have much to learn and do not have all the answers; however, many of us are committed to the children and will find pathways to success.

SUGGESTED LEARNING EXPERIENCES

1. Contact several professional organizations such as the National Council for Social Studies, the National Council of Teachers of Mathematics, or the National Council of Teachers of English to get copies of their national standards. You may also check the Internet for these standards. Examine these standards for addressing cultural diversity in curriculum and pedagogy.
2. Contact the National Council for the Accreditation of Teacher Education to get a copy of the standards for teacher preparation. Discuss the adequacy of these standards for preparing teachers for inner-city schools.
3. Examine the standards for teacher certification for your state. Discuss the adequacy of these standards for preparing teachers for inner-city schools.
4. Interview several teachers from inner-city schools to ask the following questions:
   - How long have you taught in your present school? What do you like most about your present teaching situation? What would you most like to change about your present teaching situation?
   - What was most helpful to you in learning to teach in the present context?
   - What suggestions do you have for beginning teachers at your school?

   Compare and contrast the teachers' responses to each question.

Chapter 2

Becoming a Reflective Practitioner

Etta R. Hollins
Wright State University, Dayton

FOCUS QUESTIONS

1. The previous author describes an intuitive approach to professional development. The author in this chapter proposes an approach employing inquiry and reflection. How will you decide which approach is most appropriate for you?
2. How would you approach parent involvement using the approach to professional development described in this chapter?

INTRODUCTION

> . . . teaching is a complex, situation-specific, and dilemma-ridden endeavor.
> —Sparks-Langer and Colton (1991, p. 37)

In the preceding chapter, the complex, context-specific nature of teaching is evident in K. Hollins' description of her experiences in an urban inner-city third-grade classroom. The social dynamics and pedagogical and contextual issues with which she grappled, and the pathway that led to her success were clearly dependent on her ability to relate the knowledge she had acquired about instruction to the context and population of students in her classroom. In order to plan productive learning experiences, it is necessary to have sufficient knowledge of the students' home-culture and experiential background and the specific ways in which these factors have

11

influenced how the students learn. The ability to make authentic linkages between approaches to instruction and the learning propensities of a particular group of students requires both inquiry and reflection.

In Hollins (1996), I provide an approach and guidelines for inquiring into students' experiential backgrounds. I refer to this approach as *reflective interpretive inquiry* (RIQ). This approach entails examining your own beliefs about the specific population of students in the class, about instruction, and about the social context within the classroom; the nature of the experiences your students have had within and outside of school; the students' ethnic and cultural backgrounds; the social and political dynamics of the local community; and the social and political status of the particular ethnic group and local community within the larger societal context.

The purpose of this chapter is to help you become a reflective practitioner. This chapter addresses the characteristics of reflective thought and behavior, collaborative approaches to reflective practice, and tools that facilitate reflective practice. Richert (1990) explains that as

> the ability to think about what one does and why—assessing past actions, current situations, and intended outcomes—is vital to intelligent practice that is reflective rather than routine. As the time in the teaching process when teachers stop to think about their work and make sense of it, reflection influences how one grows as a professional by influencing how successfully one is able to learn from one's mistakes. (p. 525)

This chapter explains how to use this book as a tool for becoming a consciously reflective practitioner. It helps you understand the content and process of and approaches to reflective practice, and outlines tools that can be employed to facilitate its application to professional growth.

COMPONENTS OF REFLECTIVE THOUGHT AND BEHAVIOR

There are two components of reflective thought and behavior—perception and practice. Perception is based on three components: an individual's experiential background, professional knowledge and competence, and vision of the impact of school practices on the society. Reflective practice involves two related aspects: process and focus. Process refers to how reflective practice is done. Focus refers to the content involved or what is being reflected on.

Perception

Perception arises from an individual teacher's unique understanding of the world derived from background experiences, professional knowledge and competence, and a vision of the impact of school practices on the society. Perception frames professional practice.

Background Experiences.   Background experiences that shape an individual's perception and values include initial socialization within the home-culture, contact with groups and individuals outside the home-culture, schooling, and intellectual development. Caregivers in the home-culture engage young children in a cognitive apprenticeship where habits of mind, including values and socially acceptable behaviors, are learned. During this cognitive apprenticeship, children learn how to think about and respond to those outside the home-culture. Some children will learn healthy ways of relating to those different from themselves, whereas others will develop prejudices and stereotypes. Different children will have different experiences as they take their particular home-culture to school. Some will experience school as an extension of the home-culture, whereas others will experience conflicts between the home-culture and the school culture in practices and values. The habits of mind learned in the home-culture may be incongruent with those that form the basis for traditional pedagogical practices. In such cases academic problems may be the consequence.

As children mature, what was learned from initial cognitive apprenticeships and early experiences become the foundation for adult perception. Classroom teachers who are unaware of these influences may be limited in their ability to respond to different populations of students and to different learning or school contexts. Sparks-Langer and Colton (1991) point out the importance of teachers engaging in "metacognition—self-regulated, purpose-driven behavior" (p. 30). This means developing an awareness of the influences on one's thinking as well as the cognitive processes used in making decisions. In the final chapter of this book, Abell describes five evolutionary stages in the ability to recognize cultural and ethnic differences. This discussion is intended to help you identify your own stage of development and plan for growth.

Professional Knowledge and Competence.   There is a reciprocal relationship between an individual's experiential background and values, and the acquisition of professional competence. This means that the way an individual interprets new information is influenced by prior knowledge and experiences and the extent to which metacognitive competence has been acquired. Likewise, acquiring new information may contribute to a reinterpretation of prior knowledge and experiences. Teachers who have developed metacognitive competence are less bound by their prior experiences and are better able to engage in self-regulated, purpose-driven behaviors that enhance reflective practice. For example, teachers from a particular cultural background may interpret instruction from this particular perspective. This might benefit some learners more than others. Those who are aware of this factor can more readily make adjustments than those who are not.

There are four components of the professional knowledge and competence necessary for reflective practice: pedagogical content knowledge, knowledge of characteristics of learners, knowledge of teaching contexts, and knowledge of educational purposes, ends, and aims (Shulman, 1987). *Pedagogical content knowledge* refers to teachers' special understanding of a discipline as it relates to the structure of the curriculum to be taught and the approaches to be employed in planning, organizing, and presenting appropriate and productive learning experiences for students. *Knowledge of characteristics of learners* refers to understanding the relationships between learners' prior knowledge and schooling experiences, their cognitive and physical propensities, and their cultural and experiential backgrounds and productive classroom learning experiences. Teachers with the appropriate knowledge are able to draw upon the characteristics of their students to make learning meaningful and to develop a comfortable and supportive classroom context. *Knowledge of teaching contexts* refers to understanding the relationship between approaches to facilitating learning and a positive and supportive social context in the classroom, and the characteristics of the learners, the social relationships and interactions among the learners and the teacher, the school culture, and the societal values that influence schooling. *Knowledge of educational purposes, ends, and aims* refers to understanding the prevailing ideology that forms the basis for school practices including daily rituals and routines, instructional approaches, and curriculum content. This knowledge includes understanding the potential impact on the society of the knowledge, habits of mind, values, and social behaviors learned in school.

In chapter 5 McElroy and I illustrate the importance of professional knowledge and competence in teaching a science lesson to inner-city students. McElroy reflects on and describes his own teaching behavior and the responses of the students in order to better understand and develop meaningful and productive learning experiences. According to Sparks-Langer and Colton (1991):

> stories written by and about teachers form the basis of narrative inquiry. The participants in such inquiry construct and reconstruct narrative plots to gain a deeper understanding of their experiences. In this view, therefore, the process of reflective thinking is seen as narratives or stories with settings, plots, and characters. (p. 42)

McElroy and I draw on the research literature for a deeper understanding of the results of this narrative inquiry. This allows for a comparison of our findings with those of other researchers.

Vision of the Impact of School Practices on the Society. Teachers shape the future of the society. Their work has a significant impact on their students' lives in terms of academic competence, social participation, and value perspectives. In my view, teachers have a moral obligation to provide the best possible instruction and support for their students' growth and development in these areas. It is important for teachers to have a vision of how their classroom practices influence or shape students' development. For example, to what extent will your students reach a level of academic competence that will allow them to understand the structure of the discipline, how to conduct inquiry in the discipline, and how knowledge in the specific discipline contributes to understanding and improving the human condition? Will your students understand how and where the knowledge they acquire is used in the society or the professions? Will your students acquire enough academic competence to transfer what has been learned from one situation to another? What will your students learn about living in a culturally diverse and democratic society?

School practices legitimate specific knowledge, perspectives, values, and social relationships among people and institutions. These school practices are evident in classroom instruction, including the way in which a teacher frames the curriculum content, selects the teaching materials, and establishes the social context for learning. Teachers need to be aware of the value perspectives presented to their students through both the curricula and the teaching materials they use in order to avoid unknowingly perpetuating bias and prejudice. For example, Shropshire (chap. 9, this volume) discusses the controversy over perspectives represented in the history curriculum. She points out distortions and omissions that promote bias and prejudices. The proponents of each history perspective have particular societal outcomes in mind. The position presented in this book is that teachers should consciously plan their instruction and the social context within their classrooms to influence academic competence, social participation, and value perspectives that prepare youngsters to be responsible and productive citizens in a culturally diverse and democratic society.

Practice

Reflective practice in teaching is influenced by an individual's perception, which has two aspects: process and focus. The *process* of reflective teaching involves a sequence of mental operations and actions. The *focus* during reflective teaching is influenced by the stage of an individual's professional development resulting from teacher preparation, classroom experience, and the extent to which these experiences result in growth.

The Process. Employing a systematic process of reflective practice helps teachers grow professionally from their experiences. I encourage preservice teachers to:

1. Recognize and develop an accurate description of a dilemma.
2. Identify responses likely to have a positive effect on the dilemma given its characteristics, the individual's prior experiences with related situations, and what can be gleaned from formal theory and research.
3. Develop and implement a strategy.
4. Adjust or modify the strategy as necessary to effect the desired outcomes.
5. Analyze the consequences of the strategy to determine the extent to which intended outcomes were achieved.

Writing a description of a dilemma helps frame it as a solvable problem. The description should give attention to the context of the dilemma, contributing and precipitating factors, characteristics and behaviors of individuals involved and relationships among them, and the effects of the dilemma within and outside the context in which it occurs. Identifying responses likely to have a positive effect directly relates to the clarity with which the dilemma is described. When a dilemma is clearly described, its characteristics are evident and it can be more easily related to prior experiences and to formal theory and research. Developing and implementing a strategy is based on the characteristics of the situation, prior experiences, and formal knowledge. The impact of the strategy must be observed during implementation and appropriate adjustments and modification made to effect the desired outcomes. Finally, good reflective practice involves determining the extent to which the strategy was successful. This requires a thoughtful analysis of the change (if any) that has occurred by reexamining the original description of the dilemma in comparison to what exists after the implementation of the strategy.

The Focus. According to Colton and Sparks-Langer (1993):

> Experienced teachers have stored automatic scripts allowing them to handle common routines almost without conscious thought, thus requiring little if any mental effort. Novices, on the other hand, have few automatic routines and must consciously think through every decision. This certainly inhibits the mental flexibility required for excellent teaching; moreover, it's tiring. (p. 46)

This suggests that the initial goal of reflective practice for novice teachers is to develop a level of automaticity that will support advancement to the next stage of professional growth. This requires understanding your own stage of professional development and planning and monitoring your own learning experiences and progress.

Lasley (1992) identifies three stages in teacher development: Stage I: technical/survival, Stage II: task/conceptual, and Stage III: impact/dialectical. At each stage, teachers have different concerns and issues and have the capacity to engage in reflective practice with a different focus. At Stage I, teachers are preoccupied with their own competence in effectively managing the tools of the craft such as developing lesson plans that employ learning experiences and materials that keep pupils on task, meeting the administrator's expectations, and receiving a good evaluation. In essence, teachers at this stage are concerned with personal survival in the profession. Acknowledging that this is where you are and engaging in reflective practice related to the issues of immediate concern will help you advance to the next stage. For example, if you are using a journal for reflection, it may be worthwhile to document dilemmas and situations that interfere with your application of the tools of the craft and to deliberately engage in the reflective process described in this chapter. This may be a good time to form a support group with other beginning teaches who are addressing the same issues. Employing the process of reflective practice in and sharing experiences with a support group can enhance professional growth.

In Stage II, teachers have acquired a reasonable level of competence with the basic tools of the craft. They can design lessons that keep pupils engaged and maintain an orderly classroom environment. This is a great accomplishment. However, if you are at this stage, it is important to recognize the need to address the relationship between pupils' cognitive schema or experiential background, and meaningful and productive classroom learning. This is a good time to conduct action research or to begin case studies of individual pupil's responses to classroom instruction, to inquire into their thinking processes, and to attempt an understanding of how to make learning experiences more meaningful. Case studies can help you identify and respond to different patterns of students' learning and thinking. This approach is consistent with the tendency at this stage for teachers to begin to employ existing theory or develop their own theories to explain teaching, learning, and the social dynamics of the classroom.

In Stage III, teachers have acquired a level of automaticity with their craft that allows them to proceed with ease in managing the technical aspects of classroom instruction and being responsive to individual and group needs within the learning community. These teachers are responsive to their students' cultural and experiential backgrounds, cognitive schemata, learning and thinking patterns, and the social dynamics within the classroom. They are aware of internal and external forces that influence their teaching and what and how their students learn. These teachers are concerned with the moral and ethical aspects of schooling. At this stage, teacher study groups may address broader issues affecting the school, community, society, and the profession. They are concerned with improving knowledge and practice in the field and better understanding and improving the human condition.

COLLABORATIVE APPROACHES TO REFLECTIVE PRACTICE

Typically, teachers are isolated from their peers as they work in their own classrooms or teach courses. Thus, teachers usually engage in reflective practice alone. Certainly, private time is needed for reflecting on your own practice and for using tools that support reflective practice. However, a great deal can be gained from collaborating with others. Examples of collaborative approaches to reflective practice include *teacher support groups* and *study groups.*

Participating in Teacher Support Groups

Teacher support groups can be particularly helpful to novice teachers in Stage I or Stage II of professional development. These teachers can assist each other in developing proficiency with the technical aspects of their craft. The group might focus on such topics as classroom management, student motivation, or instructional strategies for a particular content or population of students. The topics must be narrowed to reveal specific dilemmas or problematic areas. This will allow teachers to share their experiences and insights in ways that promote problem solving and professional growth.

The first step in preparing to participate in a support group is to list five or six highly salient concerns, then convert them to questions that can be addressed through data collection and analysis. For example, if a lack of motivation is a concern, formulate questions such as: Can the curriculum content be reframed in a way that will make it more meaningful and interesting for the students? What learning experiences might be more meaningful and productive for the students? The practice of converting negative concerns into questions is an excellent beginning and can help foster a more positive attitude toward students. Questions generated in this way can form the basis for discussion at a support group meeting. Other teachers may have ideas and resources to share that can help address the questions. Some teachers may be willing to collaborate in reviewing the research literature for solutions or to participate in action research in their own classrooms.

When participating in a support group, it is helpful to keep a journal. The first entry in the journal may be a complete description of the composition of your class(es). You may want to keep demographic data such as your students' cultural/ethnic backgrounds, social class status, prior academic performance, and descriptions of their recent performance under your direction. Before attending a support group meeting, you might want to make an entry into your journal describing a dilemma for which you would like to solicit suggestions.

Avoiding Pitfalls.   There are particular pitfalls for teacher support groups that can be avoided by engaging a process and focus for the group's activities. One such structure might involve (a) identifying and describing dilemmas or questions related to a particular population of students, (b) determining options for addressing specific challenges or situations, and (c) evaluating approaches. The following format may be helpful for working together on challenges:

1. In a written statement, describe the challenge or concern as specifically and clearly as possible. Describe the desired outcome.
2. Convert the challenge statement to a series of questions.
3. Determine the information needed to address the challenge and identify sources for obtaining it.
4. Identify options for addressing the challenge and choose one or two approaches to be tried by several different teachers.
5. Keep accurate records of the challenges addressed, approaches tried, and the outcomes.
6. Evaluate the strengths and weaknesses of each approach. Students' responses to a particular approach may differ with individual teachers. An approach that generates the desired outcomes should be continued.

Approaches to Common Challenges.   The following examples of common challenges that combine principles of effective teaching with dilemmas teachers face in the classroom may provide a focus for support group work. Sample discussions follow each example.

Example 1: Participants raise critical questions concerning teaching and learning, engage in objective analysis of learning situations, and identify strategic approaches to instruction that lead to productive learning.

1. Productive learning requires that the teacher and students share a common frame of reference for the skill or knowledge that is the subject of instruction; otherwise, communication is seriously impaired and learning is hampered. What are some ways to establish a common frame of reference when the teacher and students do not share the same or a similar cultural

or experiential background? (For a positive example, see Moses, Kamii, Swap, & Howard, 1989, and for a negative example, see Michaels, 1981.)

2. Learning is more meaningful when the content of instruction is directly related to what is valued by adult members of the students' local community and to practices engaged in by locally respected individuals. How can teachers reframe the existing mandated curriculum to incorporate content valued by adult members of a particular community and related to practices engaged in by respected individuals? (See Wiggington, 1991, for an example.)

3. Many students, particularly those from upper elementary grades through high school, are motivated by engaging in learning experiences that replicate skills and knowledge observable in real-life occupations and professions. Many students learn advanced skills as well as basic skills through such practices. What approaches to instruction provide learning experiences that the students will view as replicas of or preparation for real-life occupations and professions? (See Wiggington, 1991, for an example; these students were engaged in photojournalism.)

Example 2: Participants identify factors that contribute to a collaborative and supportive social context for learning.

1. When teachers and their students are from different cultural and experiential backgrounds, their expectations, interpretations, and responses to social situations and interactions may significantly differ. Although these differences may not be negative, they can contribute to conflicts in interpersonal relationships. How can teachers interact with students in a way that will be interpreted by the students as appropriate adult leadership that is positive and supportive? (See E. Hollins, 1982; E. Hollins & Spencer, 1990.)

2. Some teachers believe that some students require strict or rigid discipline in the classroom. Existing research does not support this conclusion. All students need a comfortable and supportive context for learning. Too much rigidity can lead to resistance (see D'Amato, 1988; Gilmore, 1985). How can teachers develop a comfortable and supportive social context for learning that also includes a reasonable degree of order?

3. Some students can especially benefit from a classroom context that allows for frequent peer interaction and collaboration. Learning from peers can be as effective as learning from adults. Collaboration is not the same as peer tutoring or peer teaching. Collaboration means that each student applies what he or she knows in a joint effort to meet a challenge or complete an academic task. The individual members of a small group of students engaged in a particular instance of collaboration may have varying

degrees of competence. The quality of the task determines the level of involvement and extent of new learning by the students engaged in the experience. What kind of classroom learning experiences best support peer interaction and collaboration as a part of meaningful and focused learning?

4. Many students who have experienced repeated failure in school have developed negative attitudes as a psychological defense. This is a perfectly understandable human response to being forced to confront failure on a daily basis over a period of years without any indication of relief. School practices that generate failure among these students usually remain unchanged. How can teachers who have reframed the curriculum and redesigned their instruction entice these students to take a risk by trying again?

Example 3: Participants identify ways to utilize human and material resources from the students' home community to enhance classroom learning.

1. Learning and students' sense of self-worth can be significantly enhanced by exploring and acquiring more in-depth knowledge about their own community. What local community resources are available that can make learning more meaningful for students?

2. Involving highly visible and respected members of the community in school activities can provide successful role models for the students and help them visualize the positive outcomes of schooling. Direct contact with these individuals can help students with their own life goal setting and career selection. Who are the most respected individuals in the students' home community and under what conditions might they be invited to participate in school activities or classroom learning experiences?

3. Students get a sense of the value and purpose of schooling when learning experiences include analyzing and exploring options for addressing challenges that are of concern to the adult members of their local community. Engaging in dialogue with community members concerning highly salient issues and concerns increases the sense of social responsibility. What issues and concerns are the most salient for adults in the students' local home community and how can they be incorporated into the curriculum? (For an example, see Moll, 1986.)

Participating in Study Groups

Study groups differ from support groups in that the focus is less immediately personal and is not directed toward the attainment of basic professional competence. Typically, study groups are made up of teachers at Stage III in their professional development. These teachers are concerned with issues and problems associated with the profession and schools that have implications at the local, state, and national levels. These teachers look for opportunities to collaborate with others who share their concerns and interests. Examples of issues that may be addressed by study groups include statewide testing initiatives and national standards for curriculum content.

The work of teachers in study groups may appear more political than that in support groups. Efforts may be directed toward participation in planning and decision making at various levels including their own school building, district, or state and national levels.

TOOLS THAT FACILITATE REFLECTIVE PRACTICE

The essential tools for reflective practice include journals, action research and case studies, and theory. These tools support professional growth by providing teachers opportunities to document their action and thoughts for future reference and reflection, to study selected aspects of their pedagogy and students' responses, and to apply and construct theory to guide their practice.

Using Journals

The act of documentation is essential to reflective practice. It allows teachers to revisit their own actions and thoughts and to acquire important metacognitive skills. Documentation provides special opportunities for growth by serving as an easy reference for making linkages between past and present experiences. Journals are an essential tool for this purpose.

Journals are frequently used in graduate and undergraduate courses as a metacognitive tool for critical analysis of one's own thought processes, for maintaining a private dialogue about a learning experience, and for reflecting on concepts, ideas, and issues introduced in class discussions. Journals may be informal or structured to use a particular format or to respond to specific issues or questions. McAlpine (1992) discusses using journals as professional conversations by employing descriptive writing (documenting events), cathartic writing (expressing emotions), and reflective writing (probing to enhance understanding). McAlpine's discussion focuses on using journals in the context of a professional trainee and a clinical instructor where the journal is shared between the two as professional conversation. In this case, the clinical instructor assists the trainee in integrating what has been learned in course work with its application in field experiences. Journals can also be used to facilitate conversations among beginning teachers and experienced teachers in difficult or unfamiliar situations.

Teachers' use of descriptive writing in journals may be structured or unstructured. In structured journal writing, specific issues are addressed consistently and over time. This makes it easy to review specific patterns of decision making and professional growth. For example, descriptive journal writing may be focused on a particular aspect of classroom practices or on student responses to instruction or the social context in the classroom. A journal focused on students' responses to instruction may contain demographics of the class, lesson plans, samples of students' written work (including responses on tests), teachers' notes describing positive and negative patterns in lesson outcomes and students' responses, and suggested modifications for use in the future. Decisions about what should be included in unstructured journals are spontaneous. At some point when reflecting on an event or situation the teacher may decide that it should be documented in the journal.

Cathartic writing in journals is useful for clarifying and expressing emotional responses to situations. A very emotional individual can engage in self-monitoring and gain control over emotional responses. It can provide insight into one's own attitudes and value perspectives that may influence classroom practices. Cathartic writing is most beneficial when combined with descriptive or reflective writing. When used in this way, it allows one to put emotional responses in perspective and move on to developing strategies for addressing issues and solving problems.

Reflective writing is the documentation of reflective practice. It documents what one does and why, including the assessment of past actions, current situations, and planned outcomes. Reflective writing supports teachers in thinking about and making sense of their work. Reflective writing may incorporate the strategies of descriptive and cathartic writing.

Using Action Research and Case Studies

Practitioners and scholars define or describe action research in many different ways. However, for the purposes of this discussion, action research is defined as the *documentation* of specific aspects of mindful reflective teaching practices evident in a continuous cycle of planning, implementation, assessment, and reflection aimed at increasing the positive outcomes of schooling. The act of documentation serves several purposes. First, it promotes clarity in addressing problems and identifying solutions. When problems are clearly defined, viable solutions are more easily developed, implemented, and assessed. Second, documentation provides opportunities for collaboration with colleagues who share an interest in the concern. Clarity in documentation improves communication among those who share an interest in addressing an issue or problem. Third, documentation creates a record that can be reviewed and shared with others. The nature of the problem, approaches to solutions, and outcomes can be shared with those who are not directly involved in the action research study.

As you go through the cycle of reflective practice, you will observe the social context within the classroom, and your students' responses to learning experiences and to you. In situations where students' responses are not as desirable as they might be, more careful study may be warranted. You may begin by documenting the problem. If the problem is academic, the following procedure may be helpful:

1. Carefully observe the student at work or responding in class, examine work completed by the student (including test results), and talk with the student to determine the precise concept, procedure, or skill with which difficulty is experienced.
2. Document the source of the difficulty and patterns identifiable in the student's strategy for acquiring the knowledge presented.
3. Describe the relationship between the strategy used by the student and that required for succeeding with the instructional approach you are using.
4. Decide whether you will attempt to correct the strategy used by the student or change the instructional approach.
5. Carefully describe the approach you decide to implement to improve the student's acquisition of the intended knowledge.
6. Document the outcomes of your approach.

It is important to clearly define the relationship between academic learning problems and instructional approaches. This will influence the strategy selected for solving the problem. For example, halfway through the academic year you determine that a first-grade child is still having difficulty with initial consonant sounds in reading skills acquisition. You need to decide to either help the child refine auditory discrimination and build appropriate memory structures to support a phonetic approach to reading or consider changing to a visual/sight approach.

Action research studies of the social context for learning may require a slightly different approach than that used to study academic learning problems. The social context for learning is based on interactions and relationships among and between individuals and groups within the classroom. These interactions and relationships are based on past experiences, perceptions, practices, traditions, and values. At times, it may seem that a single student is responsible for disrupting the class. This is rarely the case. The relationship between an individual and a group may elicit undesirable behavior from an individual. Blaming an individual is counterproductive. Changes in the individual's response to the group or the group's response to the individual may prove effective. Working to change both responses may be even more effective. The following approach to studying the social context for learning may be helpful:

1. Carefully observe and document the targeted undesirable behavior.
2. Pinpoint, and verify through discussions with the students, the underlying attitudes, feelings, perspectives, and values.
3. Describe the relation between the value perspectives held by the students and your approach to fostering a positive social context within the classroom.
4. Solicit student input for designing a comfortable and supportive social context for learning.
5. Implement the strategy and document the outcomes.
6. Report the outcomes to the students.

It is especially important for students to be active participants in action research related to the social context for learning.

Using Theory

In the process of reflective practice, existing educational theory may be clarified and validated, or new theory may be constructed from practice. In either case, theory is employed as a tool for thinking about and making sense of teaching and learning in classrooms.

Applying Theory to Practice. Preservice teacher preparation includes courses on learning theory, methodologies that apply learning theories, and theories of instruction and teaching. Preservice teachers are expected to apply theory to practice during specified early field experiences and during student teaching. Interaction with the university supervisor and the mentor teacher provides support for integrating theory and practice during student teaching. The lessons learned during this time period should prepare the beginning teacher to independently use what has been learned about theory for reflecting on practice.

Simply put, theory is an explanation of how, why, and under what conditions a particular phenomenon exists. It may also propose a means for altering a phenomenon or situation. For example, according to Kozulin and Presseisen (1995), the central question addressed in the theory of mediated learning experience is "What is the cause of individual differences in cognitive development?" (p. 69). The proposition is that organismic and environmental (biological and social) factors are distal determinants of cognitive development, whereas mediated learning experiences, or the lack thereof, constitute the proximal factor influencing variations in cognitive development. In other words, children with similar initial cognitive functioning who are nurtured in the same environment may have differences in cognitive development resulting from variations in the extent and quality of mediated learning experiences and experiences with higher order psychological tools. A mediated learning experience occurs during a reciprocal interaction between an adult or more advanced learner and a child or less advanced learner where the child's cognitive processes are intentionally engaged in a meaningful experience to facilitate thinking that reveals underlying principles that are transferable to other situations. Higher order psychological tools include writing, numerical, and other abstract notational systems. The application of the theory of mediated learning experience to practice would, according to Kozulin and Presseisen, require "that teachers interpose themselves between the learner and the learning material, make the learning intentional, help the student extract principles embedded in the material, and help the student transfer these principles to various content areas" (p. 72).

The example of the theory of mediated learning experience used here provides a heuristic for translating theory to practice. This translation process introduces the opportunity to formulate questions to guide reflection on teaching practices. Based on this theory, at the conclusion of a learning experience the teacher might reflect on such questions as: Was the intent of the learning experience clear and meaningful enough to engage the child's cognitive processes? Did the child receive adequate guidance for accomplishing the intent? Was the child able to extract principles embedded in the material? Was the child able to transfer the extracted principles to other situations and tasks? These questions can help teachers improve their practice.

Extracting Theory From Practice. Teaching contexts significantly differ based on the population of students taught, their cultural and experiential background, prior learning or schooling experiences, practice in the use of higher order psychological tools, and level of cognitive development. This requires that teachers thoroughly understand the theories they apply in classrooms and that they are attentive to their students' responses to the learning experiences provided. After several attempts at applying a particular theory with a specific population of learners, a teacher may formulate questions that deepen understanding of the theory, extend the theory, or lead to the formulation of new theory. For example, a teacher employing the theory of mediated learning experiences may formulate the following questions in order to deepen understanding or extend the theory: What constitutes a meaningful learning experience? How might what constitutes meaningfulness vary from one population to another? Does adult guidance behavior change from one population of learners to another? Are the principles extracted from a particular learning experience expressed or represented differently by different populations of learners?

A teacher unfamiliar with the theory of mediated learning experiences may extract from her or his practice a theory explaining optimum learning conditions for a specific population. This can be done by using one instructional approach under a variety of conditions or using several different instructional approaches under the same conditions. For example, the social context (individual, small group, whole class) for learning may be held constant while varying instructional approaches (visual, auditory, kinesthetic), or the reverse may be done. The teacher may experiment with different adult guidance behaviors such as those employing inductive or deductive logic. The teacher may choose the Socratic method of questioning or present clues that allow the child to discover a principle. It is important to carefully document the learners' responses under the different conditions and with different instructional approaches. This documentation can be analyzed to formulate a theory about the optimum learning conditions for a specific population. Questions such as the following might be helpful in analyzing the documentation: What type of learning experiences are the most meaningful for this population? What social conditions best support learning for this population? What adult guidance behaviors are best for this population? What other factors within the classroom seem to influence learning for this population?

CONCLUSION

Becoming a reflective practitioner requires engaging in a continuous cycle of mindful reflective practice that makes use of the components of reflective thought and behavior, individual and collaborative approaches to reflective practice, and the tools that facilitate reflective practice. The authors in this book provide examples of reflective practice that address instructional techniques, curriculum perspectives, and a social context for learning that are responsive to students in a culturally diverse society. These examples are not presented as exhaustive. Teachers in different school contexts and with different populations of students will need to use the strategies associated with mindful reflective practice to enhance their students' learning and their own professional growth.

SUGGESTED LEARNING EXPERIENCES

1. Interview several principals from local schools as part of your investigation of the types of professional development experiences available for classroom teachers. Request written material describing the

inservice training. Ask about the approach used in the district to plan teacher inservice education. In a written report, describe the focus and approach used in the inservice education programs the principals described. Explain the extent to which teachers participate in the design of inservice education, the opportunities available for collaboration, and participating in support and study groups.

2. Request information from your local county office of education or education service district on the academic performance of students in local school districts. Based on the information you collect, develop a list of questions suitable for action research or case studies.

REFERENCES

Colton, A. B., & Sparks-Langer, G. M. (1993). A conceptual framework to guide the development of teacher reflection and decision making. *The Journal of Teacher Education, 44*(1), 45–54.

D'Amato, J. (1988). "Acting": Hawaiian children's resistance to teachers. *The Elementary School Journal, 88*(5), 529–544.

Gilmore, P. (1985). "Gimme room": School resistance, attitude, and access to literacy. *Journal of Education, 167*(1), 111–128.

Hollins, E. R. (1982). The Marva Collins story revisited. *The Journal of Teacher Education, 33*(1), 37–40.

Hollins, E. R. (1996). *Culture in school learning: Revealing the deep meaning.* Mahwah, NJ: Lawrence Erlbaum Associates.

Hollins, E. R., & Spencer, K. (1990). Restructuring schools for cultural inclusion: Changing the schooling process for African American youngsters. *Journal of Education, 172*(2), 89–100.

Kozulin, A., & Presseisen, B. Z. (1995). Mediated learning experience and psychological tools: Vygotsky's and Feuerstein's perspectives in a study of student learning. *Educational Psychologist, 30*(2), 67–75.

Lasley, T. J. (1992). Promoting teacher reflection. *Journal of Staff Development, 13*(1), 24–29.

McAlpine, L. (1992, January). Learning to reflect: Using journals as professional conversations. *Adult Learning, 15*, 23–24.

Michaels, S. (1981). "Sharing time": Children's narrative styles and differential access to literacy. *Language in Society, 10*, 423–442.

Moll, L. C. (1986). Writing as communication: Creating strategic learning environments for students. *Theory Into Practice, 25*(2), 102–108.

Moses, R. P., Kamii, M., Swap, S. M., & Howard, J. (1989). The Algebra Project: Organizing in the spirit of Ella. *Harvard Educational Review, 59*(4), 423–443.

Richert, A. E. (1990). Teaching teachers to reflect: A consideration of programme structure. *Journal of Curriculum Studies, 22*(6), 509–527.

Shulman, L. S. (1987). Knowledge and teaching: Foundations of the new reform. *Harvard Educational Review, 57*, 421–444.

Sparks-Langer, G. M., & Colton, A. B. (1991, March). Synthesis of research on teachers' reflective thinking. *Educational Leadership*, 37–44.

Wiggington, E. (1991). Culture begins at home. *Educational Leadership, 49*(4), 60–94.

Part II

USING CULTURE AS A COMPASS: CREATING CULTURALLY AUTHENTIC CURRICULUM AND PEDAGOGY

OVERVIEW

The theoretical frameworks set by the previous chapters are applied to classroom practice in this part. Through their reflective approaches to instruction, the authors illustrate how culturally sensitive curricula enhance the learning potential of students. Using their own experiential backgrounds, these teacher researchers develop instruction around the cultural context of their individual classrooms. The section begins with a look at the importance of culturally relevant materials in successful reading activities for children.

In chapter 3, Presmeg looks at culturally mediated instruction from the mathematics students' point of view. Interviewing preservice teachers about perceptions of their own experiences, she calls for the use of nontraditional approaches to mathematics in formal instruction. Presmeg then describes the barriers that need to be overcome before this approach can be put into practice. She stresses that an increasingly multicultural classroom demands a change in traditional pedagogies. Her description of the childhood experiences of four African American preservice teachers shows the importance of role models. They tell of teachers, often but not always African American, who inspired them, made learning "fun," and cared about their students. These preservice teachers, in turn, learned from those teachers with whom they had less than desirable experiences how not to teach. When they analyze their college experiences, they have difficulty finding the relevance of that work to actual teaching and often see little connection between the constructivist paradigm of the pedagogical model and the actual mathematics class. When applying their knowledge to actual problems, they see the discrepancies between learning material and relating it in any conceptual way to meaningful data. Such restrictive learning has definite educational disadvantages.

Citing Parham and Parham (1989), Presmeg identifies factors necessary for the development of positive self-concepts for African American students: parental/teacher participation, reinforced home and community mores and values, reflection of African American culture and lifestyles in curriculum, and encouragement for achievement for all. According to the preservice teachers interviewed, these factors are essential for later classroom success. The author explains the importance of positive self-concept, understanding of racism, and support.

Promoting what she terms *ethnomathematics*, Presmeg points out that each individual's experience with mathematical resources is based on a unique cultural heritage and ethnicity that can be shared with others. To illustrate, she provides a number of ethnically based mathematics problems (e.g., mathematics of baseball, cricket, sharecropping, musical instruments, bridge). The author describes the incorporation of ethnomathematics with academic mathematics through symbolism and systematization. These connections, she contends, promote equity and meaning for African American students in the mathematics classroom.

In chapter 4, Fran Davis Perkins reflects on her own childhood. She compares the distant, lackluster lives described in the children's books presented at school with the "real fun" that awaited her at home where she enjoyed rich literary experiences through family recitations, church and community events, and storytelling. Yet the familiar was never so valued as "someone else's story" presented in school. Stressing the importance of validation through identification, Perkins illustrates the ways in which students become engaged in reading based on their ability to see themselves in their texts. The more viable the reading, the more self-affirming the experience. Perkins bases her reading curriculum on reader-response theory, which purports that the more closely the reader relates to the text, the more meaningful the reading experience. The reader, then, should be engaged in a "transaction" with the literature—a difficult feat if the material is far removed from the student's life.

In an attempt to identify and describe the response patterns of low-income, third-grade African American children using self-affirming literature, Perkins conducts an experiment using books by and/or about African Americans. Each book reflects a family theme, intergenerational relationships, and an insider's perspective. She notes personal connections made by students reflecting on their experiences, feelings, and fulfillment. In addition, her research becomes a way of including family and community in literacy development. Calling for a reexamination of existing literacy programs that exclude African American literature, the author reminds us that we need choices in text selection, time to read and collaborate with others in making these literary transactions, and open discussions about diverse literature. We should select literature that reflects the child's world.

Chapter 5 looks at the characteristics of successful science teaching for African American middle-school students. In presenting our vignette, McElroy and I demonstrate an experiential lesson based on a discrepant event where the unexpected happens. We begin by presenting the literature on school failure, characteristics of effective teachers, and successful school practices. We define various theories in the literature which attempt to explain school failure among ethnic minority children. The disfavored genetic inferiority and cultural deficit models have given way to the more widely accepted theories of *cultural mismatch* (where the home-culture and school-culture are discrepant) and *contextual interaction* (where multiple factors influence outcomes). Effective teacher strategies include the use of kinship terms, cultural connectedness, warmth, control, and high expectations. African American teachers have a unique relationship with their students because of their shared community, but it is possible for such culturally congruent instruction to be applied by teachers of dissimilar backgrounds as well.

In analyzing specific school practices, we point out that the "topic-associated" culturally derived narrative style used by African American students in lieu of the "topic-centered" style used by European American students should be valued. We also note that when the relation between the school and the community becomes closer, students' performance levels in mathematics are higher. In general, when communicative behaviors are familiar to the learner, the learning process is more successful. More reflective teaching processes are required to better understand and therefore teach these children. To this end, we describe a productive science lesson that engages students in scientific inquiry—observing, interpreting, and inferring. This vignette shows the significant influence of socialization and the relation between culture and cognition. In the vignette shown, an African American teacher creates a nontraditional social context style that allows for more effective communication and enhancement of learning.

In chapter 6, Moll is concerned with the practice of teaching limited-English-proficient children a "watered down" curriculum that limits their academic achievement. He contends that "the source of students' problems in school is not to be found in their language or culture, it is to be found in the social organization of schooling." He argues that although student characteristics do matter, children who fail under traditional structures of schooling can succeed when these structures are altered to accommodate their talents and skills. He contends that just as failure is socially organized, success can be socially arranged. His data reveals that most of the writing in the homes of the limited-English-proficient students in the study was functional (grocery lists, phone messages, and occasionally, letters). Children who were more fluent in English than their parents conducted family business such as paying bills. In Moll's study the functional quality of literacy found in the home was applied to school learning. He describes a module of instruction where the youngsters conduct a survey on bilingualism that forms the basis for a report to be shared with their community. In this approach, classroom instruction is linked to the real world of the students, and they are provided the support necessary to perform at the highest level possible, regardless of English language proficiency.

In chapter 7, Pewewardy looks at the plight of American Indian students whose relationships with government and educational institutions have been negative for generations. Distrust, anger, and confusion have contributed to a schism of misunderstanding that has caused this population to have the largest attrition rate of any racial or ethnic minority in this country's schools. He describes aspects of Native American cultural and experiential background that he hopes will assist teachers in using culturally responsive pedagogy to provide successful school experiences for these students.

Pewewardy begins by stressing the diversity that exists within the American Indian population, from physical characteristics to cultural practices and language use. Differences in physical appearance within this population often elicit acts of rejection and prejudice from traditional Indian people and non-Indians. Pewewardy describes several family structures, all of which struggle with a variety of issues revolving around acculturation. For example, teachers often interpret the American Indian lack of nuclear family commitment as a negative. The neo-traditional and transitional families, bicultural families, and pan-renaissance families (those reconnecting with Indian tribal heritage) each encounter problems relative to structure, geography, assimilation, and language. Each tribe has a different identity, but most of the tribes share core values of sharing, cooperation, noninterference, time orientation, strong kinship ties, and coexistence with nature. These values, Pewewardy suggests, are what educators should ascribe to when developing cultural models for learning and teaching.

Because of the lack of viable educational studies about the American Indian and schooling, there is little to assist teachers in creating successful teaching strategies. He calls for a redefinition of qualities of the American Indian student that avoid existing stereotypes, fostering meaningful interpersonal school relationships and communicative styles, and using the child's culture as a bridge to understanding and achievement. We must move from ethnocentrism to cooperation through intertribal, intercultural, and transcultural teaching. Teachers must be able to use students' learning patterns and world views, tribal languages and Indian English in the class-room. Adaptation to local circumstances is necessary.

In discussing teachers' biases, Pewewardy warns against "dysconscious racism," which accepts dominant White norms, taking for granted "White privilege." We must prepare monocultural teachers to teach American Indian students. With proper training and appreciation of other cultures, teachers can avoid the "cultural discontinuity" that has been the order of the day for so long. We must emphasize strengths in Indian families. Culturally responsive pedagogy is possible if teachers observe Indian children in the classroom before student teaching. They should also develop respect for other cultures, knowledge of the history and culture, reflective observation and evaluation skills, community involvement, and awareness of cultural code-switching, body language, and behaviors different from children of parallel cultures. He offers a number of useful strategies for daily classroom practice.

Each of these chapters in Part II offer strategies and practices that extend the theoretical underpinnings of teaching in the culturally diverse classroom. Each has applications to other populations and each provides suggestions for working with students from racial and ethnic minority groups whose cultures have historically been ignored or undervalued. Finally, each author has argued for the inclusion in the classroom of world views other than those of the dominant culture with the promise of more successful approaches to teaching all of our students.

Chapter 3

Culturally Mediated Instruction in Mathematics: Strengths and Barriers

Norma C. Presmeg
Florida State University

FOCUS QUESTIONS

1. What principles can be developed to guide the use of authentic cultural activities and experiences to facilitate students' construction of mathematical concepts?
2. How might a teacher use *ethnomathematics* in a culturally diverse classroom setting to benefit all learners?

INTRODUCTION

Of all subjects in the school curriculum, mathematics is the one that has been traditionally considered culture- and value-free. Bishop (1988) argues convincingly that this is not the case. This is made explicit in the following statement:

> *Educating* people mathematically consists of much more than just teaching them some mathematics. It is much more difficult to do, and the problems and issues are much more challenging. It requires a fundamental awareness of the *values* which underlie mathematics and a recognition of the complexity of educating children about those values. It is not enough merely to teach them mathematics, we need also to educate them *about* mathematics, to educate them *through* mathematics, and to educate them *with* mathematics.

Teaching children to do mathematics emphasizes knowledge as "a way of doing." A mathematical *education* seems to me, in contrast, to be essentially concerned with "a way of knowing". That then speaks to me of a cultural perspective on mathematical knowledge. (p. 3)

Bishop's perspective on what it means to view mathematics as "a way of knowing" has implications for the teaching and learning of all mathematics and especially for the mathematical education of diverse populations of students who are learning together in multicultural classrooms.

This chapter examines the relationship between culture/ethnicity and learning mathematics. The chapter is divided into two parts. First, I show the need for changed pedagogical practice that incorporates elements of cultural practice in the teaching and learning of mathematics at all levels by referring to case studies of African American mathematics education students at a large state university, as well as referring to relevant literature. In the second part, two "ethnomathematics" research projects are described, one in a graduate course for prospective and practicing mathematics teachers, the other in a mathematics classroom of a secondary school with a high proportion of minority students. From these two projects emerges a philosophy in which each student's ethnicity is considered a strong resource for a mathematics teacher because mathematical elements may be developed from concomitant cultural practices. However, barriers must be overcome before culturally mediated instruction can be used optimally in mathematics classrooms. One of the largest barriers is the implicit belief still entertained by many teachers and their students that mathematics is a sterile subject that has few, if any, links with culture and everyday practice. The chapter closes with suggestions for reconciling "rigorous academic mathematics" and "mathematics of cultural practice" to benefit students in learning school mathematics.

ELEMENTARY SCHOOL EXPERIENCES
WITH MATHEMATICS

The need for change in traditional beliefs about, and pedagogy of, mathematics education was highlighted in a research project that I carried out during the summer of 1991. The Center for the Study of Teaching and Learning on the campus where I work asked me to investigate possible reasons why some of our prospective African American mathematics teachers were having difficulty in the required university mathematics courses.

Each of the four students were interviewed four times. These interviews, semistructured for comparison, had durations between 20 and 55 minutes, and all were tape-recorded and transcribed. Jinny, Jane, and Dany were prospective elementary teachers, and Cord, the only male, was preparing to teach high school mathematics (students' names are fictitious). The passion with which these African American students spoke about their school and college experiences in learning mathematics was striking.

There were two overriding themes in the students' descriptions of their schooling. First, there was the influence of role models on their decisions to become teachers. Second, this decision was influenced by both positive and negative classroom incidents that the students either experienced or witnessed. Even those incidents that seemed trivial significantly impacted their lives.

Early Experiences With Inspiring/Caring Teachers

Cord was from a middle-class home, but the predominantly African American elementary school he attended (a 45-minute walk from his home) was in "a poor kind of neighborhood" in a large city. The junior high school he attended was "all Black," and at that time he decided he wanted to teach business education. However, in the predominantly Hispanic and European American senior high school he attended, there was a teacher, Mrs. M., of whom he said, "She is the one that really inspired me in mathematics." Along with detailing how she taught particular mathematical topics, he remembered, "She would always make it so much fun to learn." In his five senior high mathematics courses, Cord's grades were two As, one B, and two Cs. As a result of Mrs. M.'s teaching, he decided to become a mathematics teacher. Although she was European American, Mrs. M. was a role model for Cord.

In contrast, the other three prospective teachers all described African American mathematics teachers as role models at some point in their education. All of the influential teachers were described as caring, whereas the university mathematics professors with whom these students struggled were characterized as impersonal.

Long-Term Effects of Negative Experiences

With regard to their schooling, Cord and Dany both had negative experiences that left deep imprints:

Cord: "My elementary experience was very bad, and that's why I decided to become a teacher. I had some good teachers, and a lot of 'em were not! It was a negative thing that happened [in fifth grade] that inspired me to become a teacher. One of my friends had asked the teacher to explain the lesson because he did not understand where she was going or how she was explaining it. And she said, 'You know, I've explained it one time and I'm not going to explain it again, whether you all learn or not! You have to realize, I wanna get my paycheck! And . . . when she made that comment, I thought . . . from that day on I just . . . wanna be a teacher, I wanna be a *good* teacher!"

And from the interview with Dany:

Interviewer: "And how did you feel about the mathematics? In elementary school?"

Dany: "I don't remember much of it [laughing]. I mean, I must have done it somehow, but . . . I remember third grade really well, and that was because we had one boy that could never do it, and . . . he would stand [next] to the board and cry. And I would be so upset . . . I would start screaming the answers, and my teacher would [say], 'Dany, be quiet then!' He'd be [adding] 10 plus 7, and, I would [say] 'It's 17!' I would just say, 'It's 17,' and I always said that. And every time she would send him to the board I'd go 'Not again!' . . . If you didn't know, you didn't know! . . . You didn't have anyone to say, 'Well, let's take out some beans and count ten of 'em, and let's count seven more and let's put them . . .' you know, we had no one, you know."

Dany's passionate description is a prelude to the students' reports of their perceptions of the university mathematics courses.

PROBLEMS WITH COLLEGE MATHEMATICS

The students described nine courses including college preparatory algebra, college algebra, college geometry, trigonometry, and calculus. Cord's case is particularly serious. In elementary and secondary school he tested exceptional in mathematics. Yet he had difficulty successfully completing the university mathematics courses. He was repeating calculus for the third time, and would repeat college geometry as well.

Cord: "Well, right now, I'm just debating my major. I'm debating whether I want to teach any more or go to another field." [He was considering another service field, public administration.]

Interviewer: "Why? Because of the math?"

Cord: "Yeah! It's just because I still have to take linear algebra, and . . . statistics, and . . . Calculus 2. So . . . I [don't know] if I wanna go through that."

Interviewer: "All this heavy math in order to be a high school teacher."

Cord: "Exactly! That's where the problem comes in. I don't see the relevance for a lot of the math, but, . . . this department has been here for a long time, they're professionals, so apparently there's some relevancy to all this that I can't see because I'm not in the classroom. So that's how I think about it."

Methodology and Relevance

When questioned, Cord explained that he had taken content mathematics courses concurrently with mathematics education courses taught according to a constructivist paradigm. He found a large discrepancy in the teaching methods employed.

Cord: "We sat [in college geometry] for 2½ hours, no, 2 hours, listening to him lecture. It killed us! And when you take classes together, like college geometry and introduction to applications for mathematics teachers [a constructivist course], so it would be like, we came from [the constructivist] course, where we interacted and we just had fun, and we could apply our learning, and then we'd go to this course where we sat there for two hours and listen to this man lecture. And, . . . we had to go through that all the time we were in [the constructivist] class, and it was just terrible! It was just, [it] made me *miserable!*"

Cord could not see why the course, college geometry, was required, if the students were also required to take the education course, teaching algebra and geometry in the high school, which was another constructivist course. He said, "To me, that is two courses that are knocking each other."

Cord: "I didn't see any relevance for college geometry. And, with talking with people in the department, you know, math education students even, nobody could remember. I, when I was in the course I tried to get help, and the people that took it before couldn't remember what it was about. Because, you take it and you get a grade, and you just do it!"

Interviewer: "So it's for the sake of the grade?"

Cord: "Yeah! Just because it's required."

Jinny was another student who spoke eloquently and repeatedly about the irrelevance of higher mathematics courses, most of which she had found "boring." She was fully convinced that higher mathematics was an instrumental subject in which rote memorization was the predominant mode of learning. Students also reported the following additional constraints:

- fast pace of pure mathematics courses (Jinny, Dany, and especially Jane, for whom lack of time was often a problem);
- large classes, which made learning impersonal (Jane and Dany);
- quantity of content matter (Jinny and Dany);
- students' excessive workload (Jinny). (Excessive workload refers to the number of courses taken and the homework assignments given.)

Application and Recall

In the second interview, students were asked to select problems from university mathematics textbooks that they had used and to solve the selected problems. Jinny and Dany recognized the material in the books, but when they attempted to solve the selected problems they were unable to do so. The students learned mathematics in an instrumental rather than a relational way (Skemp, 1976); in a procedural way, without real understanding of the concepts (Hiebert, 1986) or of why certain procedures worked; and much of this procedural learning had been forgotten. What remained was the emotion that they associated with the course.

Cord spoke vehemently about the negative effects of a restrictive mathematics syllabus, particularly at the university level: "A lot of teachers in the math department just follow the syllabus. . . . I hate syllabuses with a passion! Because syllabuses confine you too much. And it limits what the class can do."

Cord's passion was typical of all the students' reactions in this study. Students learned mathematics instrumentally, and then forgot the procedures after the final examination. The negative feelings they associate with the course, whether it was successfully completed or not, remain long after the subject matter is forgotten. "God, I hated all of this stuff," said Jinny, as she paged through a college algebra textbook.

CULTURAL HERITAGE IN MATHEMATICS LEARNING

Not all of the aspects the students identified as problematic were specific to their African American cultural background. Some psychological issues were related to the students' perceptions of themselves as learners, which often appeared to be linked to teacher expectations. According to Berry and Asamen (1989), "A person in our society often validates his identity through the evaluations of significant others" (p. 126). However, commitment to their cultural heritage was a source of strength that enabled these students to persevere and ultimately succeed in their mathematics courses. Parham and Parham (1989) conclude that four factors are necessary for the development of positive self-concept in African American children: (a) maximum participation by parents and teachers, (b) mores and values of the home reinforced in the immediate community and school, (c) African American culture and lifestyles reflected in the educational curriculum, and (d) academic achievement being encouraged regardless of social class (p. 127).

SOCIAL CONTEXTS FOR MATHEMATICS LEARNING

There is an interplay of sociocultural and psychological processes as students learn to cope with the stresses of being African American on predominantly European American university campuses (Prillerman, Myers, & Smedley, 1989). In the "high-demand and often nonsuppportive environments" of predominantly European American universities, "noncognitive, personal and contextual factors such as positive self-concept, an understanding of racism, and the availability of supportive people at the university, were more predictive of Black student retention than academic ability" (p. 200). Prillerman et al. report that adjustment styles that combined a commitment to both personal and racial group objectives were most adaptive. This commitment to racial group objectives is called *race consciousness* by Hall and Allen (1989).

In the sense of mission expressed by all the students in this study, their race consciousness was apparent. Each wanted to make a difference in the lives of African American children. This sense of race consciousness was a tremendous source of strength in the adaptations and coping required of these students in dealing with the stresses of their campus lives.

ETHNOMATHEMATICS

Definitions of Ethnomathematics

According to Ascher (1991), *ethnomathematics* is "the study and presentation of the mathematical ideas of traditional peoples" (p. 188). She describes the goal of ethnomathematics as

> broadening the history of mathematics to one that has a multicultural, global perspective . . . This broadening of perspective to include other cultures has the associated effect of enlarging the history of mathematics from dealing

primarily with the Western professional class called mathematicians to involving all sorts of people. (p. 188)

My informal definition of *ethnomathematics* has been "the mathematics of cultural practice," a definition that includes mathematical ideas based on activities in all cultures, including one's own (and not specifically limited to those of "traditional people"). The compatibility of this definition with Ascher's (1991) is reflected in her writing: "As we seek these [mathematical] ideas across cultures, we recognize that even within our own culture, mathematical ideas exist in many different contexts" (p. 187). She continues, "All mathematical ideas, in traditional cultures or otherwise, need to be viewed in cultural context" (p. 191).

Theoretical Basis

How do we incorporate culture into the way mathematics is taught in public schools and colleges or universities? In the fall semester of 1993, I developed a graduate course for prospective and practicing teachers called mathematics education and culture. One goal of the course is to enable students to develop mathematical concepts from their own varied cultural backgrounds. This research by the students, and reflections on books by Ascher (1991), Hollins (1996), Nieto (1996), and Zaslavsky (1996), encourages the broadening of beliefs about the nature of mathematics and how it should be taught. Principles used successfully in this course include the following.

1. Each student is considered to have a unique cultural heritage; each student has ethnicity.
2. Ethnicity is a mathematical resource; mathematics may be developed from associated cultural practices.
3. Students can use their ethnicity in developing mathematical activities for sharing with peers.

The affirmation of diversity (Nieto, 1996), which is implicit in these principles, has the potential for pedagogical practice that is more equitable in mathematics classrooms at the elementary and secondary school levels. After initial doubts about their ability to develop mathematical ideas from activities associated with their own cultural heritage, students successfully constructed mathematics by analyzing the patterns and order in cultural activities unique to their own ethnic heritages and backgrounds.

In fall 1995 and spring 1996, I and two research assistants interviewed seven students of diverse ethnic backgrounds who were learning mathematics together in one class. The participants were African American ($n = 3$),

Asian ($n=2$), European American ($n=1$), and Hispanic ($n=1$). The students were questioned about their heritage, hobbies, hopes (career aspirations), histories, and homelands. One goal of the interviews was to identify cultural practices that might be suitable for constructing mathematical ideas. Each student was interviewed six times. Issues discussed included perceived cultural use of mathematics, the nature of mathematics, their parents' occupations (and whether mathematics was used in their parents' work), their achievement in and feelings toward school mathematics, and perceived links between mathematics and other subjects in the school curriculum.

Based on the interview data, traditional mathematics teaching does not facilitate a view of mathematics that encourages students to see potential for mathematics in their lives outside of the mathematics classroom. All but one of the subjects interviewed had an instrumental (Skemp, 1976) view of mathematics as a "bunch" of numbers, equations, and formulas used to solve (school) word problems. These beliefs persisted even after involvement in the project and participation in one ethnomathematics lesson, in which we attempted to facilitate construction of mathematical ideas from a musical activity. Only a single ethnomathematics lesson was attempted because the teacher felt pressured to complete the syllabus and expressed impatience that the activities had taken longer than intended. Successful introduction of ethnic and home activities into mathematics classrooms requires recognition of the value of such activities. Teachers and students must change their beliefs about the nature of mathematics.

Ethnomathematics Versus Academic Mathematics

Reconciling ethnomathematics and academic mathematics requires a rene-gotiation of the classroom norms to broaden the view of what is accepted as "mathematics." D'Ambrosio (who coined the term *ethnomathematics*) and Ascher (1994) considered mathematics to be more than problem solving; however most of the participants interviewed in my high school project considered problem solving using numbers and formulas to be the essence of mathematics. Mathematical ideas "have to do with number, logic, mid spatial configuration and, very important, the combination or organization of those into systems and structures" (Ascher & D'Ambrosio, 1994, p. 37). In this conception, mathematics is not in the activities of cultural practice, but these activities have the potential for mathematics to be constructed through symbolism and systematization. Viewing mathematics in this way opens the door to a reconciliation of ethnomathematics and academic mathematics. But this view of the nature of mathematics contrasts strikingly with the students' limited opinion of what mathematics is.

It is not that the activities described by these students were not rich in potential for the fulfillment of multicultural goals such as those described by Spring (1996):

1. building tolerance of other cultures,
2. eliminating racism,
3. teaching the content of different cultures, and
4. teaching students to view the world from differing cultural frames of reference. (p. 164)

These goals resonate with most of those suggested by Banks and Banks (1995), as well as Lomotey (1990), and in literature more specific to mathematics education (Mathematical Sciences Education Board, 1990). The potential for classroom activities that might facilitate such goals was evident in the interests the students described, which included collecting dolls and postcards from other countries, coin collecting, barrel racing or horseback riding (central Florida), playing various sports, farming, singing/listening to Gospel music, cabinet making, cheerleading, writing poetry, and camping.

The project, which seemed merely to scratch the surface of a much larger undertaking, suggests that ethnomathematics, taken broadly to encompass mathematical elements in everyday activities of students, has an important role to play in making mathematics more meaningful in the lives of students. At the same time, the research suggests that literature on changing beliefs of teachers and students is relevant to this endeavor. Prospects are high for the use of ethnomathematics in alleviating some of the negative feelings that low achievers have toward mathematics. A first step in this direction is the inclusion of ethnomathematics courses in preservice and in-service teacher education because changed beliefs must begin with the teachers.

FUTURE RESEARCH DIRECTIONS

Further research should focus on the following question: How does one create a set of tools (principles) that will allow the teacher to facilitate students' construction of mathematical concepts in the sharing of cultural activities that are authentic to at least one of their peers? A cultural activity that is authentic to a student would be described in class by that student; then small group work and whole class sharing would be used to develop mathematical concepts from the activity. Students learn mathematical principles and share culture simultaneously.

Classroom norms must be renegotiated in order to provide the required "project" environment for constructing mathematical ideas from cultural activities. In essence, students should develop curriculum. Although current trends suggest teachers play a greater role in the development of mathematics curricula, what is suggested in this chapter goes a step further to include teachers facilitating the development of curriculum by students. Starting with a student's cultural activity rather than with a piece of mathematical content may be uncomfortable for teachers who are unaccustomed to such an approach, which is why the approach would have to begin in teacher preparation or enhancement courses.

Many questions remain. For instance, should it be a case of "ethnomathematics on Fridays," while "academic mathematics" is taught on the other days? To what extent should current multicultural mathematics materials (Krause, 1983; Zaslavsky, 1996) be introduced by the teacher, perhaps as an example and starting point? The approach advocated in this chapter, although promising in this initial research, has not been tested in the classroom. However, the project has shown enough promise for me to believe that there is a possible didactic interface between ethnomathematics and academic mathematics, and that pursuing such an interface is of value in the search for equity and meaning.

SUGGESTED LEARNING EXPERIENCES

1. Discuss the promises and potential pitfalls of ethnomathematics. Propose ways to avoid the pitfalls and enhance learning for students from diverse ethnic and experiential backgrounds. Explain why there might be resistance to ethnomathematics even if it improves learning for certain groups of students? Is such resistence justifiable?

2. Research the cultural practices and values of a specific cultural or ethnic group. Develop or identify and describe an approach to mathematics that takes into consideration the cultural practices and values you have identified. How would you decide which cultural values and practices have the highest salience for facilitating mathematics learning?

REFERENCES

Ascher, M. (1991). *Ethnomathematics: A multicultural view of mathematical ideas.* New York: Chapman & Hall.

Ascher, M., & D'Ambrosio, U. (1994). Ethnomathematics: A dialogue. *For the Learning of Mathematics, 14*(2), 36–43.

Banks, J. A., & Banks, C. A. M. (1995). *Handbook of research on multicultural education.* New York: Macmillan.

Berry, G. L., & Asamen, J. K. (Eds.). (1989). *Black students: Psychosocial issues and academic achievement.* Newbury Park, CA: Sage.

Bishop, A. J. (1988). *Mathematical enculturation: A cultural perspective on mathematics education.* Dordrecht, The Netherlands: Kluwer Academic Publishers.

Hall, M. L., & Allen, W. R. (1989). Race consciousness among African American college students. In G. L. Berry & J. K. Asamen (Eds.), *Black students: Psychosocial issues and academic achievement* (pp. 172–197). Newbury Park, CA: Sage.

Hiebert, J. (Ed.). (1986). *Conceptual and procedural knowledge: The case of mathematics.* Hillsdale, NJ: Lawrence Erlbaum Associates.

Hollins, E. R. (1996). *Culture in school learning.* Mahwah, NJ: Lawrence Erlbaum Associates.

Krause, M. (1983). *Multicultural mathematics materials.* Reston, VA: National Council of Teachers of Mathematics.

Lomotey, K. (Ed.). (1990). *Going to school: The African American experience.* Albany: State University of New York Press.

Mathematical Sciences Education Board. (1990). *Making mathematics work for minorities: Framework for a national action plan, 1990–2000.* Washington, DC: National Research Council.

Nieto, S. (1996). *Affirming diversity: The sociopolitical context of multicultural education.* White Plains, NY: Longman.

Parham, W. D., & Parham, T. A. (1989). The community and academic achievement. In G. L. Berry & J. K. Asamen (Eds.), *Black students: Psychosocial issues and academic achievement* (pp. 120–137). Newbury Park, CA: Sage.

Prillerman, S. L., Myers, H. F., & Smedley, B. D. (1989). Stress, well-being and academic achievement in college. In G. L. Berry & J. K. Asamen (Eds.), *Black students: Psychosocial issues and academic achievement* (pp. 198–217). Newbury Park, CA: Sage.

Skemp, R. R. (1976). Relational understanding and instrumental understanding. *Mathematics Teaching, 77,* 26–29.

Spring, J. (1996). *American Education.* New York: McGraw-Hill.

Zaslavsky, C. (1996). *The multicultural mathematics classroom: Bringing in the world.* Portsmouth, NH: Heinemann.

Chapter 4

"People Like Us": African American Children Respond to Self-Affirming Texts

Fran Davis Perkins
University of Alabama

FOCUS QUESTIONS

1. This author and the children she taught shared a common cultural heritage, which allowed her to use her own experiences as a basis for understanding the children's needs. When a teacher and the children she teaches do not share a common cultural heritage, what approaches might be used to better understand the needs of the children?

2. How does this author's discussion of the significance of African American children's literature in literacy programs contribute to your understanding of the discrepancies in reading skills acquisition for African American children as a group and middle-class European American children as a group?

3. This author's research supports the significance of including literature that validates the life experiences of African American children in literacy programs. What criteria should be used to select the literature?

INTRODUCTION

As I reflect on my own early literacy experiences in a small urban school in the South, I sometimes wonder how I ever learned to love reading. I distinctly recall reading basal reader stories about families who were so unlike mine—income, race, ethnicity, family rituals, language, and even the names of the children were unfamiliar. I eventually began to feel sympathy for the children in the stories and wondered why they never had any real fun as my siblings and I did. I seldom saw the characters in the stories playing games such as four-square, hand-game rhymes, hopscotch, jump rope (double Dutch, of course), stick ball (made from old socks with a few rocks in the middle), hide-and-seek, Red-Head Devil, 1-2-3 red-light, and dodge ball. Ultimately, I resolved in my mind that some people were destined to lead boring lives and schoolchildren were fated to read about them. Therefore, I sat anxiously through the reading group awaiting the end of the day when I could get home to some real fun.

Unlike the language learning experiences in my school, my home was filled with extremely valuable literacy experiences that were crucial to the culture of my home and community. My siblings and I were afforded the opportunities to memorize and deliver speeches (or recitations) for church and community programs. My parents' major contributions to our literacy development existed in the form of telling stories about their childhoods and encouraging us to entertain each other with our own. Subsequently, this led to my siblings and me telling our own stories (exaggerated versions of our parents', initially) for enjoyment. There was nothing as entertaining as my older sisters' renditions of poems such as "In the Morning" by Paul Laurence Dunbar and "Dreams" by Langston Hughes.

Unfortunately, very few of these literacy events were valued in the language arts programs that were prominent in my elementary school years. Although these experiences were valuable to me and a crucial part of my culture, they were never viewed as real reading by the school, my family, or me. Therefore, when given an occasional choice to read in school, I didn't. I always perceived the act of reading in school as reading someone else's story with pictures that were only vaguely connected to the words.

It was nearly two decades later when I began to observe similar attitudes in children I taught, particularly the African American children. Many of them seemed so indifferent to reading as defined by traditional basal readers. Yet, their eyes would always seem to light up when I read an occasional book by John Steptoe or Eloise Greenfield (see also K. Hollins, chap. 1, this volume). They often moved closer to me during story time when I held up any books with illustrations of African Americans. Inevitably, someone might say, "Hey, I like that book. . . . It's got people like us in it!"

THE NEED TO VALIDATE STUDENTS' EXPERIENCES

The positive responses of these young African American children to culturally affirming literature are not surprising. Many educators and scholars (Bishop, 1990; Freire & Macedo, 1987; Harris, 1990; Larrick, 1965) have argued that all learners desire and deserve to have their lives validated in the literature they read. It is equally revealing that the same children responded with apathy toward their basal reader stories. Bishop (1990) contends that "when African American children cannot find themselves and people like them in the books they read and those read to them, they receive a powerful message about how they are undervalued in both school and society" (p. 561). Consequently, they are unlikely to have much interest in reading.

Faced with the formidable challenge of meeting the needs and interests of the students, educators must begin to engage in the process of reconsidering instructional practices that perpetuate educational inequities and lack of interest in learning. Such inequities exist in curricula that exclude the voices (i.e., history, culture, experiences) of the learners. There are many vehicles that would enable teachers to effectively validate the lives of learners. Nieto (1996) suggests, for example, that teacher attitudes and behavior can set the stage for affirming student diversity. Furthermore, collaboration among students, use of varied teaching and learning styles, and diverse curricula and materials can serve as other important sources for affirming the experiences of learners.

The focus of this chapter is the use of literature as one viable means for providing children with self-affirming experiences that support literacy development. Because reading remains a primary means by which children learn about the world around them, literature is a natural context for providing children with self-affirming experiences as well as insight into the lives of others. This chapter describes responses of third-grade African American children to books by and about African Americans as they engaged in literature discussions.

A THEORETICAL BASIS FOR VALIDATING STUDENTS' EXPERIENCES

The transactional view of reading, as proposed by Rosenblatt (1978), provides a strong basis for examining the relationship among literature, literacy, and culture. She maintains that "a reader is a reader by virtue of a particular kind of relationship with the text" (p. 15). There exists a reciprocal relationship between the reader and the text; thus both contribute to the construction of meaning by shaping and being shaped by each other. Crucial to that relationship are the past experiences that the reader brings to the text. This becomes especially significant when considering the possible number of literacy programs that do not take into account the cultural experiences that the reader brings to the text.

The need for self-affirmation in learning is discussed in the writings of Freire and Macedo (1987). They maintain that failure to take into account the cultural experiences of the students may lead some to defy "curriculum and other material conditions in schools that negate their histories, cultures, and day-to-day experiences" (p. 121). As noted earlier, I observed this behavior in some of my African American students who were just not interested in reading the traditional basal stories. Yet, they welcomed stories that were more affirming, for example, *Stevie and the Train Ride* by John Steptoe, and *She Come Bringing Me That Little Baby Girl* by Eloise Greenfield. Failure to personally connect with those basal stories may have been rooted in the fact that "one of the major influences on reading comprehension (and interest) is the knowledge that the reader already possesses about the topic and the form of the text being read" (Fielding, Wilson, & Anderson, 1984, p. 151). It all seemed so logical, then, that self-affirming literature could serve as a bridge between the reader's culture and his or her literacy development.

Ferdman (1990) addresses the relation between cultural identity and literacy. He argues that cultural diversity plays an important role in influencing the relationship between literacy and the individual. He points out that "not only will cultural identity mediate the acquisition and expression of literacy, but literacy will also influence and mold the individual's cultural identity" (p. 34). Ferdman further argues that what the child experiences as owned or not owned by his or her group (culture) is the issue in literacy education today. He explains that when a child perceives a text and its contents as reaffirming to his or her cultural identity, it is more likely that the child will become engaged and individual meaning will be constructed. This is not to suggest, however, that children of color should only read about themselves. On the contrary, Ferdman (1990) and others stress the importance of inclusion rather than the exclusion that has been the practice of the past.

Sims (1983) examines self-affirming literature as it relates to the reading interests of one young girl. She conducted an interview with a 10-year-old African American girl. The purpose of the interview was for the young girl to discuss her reactions and responses to books about African Americans. The fifth grader, who was described as precocious, verbal, and a very good reader, met at the home of the researcher and discussed her list of 30 books. Sims' analyses of the typescript of the interview reveals that the young reader affirmed a desire to see and read about people like herself. She especially preferred books about African American girls.

Sims (1983) raises several issues as a result of her interviews with the young reader. First, she maintains that children should not be denied access to books that could provide important self-affirmation and possibly increase reading interests. Second, in the case of African American children responding to books that are self-affirming, there may be a case of developmental stages of response. The participant, for example, expressed a preference for reading about other middle childhood females who are strong and know what they are doing. A third issue is the extent to which the unique characteristics of African American children's literature appeals to young African American readers. Sims' analyses of books by Black authors reveals that they tend to focus on "African American heritage and history; pride in one's blackness; a strong sense of community; warm relationships, especially within the family; a sense of continuity; and the will and strength to survive" (p. 27). Consequently, African American children's desire to read about people like themselves is most likely to be met by such books, usually written by African American authors. Finally, Sims found a limited amount of research focused on African American children's responses to reading stories about characters like or unlike themselves.

Smith (1995) describes research in a fifth-grade class in a large urban school where the responses of three African Americans to a variety of texts are examined. She found that each of the three fifth-grade African American students most frequently "self-selected literature that patterned their writing after experiences, events, and texts that culturally mirrored them" (p. 574), the African American texts. Her findings were consistent with the belief that learners desire to have their lives validated in the school curriculum, especially if relevant connections are made in classroom discussions and related learning experiences. Herein lay the challenge and motivation for the study that follows.

CONFIRMING THE EFFICACY OF VALIDATING STUDENTS' EXPERIENCES

Armed with multiple copies of African American books, notepads, pencils, self-stick notes, and permission to invade a summer school remedial reading program, I descended on 10 third-grade students—all of African descent. My goal was to identify and describe the response patterns of low-income, third-grade African American children as we interacted with self-affirming literature.

A primary factor in determining the site was the current movement in education to incorporate more culturally relevant experiences in inner-city classrooms as a means to improve literacy instruction for students from urban backgrounds (Bishop, 1990; Harris, 1990). The school system from which the research site was selected enrolled a population of 89% African Americans, most of whom were from low-income families.

The school in which the study took place marked the beginning of the school system's existence. The school had recently celebrated its 100th birthday and received a historic marker for this grand event. The school is located across the street from a large housing project from which most of the student population is drawn. Nonetheless, the community takes great pride in the care of the school as evidenced by the beautification awards received because of its attractive and well-maintained grounds. The age of the school became apparent only after entering the building. Excerpts from field notes held the following reflections from the first day's observations:

> The tall, dull-colored walls were in desperate need of paint. The school would have seemed uninviting except for the brightly colored bulletin boards, covered with end-of-year student work. This large three-story building is obviously old, but very appealing despite the two to three layers of paint that showed through areas where paint was peeling.
>
> The classroom teacher welcomed the idea of using African American literature with the children. Her reply to my request to share the literature was, "It's about time!" She was known by her colleagues for her warm, caring, and energetic interactions with the children. She was described by the principal as "one of the school system's best!"
>
> The principal had an extensive history of commitment to education, the welfare of children, and good working relationships with the community. "Just because you are inner-city doesn't mean you can't succeed. . . . A lot of these kids are raised by single parents. All they need is a little tender loving care," stated the principal (Staed, 1990). She visited classrooms daily to interact with the children and their teachers. This summer program was no exception. The principal often questioned students about the books they were reading, and sincerely inquired about their families.

Eight books were selected as the primary context for student response. With the exception of one text, all were written and illustrated by African American authors and artists. They included *The Patchwork Quilt* by Valerie Flournoy, *Grandpa's Face* by Eloise Greenfield, *Aunt Flossie's Hats (and Crab Cakes Later)* by Elizabeth Fitzgerald Howard, *When I Am Old With You* by Angela Johnson, *Mirandy* and *Brother Wind* by Patricia McKissack, *Tar Beach* by Faith Ringgold, *Daddy Is a Monster . . . Sometimes* by John Steptoe, and *Two and Too Much* by Mildred Pitts Walter.

Each of the books reflected a family theme: parent(s), child, sibling, and intergenerational relationships (in both historical and contemporary settings) and was written from an insider's perspective. This was a major criterion when considering the issue of personal perspective in writing about any aspect of a given culture. This is not to suggest that only African Americans can write books in which students of the same culture can make connections that are personally and culturally affirming. Some researchers (Anderson, 1981; Sims, 1982; Taxel, 1986; Trousdale, 1990) have shown through content analyses of African American literature that numerous fallacies and distortions were present in the stories written by non-African Americans. They concluded that when books about African Americans are written by people outside the culture, there is an increased likelihood of problems associated with detailing authentic experiences.

Students were given a book, a pad of self-stick notes, pencils, and a writing pad. They were then encouraged to take the books home to read and prepare for discussions on the following school day by using the self-stick notes to mark favorite scenes, passages, or events that they wanted to share. The self-stick notes were also used to write down any interesting or difficult words that the reader wished to share or have clarified. Alternatively, the notepads could be used for reflections or any comments the students wished to discuss. My goal was to help students plan for the discussions because it had been explained to them that I would primarily observe and occasionally take the responsibility for leading some discussions and sharing my personal connections in the same way as the students. In literature discussion groups, the teacher works alongside the students, negotiating meaning and taking into account the students' perspectives. This is consistent with the research of Hepler (1982), Peterson and Eeds (1990), and Short (1986). They view literacy in terms of communities of learners in which children and teachers talk in groups to work through meanings that might not otherwise be articulated.

Self-Affirmation: ". . . Reminds Me of Me"

An analysis of students' audiotaped discussions revealed numerous personal connections, as well as requests to read "more books like these." Consistent with Rosenblatt's (1978) view of aesthetic reading, these students paid "attention to the associations, feelings, attitudes, and ideas . . . that [were] arouse[d] within [them]" (p. 25).

Personal connections made by the students were categorized into three main subthemes—personal experiences, personal feelings, and personal fulfillment. A discussion with brief examples of each type of personal response follows. Initials will replace individual names in order to preserve anonymity.

Relating Personal Experiences: "One Time When I Was. . . ." During each of the discussion groups, students made various connections with individual and family experiences. One student felt a personal connection with the slightly mischievous character Gina in *Two and Too Much* by Mildred Pitts Walter. The teacher, Ms. P., made the following observations:

> This reminds me of me when I was little. One time, when I was two, my mama went to buy a cake for somebody's birthday [someone who worked

with her]. It was a big teddy bear cake. I kept sneaking icing off [the cake].
When my mama got to work she called and said, "B.W., I'm ashamed of
you!" All the icing was gone and she was embarrassed [because she didn't
find out until they opened the box at her office].

Other personal connections were made about specific experiences with
special family members. A scene from *When I Am Old With You* by Angela
Johnson, resulted in the following discussion:

A.B.:   I'm still laughing about when they didn't catch no fish, because
        when you go fishing, you go to catch fish.
L.P.:   They just gonna hang together and talk.
A.B.:   Me and my daddy do that. Yeah . . .

For several students, *Aunt Flossie's Hats (and Crab Cakes Later)* aroused
memories of special family stories and experiences. When students were
encouraged to elaborate on the connections they were making, one sat
back smiling and responded with the following:

T.P.:   It made me feel good inside.
Teacher: Tell us more.
T.P.:   It made me feel good how she [Aunt Flossie] told the stories
          and how the story was about way back then. My mama tells
          me stories from way back then, and my grandmama.
Teacher: What kinds of stories do they tell?
T.P.:   She [my grandmama] said one time she never had no daddy
          because her daddy . . . died before she came into the world.
          And she told me all about that.

As the discussion continued, other students commented.

K.L.:   My grandmama had lots of hats.
S.T.:   My grandmama wear[s] hats to church and stuff.
Teacher: I remember my mama wearing hats to church, too.
T.P.:   My mama [has] hats everywhere—in the closet, in my room.
          But, we can't wear [them].

Eventually, the students decided to get a family member to share a story
about when they were young. The stories became a focus for discussions
as well as a way of involving parents and other family members in their
learning process.

Family Involvement and Personal Feelings. The books were shared with family members who were able to relate to the students' feelings about these culturally affirming texts and to give some insights into their own reading preferences. The students were uninhibited in sharing their personal feelings and those of family members, as the following excerpts will show.

A.B.:   Can I have one [book]? How much [will you] sell it for?

Teacher: Ill try to get a book for everyone.

B.W.:   I want *When I Am Old With You.*

L.P.:   I want *Tar Beach.*

B.W.:   My mama . . . even my grandmama liked . . . [Another student jumps in before he can finish.]

A.B.:   They really liked these books!

Teacher: What about the books you've carried home before?

S.T.:   I didn't have any like these.

A.B.:   Even my uncle liked this (pointing to *Aunt Flossie's Hats*) [be]cause he got all kinds of hats and Aunt Flossie do, too.

Teacher: Are these books like any you've carried home before?

ALL: NO!

B.W.:   The others are boring books . . . She [the teacher] give us books like *George Curious.*

A.B.:   *Curious George,* man!

B.W.:   Well, whatever it is, it's boring!

D.W.:   [Those] old boring books at school!

K.L.:   The ones we have at school be boring, too.

N.W.:   And easy, too.

Teacher: You mean that you like these books because the words are harder?

[The two girls nod their heads.]

D.W.:   You can get interested in these books instead of like when you go to the library and read a book . . . by yourself, and not discuss [it].

As indicated in this dialogue, some students responded just as favorably to the context in which the texts were used, discussion groups. When discussing their previous reading experiences in school, the students described very traditional "round-robin" reading that consisted of a read–question–answer routine.

In addition to sharing personal feelings about the books, students often shared feelings that their parents had disclosed to them. In the next example, students share some unsolicited responses about their parents' interactions with the culturally affirming texts.

B.W.:   She [his mother] really liked me bringing these books home.

A.B.:   She like[s] Black authors. She like[s] [them] for the authors and the characters. That's what she said.

B.W.:   My mama like[s] [them because] they [are] Black, too. She tell[s] me to tell her . . . all the characters' names.

Similar, but unexpected, outcomes were observed in the school's maintenance staff. On several occasions, I returned to the school and found staff members discussing the books. One woman immediately began to apologize for bothering the books. She explained that she only wanted to read them and tell her grandchild about them. Obviously, I was pleased and encouraged her to take the books home to enjoy with the child.

In another discussion, other students shared the following about an experience with several family members who became involved with one of the books:

S.T.:   We did a play!

Teacher: Who did a play?

S.T.:   Me and my mama. My mama got a part, my sister got a part, and I got a part. Then we acted [the story] out.

T.P.:   I read the story and told my mama what I liked about the story.

N.W.:   I read it with my Auntie.

T.P.:   My mama liked it.

D.W.:   My daddy said he wish[es] he had this book [when he was a child]. He liked *When I Am Old With You* the best. My mama liked this one [*Two and Too Much*] and *Daddy Is a Monster*

N.W.:   My mama liked all of them.

This excerpt serves as another example of family involvement in the literacy development of African American children. It has been assumed, far too often, that children from poor, urban backgrounds have little or no parental involvement in their education. These 10 students shared numerous examples of involving parents in their reading. In fact, two of the parents stopped by the classroom to express gratitude for these "wonderful books about Black people."

Finding Personal Fulfillment: "I'd Rather Be Reading. . . ." A further look into the students' responses revealed that they often found reading these African American texts to be a source of personal fulfillment. This theme emerged as response patterns showed that students were choosing to read these books over doing other recreational activities.

A.B.:   I'm glad you did bring these books. They (are) the only thing that can keep me off my Nintendo—reading these books.

Teacher: Keep you off your Nintendo?

A.B.:   Yeah, give it a rest so it won't blow up.

Teacher: Well, did you take breaks with other books?

A.B.:   No. I like [these books].

T.P.:   I like [them] [be]cause of the Black authors, too. And the people who wrote them did a good job of writing. . . . I just don't play with my Nintendo hardly, either. I just read these books.

A final excerpt under the theme of personal fulfillment most effectively revealed how one student felt about becoming involved with these culturally affirming books. He reflected on his previous reading experiences in school.

B.W.:   I got a question! Why [didn't] I . . . like to read and I still make straight Bs in reading?

Teacher: I'm not sure. Sometimes, I guess we do what we have to do.

B.W.:   No! You don't get it. I just like these books. If I was reading these books at my school, [I'd] make straight As!

CONCLUSION

Although the responses shared by this group of students cannot be generalized to an entire population of students, they suggest a framework for reexamining existing literacy programs that fail to acknowledge the existence of African American children, and other children of color. When literacy programs are determined and controlled by prepackaged materials, there is little opportunity for choice of texts, natural extensions of learning, or strategies for discussing and responding to texts. The structure of such programs discourages readers from taking risks because there are generally predetermined questions and answers. Even though some of the basal reading programs have increased in selections of diverse literature, the process of comprehension is still most often reduced to learning isolated skills that limit personal and literary connections. The collaborative process involved in literature discussions provides readers with opportunities to justify their interpretations, rather than try to devise a "correct" answer for the teacher. Children need time to read and collaborate with other readers in their literary transactions. The environment created by the teacher must encourage open discussions about diverse literature in which students are encouraged to take risks and make mistakes by voicing their opinions and having them challenged.

The responses of these students are not surprising. What reader wouldn't be drawn to a text that affirms personal experiences? It has been assumed for too long that many African American children from low-income backgrounds lack the literate experiences needed for success in school. Perhaps, as Dewey (1938) suggested, literacy problems occur when the school fails to connect with the children's personal experiences.

SUGGESTED LEARNING EXPERIENCES

1. Explain how a teacher might use self-affirming texts in a culturally diverse classroom setting.
2. Develop a categorized resource list of self-affirming texts for children from different cultural and experiential backgrounds.

REFERENCES

Anderson, O. S. (1981). Fiction for the young black reader: A critique of selected books. *Journal of Negro Education, 50*(1), 75–82.

Bishop, R. S. (1990). Walk tall in the world: African American literature for today's children. *Journal of Negro Education, 59*(4), 556–565.

Dewey, J. (1938). *Experience and education.* New York: Macmillan.

Ferdman, B. M. (1990). Literacy and cultural identity. *Harvard Educational Review, 60*(2), 17–40.

Fielding, L. G., Wilson, P. T., & Anderson, R. C. (1984). A new focus on free reading: The role of tradebooks in reading instruction. In T. Raphael (Ed.), *The contexts of school-based literacy* (pp. 149–160). New York: Random House.

Freire, P., & Macedo, D. (1987). *Literacy: Reading the world and the word.* New York: Bergin & Garvey.

Harris, V. J. (1990). African American children's literature: The first one hundred years. *Journal of Negro Education, 59*(4), 540–555.

Hepler, S. I. (1982). *Patterns of response to literature: A one-year study of a fifth and sixth grade classroom.* Unpublished doctoral dissertation, The Ohio State University, Columbus, Ohio.

Larrick, N. (1965, September). The all-white world of children's books. *Saturday Review,* pp. 63–65, 84–85.

Nieto, S. (1996). *Affirming diversity: The sociopolitical context of multicultural education.* New York: Longman.

Peterson, R., & Eeds, M. (1990). *Grand conversations: Literature groups in action.* New York: Scholastic.

Rosenblatt, L. (1978). *The reader, the text, the poem: The transactional theory of the literary work.* Carbondale: Southern Illinois University Press.

Short, K. G. (1986). *Literacy as collaborative experience: The role of critical thinking and intertextuality in learning.* Unpublished doctoral dissertation, Goshen College, Goshen, Indiana.

Sims, R. (1982). *Shadow and substance: Contemporary Afro-American children's fiction.* Urbana, IL: National Council of Teachers of English.

Sims, R. (1983). Strong black girls: A ten-year-old responds to fiction about Afro-Americans. *Journal of Research and Development in Education, 16*(3), 21–28.

Smith, E. S. (1995). Anchored in our literature: Students responding to African American literature. *Language Arts, 72*(8), 571–574.

Staed, J. (1990, October 15). Principle's miracle. *The Birmingham News.*

Taxel, J. (1986). The black experience in children's fiction: Controversies surrounding award winning books. *Curriculum Inquiry, 16*(3), 245–281.

Trousdale, A. M. (1990). A submission theology for black Americans: Religion and social action in prize-winning children's books about the black experience in America. *Research in the Teaching of English, 24*(2), 117–140.

Chapter 5

Productive Science Teaching for Inner-City African American Students

Keith McElroy
University of Wisconsin, Milwaukee

Etta R. Hollins
Wright State University, Dayton

FOCUS QUESTIONS

1. Are there specific approaches and teacher behaviors that can be employed in science teaching that might better facilitate learning for students with particular cultural and experiential backgrounds?
2. How can a teacher identify those aspects of students' cultural and experiential backgrounds that can be employed to facilitate teaching and learning in science classrooms?

INTRODUCTION

This chapter examines the attributes of productive science teaching for inner-city African American youngsters at the middle school level. This discussion includes a selective review of the scholarly literature addressing trends in research and perspectives that have influenced school practices for African American youngsters, a vignette from a particular instance of productive science teaching, and an analysis of the vignette. The literature in this review includes that related to school failure, characteristics of effective teachers, and research findings related to specific school practices. The vignette is selected from the experiences of the first author in teaching inner-city African American middle school youngsters.

RELATED LITERATURE

Explanations for School Failure

There are four broad categories of explanations for school failure among ethnic minority youngsters: genetic inferiority, cultural deficit, cultural mismatch, and contextual interaction.

Genetic Inferiority. The proponents of the genetic inferiority perspective contend that some races are innately inferior to others and hold little hope for changing the intellectual capacity or academic performance levels for "so-called" inferior races (Jensen, 1969; Loehlin, Lindzey, & Spuhler, 1975). The application of this perspective leads to tracking students from the same race into homogeneous groups with similar academic performance levels. Racial groups tracked in this way usually remain at the lower levels of academic performance and have few opportunities for advancement.

Cultural Deficit. The proponents of the cultural deficit perspective believe the values and practices children from some ethnic groups learn at home are deficient. These deficiencies may be inherent in the culture itself or a response to prejudice and racism within the larger society. African Americans are frequently singled out as an example of those who are culturally deficient. Proponents of this perspective have blamed the family structure (Liebow, 1966; Rainwater, 1965) and linguistic factors (Bereiter & Engelman, 1966) for the difficulties African American youngsters experience in school. Proponents of the cultural deficit perspective believe that ethnic minority youngsters' academic performance can be improved by changing the home environment or by providing adequate remediation. Headstart is an example of an approach intended to remedy the consequences of cultural deficit. The purpose of Headstart is to provide young children from low-income families, predominantly ethnic minorities, with opportunities to "catch up" with their middle-class, European American counterparts. The program is designed to help these culturally deprived youngsters learn how to learn using the European American strategies employed in public schools.

Cultural Mismatch. Proponents of the cultural mismatch perspective contend that the discrepancy between the culture of school practices and the home culture of ethnic minority students is at fault (Gilmore, 1985; Hollins, 1982; Michaels, 1981). An explanation for differences in academic performance across and within ethnic groups has been explained in different ways. For example, Ogbu (1983) argues that how youngsters from particular ethnic groups perform in school is related to their status in the larger society. He contends that those he describes as "involuntary minorities" whose history is related to being colonized on their own land or abducted and brought to this country perform the poorest. This is because of a special type of oppression that limits their self-perception to this particular geographic location. Examples of involuntary minorities include Native Americans, Mexican Americans, and African Americans. Immigrant minorities do not suffer from this type of oppression and have an external view of themselves that permits the development of a positive self-perception that supports better academic performance.

The proponents of the cultural mismatch perspective believe that ethnic minority youngsters' academic performance can be improved by incorporating critical aspects of the home-culture in school practices. For example, Au and Kawakami (1985) describe the use of "talk story," a unique communicative practice found among Native Hawaiians, to enhance reading instruction for Native Hawaiian children in elementary school. In this communicative practice the listener shows attentiveness and understanding by talking along with the speaker.

Contextual Interaction. Proponents of the contextual interaction perspective believe that the interaction of multiple factors influence ethnic minority youngsters' academic performance. These factors include the social context (the family and community) and the school context. Factors within the school that influence the youngsters' academic performance include curriculum design, instructional methodology, and materials and resources. Also, there are factors of educator preparation such as knowledge and beliefs about schooling and about the youngsters served that influence the quality of instruction provided. Student characteristics such as academic skills and knowledge, language proficiency, self-concept, life goals, motivation, and sociocultural attributes, when not appropriately addressed, may have a negative effect on academic performance (Cortes, 1986). The proponents of the contextual interaction perspective believe that academic performance can be improved through the manipulation of one or more of the multiple factors involved. There are few, if any, authenticated examples of an approach to manipulating multiple factors to enhance academic performance such as that advocated by the proponents of the contextual interaction perspective.

Characteristics of Effective Teachers

Foster (1994) reviews the research literature on African American teachers who are effective with African American students. She describes the attributes of these teachers to include the use of kinship terms or metaphors to describe their relationships with students; reliance on cultural and social underpinnings of the Black community; cultural solidarity and connectedness; warmth in personal interactions that integrates acceptance and involvement, firm control, and psychological autonomy with high expectations for effort and achievement; linking classroom content with the students' personal experiences; the use of familiar cultural patterns; and the incorporation of culturally familiar communication patterns. These effective African American teachers have strong attachments to the African American community and consider themselves to be part of it. Foster contends that cultural solidarity and connectedness support shared meanings and shared values that result in commonly held goals and mutual respect. She further points out that the relationship between these teachers and their students reflect other relationships found between adults and children in the African American community.

The use of a culturally congruent participation structure is not limited to teachers who share the cultural background of their students. Dillon (1989) reports an ethnographic study that examines the specific behaviors of a White male teacher who is effective with low-income African American students in a rural secondary, low-track English-reading class. The author states that

> results from the interpretation of the data revealed that the teacher's effectiveness was defined by his ability to do the following: (a) create a culturally congruent social organization in his classroom that accounted for the cultural backgrounds of his students, and (b) vary his teaching style to allow him to effectively communicate with his students during lesson interactions resulting in increased opportunities for student learning and improved student attitudes toward learning and school in general. (p. 227)

This study clearly points to teaching behaviors that have a positive impact on academic performance without changing the social class or ethnic orientation of the learners. These teaching behaviors can be understood and performed by others.

Specific School Practices

The Culture of Instruction. Sarah Michaels (1981) reports on a study in which the culture of instruction interfered with African American children's access to learning. In this particular study the children were engaged in "sharing time" where each gave an account of an experience or event. The teacher expected the children to use a topic-centered style for story telling, although this was not clearly stated. The African American children used a "topic-associating" style. The teacher expected a lexically explicit and thematically connected narrative, rather than a series of temporally contiguous events. The teacher did not recognize the structure used by the African American children in their narratives and was unable to support them in acquiring the topic-centered style. Her constant interruptions, which were intended to restructure the children's narratives, confused and frustrated them. Michaels interprets the sharing time as "a kind of oral preparation for literacy." Based on this interpretation, it is unlikely that the teacher would be able to support the African American children in acquiring important prerequisite skills for literacy development.

African American children with experiences like those in Michaels' study may be at risk for placement in low-ability groups resulting in an accumulative deficit in acquiring literacy and other basic skills at subsequent grade levels. Children placed in low-ability groups, especially those for whom such placements result from teachers not understanding their linguistic styles and learning preferences, may lose confidence in their ability to do school work. Although they may be unable to overcome the barriers of inappropriate pedagogical practices, many of these children may realize that they are not inept and resist such labels and placements. This resistance may be overt, such as defiant and disruptive behavior, passive, such as refusing any attempt at school work, or self-validating, such as labeling academic success and other group behaviors as "acting White." These behaviors may be described as intuitive and common psychological defenses used to protect feelings of self-worth in situations of repeated failure over which the individual has very limited control or influence.

Demands for Social Conformity.   Even in situations where African American youngsters are able to overcome the barriers of pedagogical practices such as that described in the Michaels study, school personnel may limit access to learning by requiring even further conformity in social interactions and behaviors. For example, Perry Gilmore (1985) reports on an elementary school setting in which African American students are denied full access to literacy based on teachers' assessments of their "attitude," which refers to their conformity to the prevailing ethos of the school. African American children are admitted to the special academic programs and higher track classes only if they display the "right attitude." Those who displayed the required competencies but lacked the right attitude were denied admission, whereas their less competent peers who displayed the right attitude were admitted. The behaviors most often rejected by the teachers because they are associated with displaying a bad attitude are considered a regular part of the African American communicative repertoire and style (i.e., stylized sulking interpreted by teachers as rebellion). The children's chorally chanted rhymes accompanied by handclaps and "steps" were likewise considered inappropriate and were also banned from the school, although they are obviously an accepted part of African American children's culture.

"Ability" and Prerequisite Learning.   Robert Moses and his colleagues (Moses, Kamii, Swap, & Howard, 1989) found that African American students did not have equal access to high-level mathematics based on teachers' perception of ability and prerequisite skills and the children's lack of self-confidence. The children had internalized messages from the school

environment and the media indicating that they were unable to perform academically. Moses and his colleagues were able to increase access to higher level mathematics and the students' academic performance by changing the relationship between the school and the community, the culture of the school, and methods of instruction.

Alternative Approaches to Schooling. An alternative approach to schooling that has proven effective for African American students is that employed in Chicago's Westside Preparatory School, founded by Marva Collins. Cultural congruence in instruction has been described as one factor contributing to the school's success with urban African American youngsters who were failing in public schools (Hollins, 1982). Cultural congruence is the process of incorporating values and practices from the learner's home-culture into instruction.

According to Hollins (1982), in the Westside Preparatory School, Marva Collins incorporates aspects of African American communicative behaviors. For example, she teaches the concept of analogies using examples from the students' language, and explains how the concept can be applied to school learning. She uses the audience participatory structure employed in many church meetings and other large gatherings of African American people. Making connections between communicative behaviors familiar to the learner and the learning process appears to enable the youngsters to use what they bring to school to increase the effectiveness of instruction.

THE NEED FOR FURTHER STUDY

There is a need for inquiry that reveals salient attributes of productive teaching in specific content areas for African American youngsters at the middle school level. Such inquiry has the potential for revealing the relations between productive instructional strategies for African American youngsters employed in different situations and further clarifying the relationship between cultural practices and values and classroom instruction. Although the scholarly literature reviewed in this chapter reveals important insights about productive instruction for African American youngsters, it does not include vignettes from productive science teaching for middle school youngsters. Short vignettes such as the one presented in this chapter provide opportunities to establish clarity of meaning and interpretation.

THE REFLECTIVE PRACTITIONER

Reflective practice involves ongoing critical examination of approaches to instruction, learners' responses to instruction, and social relationships within the classroom. The focus of this investigation was to better understand how to engage inner-city African American youngsters in meaningful and productive learning of science content and to determine the value of a specific approach to instruction—the use of discrepant events. This was an attempt to apply what Richardson (1994) refers to as "practical inquiry" directed primarily at understanding and improving one's own practice, as opposed to "formal research" aimed at contributing to a knowledge base.

PRODUCTIVE SCIENCE TEACHING: A REFLECTIVE VIGNETTE

The setting for this inquiry was an inner-city middle school where the enrollment was predominantly African American. This school served as a professional development school for Michigan State University. At the time, the investigator, Keith McElroy, was a graduate student in a doctoral program. In preparation for this study a series of inquiry lessons specifically for use in an inner-city middle school science classroom were developed. The teachers in the professional development school viewed the investigator as a member of the faculty at the university because of his work with preservice and in-service teachers. This study provided an opportunity for public school teachers to observe a "university professor" engage in the practice of teaching children. This was a high-risk opportunity. If successful, the lessons could serve as models of productive practice and a validation of some of the content presented in university courses in teacher preparation programs. If unsuccessful, the lessons could serve to reinforce stereotypes of university professors as more knowledgeable about theory than about professional practice. In this vignette the investigator presented a lesson titled "The Inverted Cup of Water" (see Fig. 5.1), which is a discrepant event.

Materials:
1. A transparent plastic cup.
2. A plastic card (slightly larger than the mouth of the cup).

Procedure:
1. Fill the cup half full of water.
2. Place the plastic card on the cup.
3. Put one hand on top of the card and invert the cup while holding the card in place (do this over a sink or large container to catch any water drippings).
4. Slowly remove the hand holding the card in place.

FIG. 5.1. The inverted cup of water.

The students gathered around a long narrow table. The investigator held a transparent plastic cup in one hand and a plastic card in the other. "[This] is a plastic cup. [This] is a plastic card. I'm going to . . . fill the cup [halfway] with water and place the card on top of the cup. Watch what happens when I invert the cup and slowly remove my hand." The students watched attentively. "Why doesn't the water spill out?" the investigator asked, attempting to guide the students toward an intuitive understanding of how the concept of air exerting pressure explains what kept the water in the inverted cup. "I know why! I know why!" One student, Sara Lee, spoke with excitement and pride as she shared her ideas about this puzzling phenomenon. "The water doesn't spill out because gravity is holding the water in the cup." When Sara Lee finally finished her explanation, the investigator smiled and looked into her eyes. Sara Lee sat in the front of the classroom, upright and proud. Even though Sara Lee's explanation was not scientifically correct, she was engaged in scientific inquiry and actually practicing the science processes of observation, interpretation of data, and inference. Not knowing quite what to say, the investigator slowly lifted his gaze toward the 33 pairs of eyes that were in varying states of alertness and aimed in his direction. They were silent and expectant. "Okaaaaay, Sara Lee," the instructor acknowledged hesitantly. "Who else has an explanation?" Immediately, four or five students shouted their explanations about why the water did not spill out of the inverted cup. "Wait, wait," the investigator said. "I want to hear what others have to say."

The other explanations were not scientifically correct either, but collectively, the investigator sensed something interesting was close at hand. The students were trying to make sense of this phenomenon. Prior to this lesson, the investigator contemplated why students' explanations for natural phenomena were usually not scientifically correct. The students' confused accounts presented a marvelous opportunity to understand this issue more fully and perhaps to inform future instruction.

"Sara Lee, would you like to give it another try?" the instructor asked. Another opportunity to respond could enable her to make better sense of her observations, and give the instructor time to ask more specific questions. The investigator was careful not to obscure her ideas by reinterpreting her explanation. In order for students to understand how the world worked, they had to grapple with their own ideas. Sara Lee sighed quietly, and the instructor reassured her that although this was difficult, she should try her best. Sara Lee glanced back at the rest of the class. Other students continued to try and offer their own accounts about why the water didn't spill out of the inverted cup. Jimmy, in the back, pounded out a rhythm on the desktop with his palms and knuckles. The investigator continued posing questions to Sara Lee. The class maintained a high level of interest; this opportunity to build understanding of this phenomenon might never be better. The students had barely scratched the surface but were making interesting progress.

"Sara Lee," the investigator asked, "have your ideas changed now that you have heard others' ideas about why the water didn't spill out of the inverted cup?" The investigator moved toward the center of the classroom with his right hand raised. With his left hand, he put his finger to his lips. These simultaneous nonverbal signals requested that the other students listen to what Sara Lee had to say, because she might say something important. Sara Lee sighed again, this time in loud exasperation. "I already told you!" Still excited, the investigator tried to think of another way to carefully move the class along. Standing in the center of the room with his right hand raised and his eyes comforting the students, he challenged the students to try the discrepant event themselves. Soft jazz music facilitated their engagement. As the students engaged in the activity, the investigator walked around the room from group to group and encouraged the students to keep thinking. Proudly, the investigator gazed around the room at the groups of delightful young men and women intently trying to explain the phenomenon. Finally, Sara Lee made an important discovery. An expression of delight filled her face. She filled the cup halfway with water and placed the card on top of the cup. She then placed one hand on top of the card and turned it sideways. The water did not spill out. Sara Lee stood and said excitedly, "Hey look! Whatever is holding the water in the cup, does it in all directions." Her discovery appeared to propel the group along. Eagerly they tried to explain the occurrence to the other members of their group.

The students did not determine that air pressure was holding the water in the cup. However, they were talented problem-solvers, making observations, interpreting data, and making inferences.

MAKING INFERENCES FROM THE VIGNETTE

How youngsters go about learning is significantly influenced by socialization within the home-culture. In their own culture youngsters learn what to attend to and what to ignore in understanding and making sense of the world around them. In essence, culture can be defined as cognition. Establishing this understanding of culture clarifies the need for making meaningful linkages between what youngsters already know or learn outside of school and what they are expected to learn in science classrooms.

The lesson in the vignette had several important features: (a) the materials used were familiar to the students, (b) the phenomenon presented appeared contradictory to what was expected, thus actively engaging students in the inquiry process, and (c) the students were invited to actively engage in examining the phenomenon. These features allowed the students to apply and practice the scientific approach to inquiry without direct instruction in what it is and how it works. These features seem important in teaching science to any group of middle school students. However, closer examination reveals a social context created by the teacher that is nontraditional and consistent with aspects of existing research.

For example, the teacher's performance in our vignette reveals behaviors consistent with Foster's (1994) description of characteristics of effective African American teachers working with youngsters from their own culture. The teacher in our vignette establishes a very personal relationship with the students that is supportive, positive, encouraging, and that allows the students the psychological autonomy to express their own thoughts and engage in scientific inquiry without experiencing a negative evaluation from the teacher. The teacher's behavior is challenging and engaging, encouraging youngsters to collaborate and build on each others' ideas, rather than competing to see who can get the answer first.

The teacher's behavior in the vignette is also consistent with that reported by Dillon (1989). The teacher in our vignette did not force the students to conform to a predetermined format, such as turn-taking, for their interaction. Instead, he encouraged the students to listen to each other to determine whether reasonable answers were proposed. This teacher's playfulness as he moved about the room helped to maintain a relaxed, yet focused, approach to learning in the classroom.

SUGGESTED LEARNING EXPERIENCES

1. After reading the vignette these authors present, what inferences can you make about productive approaches to instruction in this particular context? What additional information would help you in planning instruction for the students in this classroom?

2. Given the fact that teachers from different cultural and ethnic groups receive the same preservice teacher preparation, explain the extent to which similarities in cultural and experiential backgrounds between the teacher and the students in the vignette can be expected to influence practices and outcomes in the classroom.

REFERENCES

Au, K. H., & Kawakami, A. J. (1985). Research currents: Talk story and learning to read. *Language Arts, 62*(4), 406–411.

Bereiter, C., & Englemann, S. (1966). *Teaching disadvantaged children in the pre-school.* Englewood Cliffs, NJ: Prentice-Hall.

Cortes, C. E. (1986). The education of language minority students: A contextual interaction model. In *Beyond language: Social and cultural factors in schooling language minority students* (pp. 3–34). Sacramento: Bilingual Education Office, California State Department of Education.

Dillon, D. R. (1989). Showing them that I want them to learn and that I care about who they are: A microethnography of social organization of a secondary low-track English-reading classroom. *American Educational Research Journal, 26*(2), 227–259.

Foster, M. (1994). Effective Black teachers: A literature review. In E. R. Hollins, J. E. King, & W. C. Hayman (Eds.), *Teaching diverse populations.* Albany: State University of New York Press.

Gilmore, P. (1985). "Gimme room": School resistance, attitude, and access to literacy. *Journal of Education, 167*(1), 111–128.

Hollins, E. R. (1982). The Marva Collins story revisited. *Journal of Teacher Education, 32*(1), 37–40.

Jensen, A. R. (1969). How much can we boost IQ and scholastic achievement? *Harvard Educational Review, 39*, 1–12.

Liebow, E. (1966). *Tally's corner.* Boston: Little Brown.

Loehlin, J. C., Lindzey, G., & Spuhler, J. N. (1975). *Race differences in intelligence.* San Francisco: Freeman.

Michaels, S. (1981). "Sharing time": Children's narrative styles and differential access to literacy. *Language in Society, 10*, 423–443.

Moses, R. P., Kamii, M., Swap, S. M., & Howard, J. (1989). The algebra project: Organizing in the spirit of Ella. *Harvard Educational Review, 59*(4), 423–443.

Ogbu, J. (1983). Minority status and schooling in plural societies. *Comparative Education Review, 27*(2), 168–190.

Rainwater, L. (1965). *Family design.* Chicago: Aldine.

Richardson, V. (1994). Conducting research on practice. *Educational Researcher, 23*(5), 5–10.

Chapter 6

Writing as Communication: Creating Strategic Learning Environments for Students*

Luis C. Moll
University of California, San Diego

FOCUS QUESTIONS

1. The author explains the source of academic failure for students from different experiential, linguistic, and social backgrounds as the social organization of schooling. How might teachers identify factors in the social organization of schooling that are most likely to contribute to academic success?
2. The author calls on Vygotsky's theory of proximal development to explain the relation between school learning and the home-culture. Can you identify and explain the application of other theories or principles of learning to designing instruction for learners from diverse cultural and experiential backgrounds?

Many social factors influence the building of literacy in the classroom. One of these is the set of assumptions educators make about the relationship of children's proficiency in English to instructional reading and writing programs. Too often, educators assume that a child's level of oral proficiency in English indicates a similar level of proficiency in reading and writing.

*Source: Moll, Luis C. (1986). Writing as communication: Creating strategic learning environments for students. *Theory Into Practice*, 25, 102–108 (Theme issue on "Building Literacy"). Copyright © 1986, College of Education, The Ohio State University. Reprinted with permission.

For example, in classroom studies I conducted with my colleague Stephen Diaz (Moll & Diaz, in press-a), we documented the tendency to reduce the curriculum's level of complexity to match limited English speakers' levels of English proficiency; thus relegating children who were competent readers in Spanish (and conversationally fluent in English) to very low-level English reading lessons.

Recent research has documented the importance of selecting a level of instruction that can academically challenge students (see, for example, Gallimore, 1985; Graves, 1982; Vygotsky, 1978). Children's literacy development is fostered when they engage in literacy activities that require them to go beyond what they are already capable of doing by themselves. Conversely, if instructional activities do not require children to go beyond what they can accomplish independently, literacy development is likely to be hindered. Thus, the role of educators is to help children achieve beyond their current levels of development.

The problem of instructional bias and of watering down the curriculum is, of course, not limited to non-native English speaking students; it may occur in the education of speakers of non-standard English dialects or of students whose language or cultural behavior does not conform to that of the dominant society. In fact, as Anyon (1980), among others, has shown, watering down the curriculum may be viewed as part of a broader stratification of instruction across social class groups.

This article illustrates one type of instructional bias that can hinder literacy development; namely, teaching to children's low level of English. Limited-English-proficient (LEP) students have a persistent, high rate of educational failure that makes them among the most problematic groups for educators. Students who are from non-English-language backgrounds drop out at nearly twice the rate of students from an English-language background (Steinberg, Blinde, & Chan, 1984). Although it would be justifiable to focus solely on the problems faced by students of non-English language backgrounds, given the large number of such students in urban public schools, it is important to remember that the instructional biases they face are but one illustration of a broader problem of reducing selectively the instructional level of literacy curricula.

THE SCOPE AND NATURE OF THE PROBLEM

The instructional bias described above—teaching to children's low level of English—is found even in bilingual programs and regardless of the children's academic competence in their first language. In some schools the Spanish-language curriculum is so impoverished that children cannot function in the more advanced English-language lessons except at the lowest levels available. In writing instruction for secondary level limited-

English-proficient students, writing is often used primarily in response to test items or worksheets, to the exclusion of more demanding expository writing (Moll & Diaz, in press-b).

More recently, this same phenomenon has become evident in computer instruction. Poor and LEP students do drill and practice; affluent and English-fluent students do problem solving and programming (Boruta, Carpenter, Harvey, Keyser, Labonte, Mehan, & Rodriguez, 1983; Mehan, Moll, & Riel, 1985). In all cases, students are locked into the lower levels of the curriculum.

Part of the problem is the overwhelming pressure to make LEP students fluent in English at all costs. Learning English, not learning, has become the controlling goal of instruction for these students, even if it places the children at risk academically. This emphasis, usually based on the assumption that a lack of English skills is the primary if not sole determinant of the children's academic failure, has become yet another mechanism to preserve the educational status quo and contributes greatly to the oppressive failure rate of Latinos and other minority youth in schools (cf. Cummins, 1981). This argument does not negate the goal of children mastering English and achieving academically in that language. Parents and teachers want that; it is clearly an important goal. My concern is with the pedagogy.

The pedagogical justification for the reductionist practices described above is as follows: These children need to learn how to deal with English-language schooling; therefore it is imperative that they learn English as soon as possible; otherwise they may never be able to benefit from instruction. Thus, when faced with LEP children, usually at different levels of English-language fluency, the rationale makes it seem quite reasonable for teachers to group children by fluency and adjust the curriculum accordingly, usually starting with the teaching of the simplest skills—at least until the children know sufficient English to benefit from more advanced instruction. Of course, learning English will take some time, and the students may fall so far behind academically that failure is guaranteed. That risk seems unavoidable to those who advocate this approach.

THEORETICAL CONSIDERATIONS

Recent classroom ethnographies, as well as other types of observational studies, point out the strong connection between social interactions that make up educational events and academic performance (e.g., Au, 1980; Diaz, Moll, & Mehan, 1986; Erickson & Mohatt, 1980; Mehan, 1979). These studies argue that what goes on in the classroom counts, and that it counts a lot. They shift the responsibility for school failure away from the characteristics of the children and toward a more general societal process. The source of students' problems in school is not to be found in their language or culture; it is to be found in the social organization of schooling.

While student characteristics do matter, when the same children are shown to succeed under modified instructional arrangements it becomes clear that the problems minority children face in school must be viewed as a consequence of institutional arrangements which ensnare certain children by not capitalizing fully on their talents and skills. This conclusion is pedagogically optimistic because it suggests that just as academic failure is socially organized, academic success can be socially arranged.

The work of Vygotsky (1978) provides a source of ideas for developing effective teaching and learning environments. His ideas are a powerful supplement to ethnography because they specify practical steps to take advantage of the interactional patterns that ethnographic studies so aptly describe. A full discussion of Vygotsky's theory is obviously beyond the scope of this paper (see Laboratory of Comparative Human Cognition, 1983; Wertsch, 1985), but several theoretical concepts central to its argument are summarized below.

Humans are inescapably social beings. Because all learning occurs in social and historical environments, these environments play a critical role in an individual's learning and development. Human beings themselves, through their social interactions, create the social environments in which they function and in which they learn; thus, social interactions are the primary mechanism through which human beings create change in environments and in themselves.

Vygotsky (1978) points out that these individual–environment interactions are rarely direct. Humans use tools (e.g., speech, reading, writing, mathematics, and most recently, computers) to mediate their interactions with their physical and social environment. A fundamental property of tools (be it speech or writing) is that they are first used for communication with others—to mediate contact with the world. Much later they are used to mediate interactions with self, as we internalize their use and they become part of our behavioral repertoire. Thus, Vygotskian theory posits a strong connection between intellectual activity and external, practical activity mediated by the use of "psychological tools" such as literacy.

The point, however, isn't simply that all learning takes place in a social context and that the use of tools is a prominent characteristic of human beings, but rather that the path of intellectual development moves from the social to the individual. The intellectual skills children acquire are directly related to how they interact with adults and peers in specific problem-solving environments (Vygotsky, 1978). Children internalize the kind of help they receive from others and eventually come to use the means of guidance initially provided by others to direct their own subsequent problem-solving behaviors. In other words, children first perform the appropriate behaviors to complete a task with someone else's guidance and direction (e.g., a teacher or peer) before they complete the task competently and independent of outside direction or help.

Vygotsky elaborates the instructional implications of this connection between social interaction and individual psychological action through his concept of a zone of proximal development. This zone is defined as the distance between what children can accomplish independently (the actual developmental level) and what they can accomplish with the help of adults or more capable peers (the proximal developmental level). Vygotsky suggests that the proximal level reveals, in a real sense, the child's future; the skills or behaviors that are in the process of developing or maturing.

For instruction to be effective it must be aimed at children's proximal level, at the future, and social interactions within the zone need to be organized to support the children's performance at the proximal level until they are able to perform independent of help (upon internalization). Instruction aimed at the actual developmental level is ineffective because those behaviors have already "matured" and been mastered by the children. Similarly, aiming instruction beneath the actual developmental level or way beyond the proximal level is equally ineffective. The "trick" is to aim instructional activities proximally, while providing the social support or help to facilitate performance at those levels.

TEACHING WRITING IN A BILINGUAL COMMUNITY

The study described below formed part of a larger project designed to explore ways of using information from home and community contexts in classroom practice (for details, see Moll & Diaz, in press-b; Trueba, Moll, Diaz, & Diaz, 1982). The purpose of the study was to foster instructional change as well as to document the teaching practices that make such changes possible. Twelve teachers participated, each agreeing to implement a minimum of six writing modules. These modules consisted of a series of writing activities intended to facilitate the use of community data in practice. In other words, they served as the vehicles to experiment with the use of community data in the classrooms, a sort of mediating device between community and classroom realities. The teachers also kept journals which provided data on the instructional practices of different teachers over time.

As with other community-based studies (e.g., Heath, 1983; Language Policy Task Force, 1982), field observations revealed the diversity that characterizes community life. Several factors, especially immigration, constantly molded the social configuration of the community. This diversity was most evident in the different arrangements families adopted in their attempts to adjust to social and economic realities. These arrangements ranged from so-called traditional families, with clearly demarcated roles and responsibilities for family members, to families where the father was missing and the offspring assumed adult roles. Often, depending on the families' English-language fluency, the children took responsibility for transactions with important social institutions (e.g., paying bills or answering school-related inquiries). In short, the social, economic, and linguistic demands of life in the community were met with familial flexibility and adjustment of roles and responsibilities as necessary for survival.

Most of the writing observed in the homes was functional and practical. It included preparing shopping lists, taking phone messages, and occasionally writing a letter. However, most literacy events in the homes were organized around school matters, especially homework (see also McDermott, Goldman, & Varenne, 1984). For purposes of the study, this was good news because homework assignments is one activity well within the teachers' purview.

Two additional points, both of which have practical consequences for schooling practices, became clear through our observations. Despite the lack of extended writing events in the home, and for that matter in the community, parents and other community members repeatedly expressed their belief in the value of education. They viewed writing as an essential element of a good education, a skill that must be developed in school. Also, there was broad concern about the social issues that permeated community life, such as immigration, unemployment, the need to learn English, and the like. As the project proceeded, we began to view the teaching of writing in the context of the community, and to organize writing instruction responsive to the concrete circumstances encountered.

Despite the bilingual character of the surrounding community, for the most part schools excluded the use of Spanish from the curriculum. No bilingual classes were offered, thereby eliminating the possibility of capitalizing on the students' Spanish oral language and literacy skills to develop their English language skills.[1] As a group, the students scored among the lowest on tests of writing achievement, and the teachers had received little or no training in the teaching of writing. Predictably, formal writing instruction was an infrequent classroom activity. This was particularly true with limited-English-proficient children. Most classroom writing was in response to tests or homework assignments with the teacher as the primary audience and evaluator. Writing was rarely used as a tool of communication—to convey opinions or ideas, or to analyze and explore social issues.

CONNECTING SCHOOL AND COMMUNITY
THROUGH CLASSROOM PRACTICE

Because homework assignments created frequent opportunities for literacy to occur in homes, we set out to organize writing instruction that included assignments that not only produced literacy-related interactions in the home, but involved parents and other community members in the development and conduct of instruction.

The module reviewed below was conducted in one of the English-as-a-Second-Language (ESL) classrooms. It illustrates one good way to capitalize on extracurricular sources to help develop the English writing of limited-English-speaking students. From a theoretical perspective, individual differences between LEP and other students refer to the different ways students may enter a writing activity and the nature of the help needed for them to perform at the most advanced level possible. Whether or not students are fluent in English, instruction should be organized for them to engage in the same basic educational activity: writing for communication. Given their English language difficulties, LEP students may contribute differently to the completion of the activity than regular students, and the teacher may have to provide more structured help, but both sets of students participate in comparable, demanding intellectual activities. Regardless of language differences, the higher order goal of classroom writing should remain the elaboration of thinking through communication; the mechanics of writing should be taught in the service of this goal.

Classroom Implementation

In the following example, the theme for writing was bilingualism. The teacher and students had expressed much interest in this topic and had written about bilingualism in a preceding module. The teacher's journal describes the sequence of events:

> Today, half way through the period, we began this module by reviewing the writing we had done. I spent most time asking them about their last "bilingualism" papers, and they remembered a lot about them. We reviewed and I listed on the board that that paper had been expressive in nature, *their own feelings and opinions.* That was readily accepted.
>
> I told them the (next) module was going to be concerned with information, opinions, feelings, etc., that would be gleaned from *other* sources besides themselves. They looked at me with blank faces. Then I started to discuss and probe the meaning of "survey" and "questionnaire" with them. They loved that. I gave examples of TV polls, of Cola tests, etc. Jorge and Lisa called out, "Does that mean we're going to do that?" They all were kind of excited or at least interested when I said "yes."
>
> I "fed" them the beginning questions for their questionnaires, ones I wanted to make sure *all* asked. I gave them three they *had* to use, and two more samples they could choose. The assignment was explained as follows: These three questions all must ask:
>
> A. What language do you speak best?
> B. What language do you read and write best?
> C. Do any members of your family who live with you speak another language besides English?

Two more questions were optional:

D. Would you be willing to take classes to become bilingual?
E. What career do you foresee in your future in which you would benefit by being bilingual?

Each student was required to ask:

A. Two adults not working on campus.
B. Two adults who do work on campus.
C. Three students whose first language is English.
D. Three students whose first language is other than English.

Homework for tonight was to invent three additional questions related to bilingualism and people's opinions about it.

The module continued the next day as the teacher got the students to generate additional survey questions, such as "Are your closest friends bilingual?" "Do you think speaking another language is important?" "Is it comparatively hard for you to learn another language?" Knowing her students would need further guidance in conducting the survey, the teacher spent part of the lesson clarifying examples and general concerns. She was particularly surprised at the interest generated by the students interviewing adult respondents.

> The students were buzzing when they came in and they buzzed all along! Some had never had occasion to speak to adults other than their teachers here and a few . . . were itching to show me (one of the adults') responses. . . . I instructed that all future entries must be in students' own handwriting and that they were to ask the questions orally, explicating if necessary since a few answers were not directed appropriately. The students didn't even moan at that; they thought that was logical for practicing oral English.

The teacher structured help to move the students along and to maintain their interest in quite an involved writing activity.

> The projects are shaping up and they seem to have a clear idea of what they are doing at this step, so I decided today to introduce the next step. Most had time in class to start formulating a "Results" page. I just put a suggested format on the board and explained after they had gotten their results, they could fill in the results chart.

At each step of the way the teacher made sure that the students stayed in contact with the goal of the lesson. The tasks necessary to complete the module were done to accomplish a specified and mutually understood goal. At no time were the students relegated to doing writing exercises unrelated to the purpose of the writing activity.

When the students showed signs of taking over the activity without the need for highly structured supervision, the teacher became less directive and had the students assume most of the responsibility for completing the necessary tasks.

> In class, there was a lot of constructive communicating going on—students asked each other "how to say" this and that, and asked me (usually) "how do I do it?" After I had already explained the questions they had a difficult time getting going, but I decided not to hand-feed them this time, but instead to let them muddle through. I answered specific questions today, but I didn't volunteer the questions, if you know the difference. I sent them home to finish by Monday.

The students returned Monday with their papers in different stages of completion. The teacher selected one of the more complete papers and placed it on an overhead to show it to the class. They edited the paper together, clarifying the type of paper required in the module. The balance of the time was used to write more drafts and to revise those already turned in.

Writing Samples

Below are two unedited examples of students' writing in their second language. Despite obvious errors, writing these essays created exceptional opportunities for teaching that otherwise would not have occurred.

> Student A:
> The people in cy comminuty think that being bilingual is very important for several good reasons. Firts, I felt very proud doing the Survey. the people in our commuinity feel very proud of them self that they speak Spanish and Eanglish because they can talk with there friends in any of those two len-guages. Secondly, the people I ask Some were bilingual students and adults 60% were bilingual people and 40% weren't bilingual people. Also, I ask a teacher and a student if they would be wiling to work as a bilingual person and they said no and then I ask a Student this qiestion Do you think Speaking Another lenguage is important and he said no that amazed me because I never herd one person that thinks that speaking another language ain't important. finally, I ask a teacher that What career was he interested in that would require a 2nd language and he said no common and he told this I don't know What lauguage I'm interestes that would require a 2nd lenguage because I don't know it and I ask two Students this question what career are yo interested in that would require a 2nd language and 50% said Fransh 10% said Germen 10% said Italian and 20% said no coman as you can see I was having fun.

Student B:

I found that people in our community feel good about belingualism for several good reasons. They think it it very important because they can communicate with other people. The people I asked are 60% students, 40% adults, 70% are Spanish speakers, 20% were English speakers, 70% can write and read English, 20% can write and read Spanish well. Most of the people told me that in there house can speak English and Spanish. The people I ask the questions, answers me very polite and they said the questions were very interesting. Some person said that these project was very good for me and interesting for him. When he said that I feel very good about the work I was doing. The most interesting thing that I found wat that the people like the project. Most of the people said that they were willing to take classes to become totally belingual because it could help them right now and in the future. The students I ask said that they have only friends that speak only Spanish and English not othey language. The adults I ask said that been belingual is very important for them because they can communicate with more people and they can have more opportunitis for some jobs that othey people do I feel very good about the way people answer me.

Obviously, the students still have considerable difficulty writing in English. But the teacher managed to organize lessons that minimized the constraining influence of their English-language difficulties while maximizing the use of the students' knowledge of the topic and other experiences. Students who otherwise would do little, if any, classroom writing were able to produce essays in their second language that incorporated information collected from their community.

THEORY AS A GUIDE TO ACTION

Instructional change may occur in several ways and can be facilitated by researchers and teachers working together to explicitly shape instruction. In the example included in this article, a homework assignment was purposely chosen because field reports identified homework as an important family literacy event (see also McDermott et al., 1984). The idea was to have the students collect information about a specific theme from their elders and then use this information to increase the students' and teachers' knowledge about a topic. The homework assignment served as one of the mediating steps to writing and illustrates the usefulness of extracurricular sources for the development of writing.

These advantages notwithstanding, instruction still has to be organized so that writing becomes a means of achieving social and academic goals. The concept of a zone of proximal development provides an interactional frame to turn classroom writing into communicative activities that not only address social issues, but into which teachers can embed the basic writing skills they are interested in teaching. In the cited example, students were required to interview adults and other children regarding their views on bilingualism. This information was needed to expand a paper written by the students in the preceding module by including additional details not immediately available within the classroom. The activity of collecting extracurricular information for use in writing is clearly an advanced, demanding task for secondary school students. However, this task can be accomplished with the assistance of more knowledgeable persons, in this instance the teacher and the parents. The teacher bridged the distance between what the students were able to do individually and what the writing task required by providing them with strategic help to facilitate a capable performance at higher levels.

The teacher helped the students put together a questionnaire to structure data collection and gave them suggestions on how to gather data. Once data were collected, she organized classroom discussions to assist the students in extracting relevant information and helped them include this information in their writing. This teaching activity is an illustration of aiming instruction at the proximal level. The goal of instruction is calibrated to be in advance of what the students are individually capable of doing, not accommodated to the student's low level of English proficiency. This proximal goal is achieved by linking instruction to the real world and by providing students with the instructional support necessary to perform at the highest levels possible, regardless of English language proficiency. The process is greatly facilitated by teaching writing as communication about the world, rather than as a decontextualized skill.

NOTE

1. For a case study regarding the importance of Spanish literacy skills in English language instruction, see Moll & Diaz, in press-a.

SUGGESTED LEARNING EXPERIENCES

1. Based on the research presented in this chapter, develop another module of instruction for limited-English-proficient students.
2. The author of this chapter uses Vygotsky's theory of proximal development to explain the outcomes of his study. Identify and describe another theory that might be used in this situation.

REFERENCES

Anyon, J. (1980). Social class and the hidden curriculum of work. *Journal of Education, 162*(1), 67–92.

Au, K. (1980). Participation structures in a reading lesson with Hawaiian children: Analysis of a culturally appropriate instructional event. *Anthropology and Education Quarterly, 11*(2), 91–115.

Boruta, M., Carpenter, C., Harvey, M., Keyser, M., Labonte, J., Mehan, H., & Rodriguez, D. (1983). Computers in schools: Stratifier or equalizer? *The Quarterly Newsletter of the Laboratory of Comparative Human Cognition, 5*(3), 51–55.

Cummins, J. (1981). The role of primary language development in promoting educational success for language minority students. In *Schooling and language minority students: A theoretical framework* (pp. 3–50). Los Angeles, CA: Evaluation, Dissemination, and Assessment Center, California State University.

Diaz, S., Moll, L. C., & Mehan, H. (1986). Socio-cultural resources in instruction: A context-specific approach. In *Beyond language: Social and cultural factors in schooling language minority students* (pp. 187–230). Los Angeles, CA: Evaluation, Dissemination, and Assessment Center, California State University.

Erickson, F., & Mohatt, G. (1980). Cultural organization of participant structures in two classrooms of Indian students. In G. Spindler (Ed.), *Doing the ethnography of schooling* (pp. 132–274). New York: Macmillan.

Gallimore, R. (1985). *The accommodation of instruction to cultural differences.* Paper presented at the University of California's Conference on the Education of Linguistic Minorities, Lake Tahoe, CA.

Graves, D. (1982). How do writers develop? *Language Arts, 59*(2), 173–179.

Heath, S. (1983). *Ways with words: Ethnography of communication in communities and classrooms.* New York: Cambridge University Press.

Laboratory of Comparative Human Cognition. (1983). Culture and cognitive development. In W. Kessen (Ed.), *Mussen handbook of child psychology* (Vol. 1, pp. 295–356). New York: Wiley.

Language Policy Task Force. (1982). *Intergenerational perspectives on bilingualism: From community to classroom.* New York: Centro de Estudios Puertorriqueños, Hunter College.

McDermott, R. P., Goldman, S., & Varenne, H. (1984). When school goes home: Some problems in the organization of homework. *Teachers College Record, 85*(4), 399–408.

Mehan, H. (1979). *Learning lessons.* Cambridge, MA: Harvard University Press.

Mehan, H., Moll, L. C., & Riel, M. (1985). *Computers in classrooms: A quasi-experiment in guided change* (Final Rep. No. NIE-G-83-0027). Washington, DC: National Institute of Education.

Moll, L. C., & Diaz, S. (in press-a). Bilingual communication and reading: The importance of Spanish in learning to read in English. *Elementary School Journal.*

Moll, L. C., & Diaz, S. (in press-b). Teaching writing as communication: The use of ethnographic findings in classroom practice. In D. Bloome (Ed.), *Language, literacy and schooling.* Norwood, NJ: Ablex.

Steinberg, L., Blinde, P. L., & Chan, K. S. (1984). Dropping out among language minority youth. *Review of Educational Research, 54*(1), 113–132.

Trueba, H., Moll, L. C., Diaz, S., & Diaz, R. (1982). *Improving the functional writing of bilingual secondary school students* (Cont. No. 400-81-0023). Washington, DC: National Institute of Education.

Vygotsky, L. S. (1978). *Mind in society.* Cambridge, MA: Harvard University Press.

Wertsch, J. W. (1985). *Vygotsky and the social formation of mind.* Cambridge, MA: Harvard University Press.

Chapter 7

Culturally Responsive Teaching for American Indian Students*

Cornel Pewewardy
The University of Kansas

FOCUS QUESTIONS

1. This author points out the diversity among different populations of American Indians. Despite this diversity, dismal school performance is widespread for American Indians as a group. How might classroom teachers identify pathways to success for American Indian students?

2. Every teacher brings into his or her classroom biased perspectives and preferences for specific approaches to instruction. How might teachers deal with these factors when teaching youngsters from cultural and experiential backgrounds different from their own?

INTRODUCTION

Historically, American Indians have had negative relationships with government agencies, and many Native people are likely to be realistically cautious with White authorities. The problems are vast and based on 500 years of mistreatment of Native peoples. This is understandable considering

---

*The terms *Indian, Native, Native Peoples,* and *Native American* are used many times when referring to the same population. However, I have found that *American Indian* and *Alaska Native* are the preferred terms because of the precise reference to Indian groups in this country and the confusion over someone misidentifying themselves in the U.S. census count.

the destruction of culture, language, and human lives inflicted on all Indian populations throughout U.S. history. Early educational history of American Indians is about how non-Indian policymakers sought to use the schoolhouse, specifically the boarding schools, as an instrument for acculturating Indian youth to "American" ways of thinking and living (Adams, 1995). As a result of this experience, intergenerational distrust of non-Indians may be combined with anger and confusion. Indian peoples realize the atrocities that have been committed against them far better than the greater society. Even today, in government, education, films, sports competitions, and society in general, Indian peoples are presented in a derogatory fashion (Roop, 1993).

This chapter presents particular aspects of American Indian students' cultural and experiential background that will help teachers employ culturally responsive pedagogy, and assists teachers in identifying pathways to successful teaching and learning for these students. This requires that teachers acquire a realistic and contemporary understanding of the conditions and lifestyles of American Indians.

Life in the United States continues to be difficult for American Indians. American Indians suffer from the highest unemployment rates and conditions of greatest poverty in the United States. Average family incomes may be as low as $900 per year, and unemployment rates can run as high as 90%. Deaths related to alcoholism are four times higher for American Indians than for the general population; 70% of all treatments provided by physicians at Indian Health Service clinics are for alcohol-related disease or trauma. It is estimated that alcohol is a factor in 90% of all homicides involving Indians and in most suicides and accidental-injury deaths (Mancall, 1995; Unrau, 1996).

American Indian and Alaska Natives are the most devastated groups among adolescents in the United States. According to a recent study conducted by Blum, Harmon, Harris, and Resnick (1992) at the University of Minnesota, nearly one in six Indian adolescents has attempted suicide. This is four times the rate for other teenagers. Indian young people are more likely to come from broken homes or to abuse drugs, and 20% describe their health as poor. American Indian/Alaska Native adolescents reported high rates of health-compromising behaviors and risk factors related to unintentional injury, substance use, poor self-assessed health status, emotional distress, and suicide. Many Native children living in communities under these conditions develop negative images of themselves and their societies. These views and experiences are often correlated with their economic status (Szasz, 1992).

American Indian students comprise 1% of the student population in the United States. In Grades Kindergarten through 12, about 85% of Native students currently attend public schools, with the Bureau of Indian Affairs and private schools still enrolling significant numbers. American Indian and Alaska Native students have the highest dropout rate of any racial or ethnic group in the United States, almost twice that of White students (Hillabrant, Romano, Stang, & Charleston, 1992; Johnson, Dupuis, Musial, Hall, & Gollnick, 1996).

DIVERSITY WITHIN THE AMERICAN INDIAN POPULATION

The American Indian population is very diverse and composed of many regional and cultural subgroups and tribes. The U.S. government recognizes 177 different tribes, each with its own culture and varying degrees of traditionalism, acculturation, and educational levels. To better understand and appreciate cultural differences, it is important to embrace the idea that differences are neither good nor bad. This is especially true for teachers trying to understand the cultural identity of their students. For example, Indian students who are talented in traditional modes of expression for a particular American Indian society, such as in the areas of art, dance, or even athletics, probably will be supported in the development of their talents by parents and relatives. Those students who come from families adhering to a conservative and traditional American Indian culture may experience difficulties within and outside the family if they do not conform to established norms.

Physical Characteristics

Indian students are often thought to have specific physical characteristics such as black hair and eyes, dark brown skin, and high cheek bones. Trimble (1981) indicates that for many, it is difficult to accept as an Indian an individual who has light hair, blue eyes, and fair skin. However, the reality is that Native people display a wide range of phenotypic characteristics in terms of body size, skin and hair color, and facial features. Conflicts in identity are often great for individuals who do not fit the traditional physical stereotypes. They may meet with prejudice and rejection from authentic, tribal Indians and non-Indians alike.

Family Structure

American Indian family structure is derived from the tribal village structure in which residents were members of an extended kin system. Villages were considered sacred societies and elders assumed respected roles because their accumulated wisdom was necessary to interpret lives and relationships according to a sacred context.

The Indian family structure varies from tribe to tribe. However, some generalizations can be made. For most tribes the extended family is the basic model. Indian children are often raised by relatives such as aunts, uncles, and grandparents who live in separate households. The concept of the extended family is often misunderstood by those not familiar with Indian cultures, especially those who operate under the concept of the nuclear family. The extended family structure often includes the second cousin and sometimes informal adoptions outside the family. It is not unusual to have youngsters stay in a variety of different homes. Difficulties can arise when teachers think that only the parents should raise and be responsible for Indian children.

The traditional American Indian family is the benchmark for any discussion of American Indian family types. Modal behaviors common within family types include language of preference, religious beliefs, attitudes about land, kin system structure, and health behavior. The spectrum of types does not necessarily imply a linear phenomenon. In many instances, modal behaviors change for different situations, and families can move in either direction along a continuum.

Neotraditional families emerge most commonly through mass religious conversions organizing into close kin and village structures and simply adopting new ritual procedures for sacred beliefs. Transitional families emerge through geographic relocation away from extended kin systems attempting to retain modal behaviors similar to traditional groups. Bicultural families make important shifts away from traditional modal behaviors. Often, bicultural families do not transmit specific traditional knowledge across generations; parents may understand their native language, but not use it in the home; and many have converted to non-Indian religions. Acculturated families are assimilated and represent the most extreme departure from traditional lifestyles. In acculturated families the English language is used by both parents and children; nuclear households are the preferred family structure; and peer relations generally are with non-Indians for both parents and children. Pan-renaissance families emerge as important cultural revival responses when external forces place families and individuals in jeopardy. The emergence of such families and groups is not unique to contemporary American Indians.

Cultural Identity

The tribe is of fundamental importance to cultural identity. For those Indians living on tribal reservations and for those living in urban areas, the relationship with their tribal affiliation is strong and very different from that among non-Indians. Indian people see themselves as an extension of their tribe(s). This tribal identity provides them with a sense of cultural belonging and family security. Social stratification and honors are obtained by maintaining tribal norms and conformity. Many Indian people who leave the reservation to seek greater opportunities sacrifice cultural knowledge and tribal language. In the past, the tribe, through the extended family structure, was responsible for the full development and education of all the children.

Typically, cultural identity is associated with a shared set of beliefs and values. However, the great diversity and variation among American Indians make it difficult to describe a common set of values that encompasses all groups. In a very general sense, most tribal groups share core values such as sharing, cooperation, noninterference, time orientation, extended family structure, and coexistence with nature.

Identifying the basic components of self-esteem to be significance, competence, power, and virtue, Brendtro, Brokenleg, and VanBocken (1990) explain the power of the circle of courage to reclaim those Indian youth who have experienced the ecological hazards of destructive relationships, climates of futility, learned irresponsibility, and loss of purpose commonly experienced in the American paradigm of public education. Traditional Native worldview nurtures "significance" in a cultural milieu that celebrates the universal need for "belonging"; "competence" is insured by guaranteed opportunities for "mastery"; "power" is fostered by encouraging the expression of "independence"; and "virtue" is reflected in the preeminent value of "generosity."

Charleston (1994) asserts that:

> Public schools need to teach the reasons for the hundreds of treaties and agreements between the various tribes and the United States, the thousands of acts of Congress, and the countless court cases that constitute the present complex body of federal Indian law. All of our people need to learn that the tribes and Native nations of this land have Constitutionally-based government-to-government relationships with the federal government and that no other group of people in the United States has this special relationship. Non-Native people must learn to respect the fact that, as members of tribes, American Indians and Alaska Natives are different from all other citizens of the United States; they have dual citizenship: tribal and United States citizenship. (p. 29)

Ironically, Indian people are not accepted as experts on their own culture, or themselves. Usually someone else "defines" the Indian. The process of defining and maintaining "self" is the challenge that American Indians have faced in all the political, economic, social, and cultural realities of the last two centuries. The continual process of self-knowledge, self-actualization, and self-worth is the foundation of cultural survival for many Indian people.

Tribal Language Versus English

Tribal language is a very important support system for youth because it transmits culture. How the mind creates language may have much to do with culture. Many tribal languages are "free-word-order" languages that allow phrase order to vary. For example, Comanche words from different phrases can be scrambled together: *This man caught a fish* can be expressed as *Man this fish caught, Man fish caught this,* or any of the other four orders, all completely synonymous.

In contrast, Pinker (1994) contends that English is an "isolating," "accusative," "subject-prominent" language, as well as a "fixed-word-order" language where each phrase has a fixed position. (English is an "SVO" language, with the order being subject–verb–object [*Dog bites man*].) And, of course, a glance at the grammar for any particular language will reveal dozens or hundreds of idiosyncrasies. It is important to remember that language is functional. One language or linguistic form is not inherently better than another. Teachers need to study American Indian languages so that they can support students in maintaining their native language while acquiring competence in standard English.

CULTURALLY RESPONSIVE TEACHING DEFINED

Unfortunately for American Indian students, the schools they attend and the teachers who serve them are almost never represented in sufficient numbers in national educational studies to permit reliable and valid generalizations about their characteristics. Furthermore, because of factors such as tribal and linguistic diversity, geographic dispersion, and preponderance in remote rural areas, the cost has prohibited the inclusion of representative samples of American Indian students and Alaska Natives in national educational studies. One exception is a report by Pavel, Curtin, Christenson, and Rudes (1995) that provides data on schools and staffing that is national in scope. The information provided in this report is particularly helpful in understanding the academic performance and condition of schooling for these youngsters.

Hilliard (1989) contends that the lower level of achievement of minority students is a function of systematic inequalities in schooling. These inequalities are exacerbated by misjudgments of students' intellectual capabilities. Teachers must abandon the deficit view of Indian students that permeates educational thinking. Moreover, a challenging and rigorous curriculum that extends children's thinking beyond that which is already known to them must be implemented. Delpit (1988) advocates the fostering of more meaningful interpersonal relations in schools, affirmation of the beliefs that all students are capable of learning, the establishment of high academic standards for all students, and the use of students' communicative styles in teaching. Delpit believes that academic success demands the acquisition of the mainstream culture, which means, in part, acquiring the communicative codes of those in power. She contends that those who have not been socialized into the culture of power should be taught explicitly the means of access to power, including the linguistic forms, and ways of speaking, writing, and interacting used by the powerful. Equally important, the students should be taught to value ethnic distinctions and be helped to learn that the culture of the group in power, although instrumental in the society, is not intrinsically superior to the cultures of the less powerful underrepresented groups. This requires that teachers use culturally responsive pedagogy.

According to Smith (1991), culturally responsive teaching uses the child's culture to build a bridge to successful academic achievement. Culturally responsive teaching places other cultures alongside middle-class mainstream, macrocultures at the center of the classroom instruction paradigm. The bridge developed through the use of culturally responsive pedagogy leads to more than improved academic achievement. For example, it encourages deeper study of one's own culture and/or the study of other cultures. Ultimately, it can lead away from ethnocentrism toward a common national destiny. Most importantly, the teacher and the student cross the bridge together, hand in hand, intertribally, interculturally, and transculturally.

Culturally responsive teaching is especially pertinent in an increasingly diverse society. It means responding in educationally constructive ways by employing cultural patterns that influence the behaviors and mental ecology of the classroom (Bowers & Flinders, 1990). For teachers of American Indian students, to be "culturally responsive" is to be sensitive, aware, and capable of employing cultural learning patterns, perspectives, family structure, multiple worldviews, tribal languages, and Indian English in the teaching, learning, and mental ecology of the classroom. It is important to think multiculturally, rather than monoculturally, and to be aware of one's own development as a teacher within a culturally diverse society.

Culturally responsive pedagogy is an important aspect of the multicultural educational reform presently taking place in the nation's schools. Essentially, it is at the heart of all good teaching. It helps teachers meet the needs of each individual in the classroom by addressing their cultural and experiential backgrounds and the special expertise each has developed. Culturally responsive pedagogy requires adaptation to local circumstances (Cole & Griffin, 1987; Diaz, Moll, & Mehan, 1986; Gallimore, 1985; Jordan, 1985; Nelson-Barber & Meier, 1990). A part of this adaptation is based on understanding diversity within, as well as across, cultural groups. However, teachers' biases may be a barrier to using culturally responsive pedagogy to support American Indian students' learning in school.

TEACHER BIASES

Sleeter (1992) argues that White teachers bring to the teaching profession perspectives about the meaning of race based on their own life experiences and vested interests. She further points out that "what White people know about the social world is generally correct, but only for understanding White people" (p. 211). Sleeter contends that a predominantly White teaching force in a racist and multicultural society is not good for anyone, if the goal is to have schools reverse rather than reproduce racism. Speaking to predominantly White teachers at an in-service session in 1994, Sleeter suggested that Whites should address White racism. She asserted that "our Whiteness seemed to be invisible to us—we could discuss our religious, ethnic, and social class differences, but not our common Whiteness or the privileges we gain from White racism."

Sleeter (1992) refers to the perspective of most White teachers about race as *dysconscious racism*, a term she borrowed from Joyce King. King (1991) argues that

> Dysconscious racism is a form of racism that tacitly accepts dominant white norms and privileges. It is not the *absence* of consciousness (that is, not unconsciousness) but an *impaired* consciousness or distorted way of thinking about race as compared to, for example, critical consciousness. (p. 135)

McIntosh (1989) affirms this view as she reflects that her schooling gave her no training in seeing herself as an oppressor, as an unfairly advantaged person, or as a participant in a damaged culture. She contends that "whites are carefully taught *not* to recognize white privilege . . . I have come to see white privilege as an invisible package of unearned assets which I can count on cashing in each day, but about which I was 'meant' to remain oblivious" (p. 1). Also, Stalvey (1989) asserts that she

> was conditioned *not* to notice who *wasn't* there. . . . The people I knew didn't practice discrimination; none of us suspected we were co-operating with it. We were like first-class passengers on a ship; comfortable with our privileges. We didn't know—or perhaps want to know—what went on below the decks on which we danced. (p. 16–17)

Whites rarely connect ethnicity with social structures such as friendship groups, occupation, or political organizations. Howard (1993) posits that the United States was never a White European Christian nation and is becoming less so every day. Most public school educators know the curriculum has to change to reflect this reality, but many guardians of the traditional canon still find it frightening to leave the Old World. There is a dire need to articulate clear self-interest arguments for Whites combating racism. According to Terry (1975), Whites need to understand more sharply how racism destroys them as well as others in the society. The challenge in the late 1990s, therefore, is preparing monocultural teachers to teach American Indian students. Monocultural schools may no longer be the locus of teacher placements (Aaronsohn, Carter, & Howell, 1994). The simple statements that all students, regardless of their ethnic or racial backgrounds, should have the opportunity to learn about their own culture and the culture of others forms the basic tenet of multicultural education.

Those who teach American Indian students need to be aware of their own cultural biases. This includes many Indian teachers who are products of monocultural teacher preparation programs based on western and northern European values and influences. For example, many teachers still expect Indian students to establish constant eye contact with them, to openly discuss inner feelings, to verbalize concerns outwardly, defend their answers, challenge their classmates, be aggressive in class, speak standard English, as well as participate fully in class. Where issues of trust have not been dealt with, many Native students often will not display the expected behaviors that are based on European American, middle-class norms.

Ogbu (1992) notes that students from involuntary minority groups are torn between school expectations and the failures and frustrations of their community and personal affiliations. According to Ogbu (1992),

> An involuntary minority student desiring and striving to do well in school is faced with the conflict between loyalty to the minority peer group, which provides a sense of community and security, and the desire to behave in ways that may improve school performance but that the peer group defines as "White." (p. 10)

For Indian students, "acting White" should not be a requirement for achieving the desired learning outcomes. Among Greenberg's (1992) suggestions for productive teaching for American Indian students is the idea that classrooms should be inclusive.

As teachers examine their attitudes and beliefs, they should cautiously avoid either a guilt reaction as in "We WASPs are immoral about minorities" or a defensive posture as in "It's not my fault that millions of American Indians are no longer here as a result of a national holocaust framed from

U.S. colonial policy." We must critically analyze the Doctrine of Discovery and Manifest Destiny ideologies—the exploration and settlement of an already occupied land with little regard for rights of occupants—of this country and the meaning of progress and success. Therefore, we must ask ourselves, "Whose progress?" and "Whose success?" During the pursuit of happiness of everyday life, it becomes a lifelong learning journey to study reasons why there are "haves" and "have nots" in U.S. society. Guilt reactions and defensive postures block analytical thinking and impede resolutions to these inequities. A multicultural education is, therefore, just as essential to the child of the dominant society as it is to the American Indian child (Gilliland, 1992).

APPLYING CULTURALLY RESPONSIVE PEDAGOGY

Long before coming to school, many White, middle-class children have learned to accept the authority of the teacher as that of an adult who commands respect. They understand that they are to speak only when given a turn to be verbally expressive, to respond to display questions, to value individual competition, to use topic-centered narratives, and to think linearly. For these children the school experience is an extension of the home experience. Such is not the case for many Indian children where the classroom experience often clashes with that of the home and community. Unfortunately, teachers who lack intercultural communication training (Brislin & Yoshida, 1994) and culturally responsive teaching abilities often view the response of Indian children to this unfamiliar cultural context as academic incompetence.

When American Indian students are confronted with predominant White, middle-class cultural norms and behavioral patterns within public schools, the result is usually cultural discontinuity or lack of cultural synchronization between students and their school. Irvine (1990) contends that when there is cultural mismatch between students and their school, the inevitable occurs: miscommunication and confrontation among the students, teachers, and the home, and hostility, alienation, diminished self-esteem, and eventual school failure. Marginal tribal language and/or Indian studies programs will not attract alienated Indian students who have few tangible connections to tribal culture (Pewewardy & Willower, 1993).

Culturally responsive teachers focus on the strengths that exist in Indian families while using a culturally accepted group pedagogy to promote social cohesion. Tribal culture can be used to strengthen group ties. For many Indian students, tribal identity is built through their participation in cultural activities such as intertribal powwows, feasts, special events at school, and cultural gatherings. In teaching American Indians, it may be necessary to explore issues of Indian–White relationships, to identify the individual's value structure, and to investigate issues of culture conflict and identity. Biracial and blended families may do well with traditional American methodology and pedagogy of teaching; however, traditional Native students may first have to deal with issues of trust and may respond best to a combination of student-centered instruction with behavioral approaches that are culturally responsive.

Preservice Teacher Education

In order to fully understand and be able to apply culturally responsive pedagogy for American Indian students, preservice teachers should (Pewewardy, 1994):

- Have classroom experience with Indian children before student teaching.
- Understand and respect students' cultural knowledge base.
- Study the history and culture of Indian children including their values, stories, music, and myths, as well as study racism/sexism from both cognitive and affective worldviews.
- Be reflective practitioners and develop observational, empirical, and analytical skills necessary to monitor, evaluate, and revise continually their respective teaching styles.
- Acknowledge the cognitive worldview of Indian children.
- Know how to include Indian parents and respective communities in the decision-making process.
- Understand the cultural code switching, dialect, and/or Indian English of the students.
- Understand students' interpersonal behaviors in such areas as body language, eye contact, silence, touch, public space, and facial expression.
- Overcome fear, apprehension, and overreaction related to Indian children's styles of personal presentation.
- Acquire clinical experiences in schools that have strong support systems.
- Be aware of cultural differences when evaluating students.

Teaching Indian Students

Guidelines for teaching Indian students include the following:

1. Indian students should not be stereotyped or all placed in the same category. In some cases, ethnic background is the only constant. Many Indian students have middle-class backgrounds; therefore, they may demonstrate many of the same behaviors as other students who hold middle-class values. The major difference is that these students may receive pressure to "act Indian."

2. In social studies lessons Indian students should not have to defend the Native perspective of the Bering Strait theory in class or to their teachers. Do not assume that Indian students are well acquainted with their tribal heritage and culture, speak their tribal language, or affirm their Indian identity.

3. Teachers should not call on their Indian students in class as "Indian boy" or "Indian girl."

4. Students should not be reprimanded publicly. If there is a need to reprimand a student, it should be done in private. Even the most mild-mannered Indian students are likely to fight back when embarrassed in front of their classmates.

5. Whenever possible, do not bring attention to foul language, especially if it occurs in jocular, good-natured ribbing sessions. These sessions are often an important rite of passage in Indian youth culture and critical to the development of peer and social relationships.

6. A lack of family involvement should not be assumed to mean that the families are not interested in the welfare of the student. Many Indian families will not become involved in the school because they do not know what to do; they feel that they do not have the appropriate skills, they work several jobs, or they feel uncomfortable in the area of intervention or in the presence of what may be perceived as a White authority figure.

7. Teachers should not take everything personally. There are times when things will not proceed as planned. At times, teachers may feel that it is their fault that students are demonstrating certain behaviors. In such cases, teachers feel that the negative behaviors are directed toward them, rather than toward the situation. Consequently, the relationship between the teacher and student may begin to deteriorate. If it is allowed to continue, this relationship will most likely develop into a negative situation.

8. Teachers should not try to take on the behaviors of the students. It is important to understand the students and make every attempt to help them.

9. Avoid correcting students' verbal language during conversation. Assist Indian students in using their own language as a vehicle to learning standard English.

10. Teachers should be familiar with the topic-centered and/or topic-associating strategies students use to construct their narratives during "shar-

ing time," a recurrent classroom event in which students are expected to tell their classmates and teacher about some past experience. Most Indian students favor topic-associating, whereas many White students prefer topic-centered styles of storytelling.

Principles for Culturally Responsive Teaching

The following principles are offered to guide culturally responsive teaching. Culturally and linguistically different students learn best when:

1. Teachers use students' prior cultural knowledge as a foundation in the teaching and learning process.
2. Classroom practices are compatible with students' language patterns, cognitive functioning, motivation, and the social norm and structures to which they are accustomed.
3. Assessment practices and procedures reflect the diversity of student strengths and an appreciation for multiple intelligences.
4. The attitudes, beliefs, and actions of the school model respect for cultural diversity, celebrate the contributions of diverse groups, and foster understanding and acceptance of racial and ethnic plurality.
5. Teachers value cultural knowledge, view students as assets, and integrate them into classroom instruction.
6. Teachers act as cultural mediators, and provide assistance through the use of questions, feedback, and scaffolding.
7. Schooling provides children with the knowledge, language, and skills to function in the mainstream culture but does not do so at the expense of the students' Native language and original cultural orientation.
8. Schooling helps children participate in multiple cultural or language domains (arenas) for different purposes without undermining their connection to their original culture.
9. The community and the home validate and support the academic success of their children.

CONCLUSION

An examination of the problems associated with designing, implementing, pluralizing, and evaluating an educational curriculum that is culturally responsive for Native students is likely to spark heated discussion and provide a firsthand view of the obstacles to educational reform. Only when values, ideologies, and culture are penetrated, however, can reform begin.

In the reformed public schools, Native students have the opportunity to learn together and develop socially, culturally, and academically. The isolation of Native students must end. Because most Native children attend public schools, it seems that education will continue the method of integrating children into the society. Therefore, we must socialize our children for effective living in the 21st century by transforming the transracial American nation even as it transforms and absorbs them. Continued change and development for teaching American Indian students requires a broader perspective. Native children (like all children) must see themselves as contributing to the entire human process. They must see themselves as participants, rather than spectators. All resources must be incorporated into a systematic regional approach to teaching Native students. The sustaining of a social and cultural impetus for the education of our children must come from the theorists, activists, practitioners, and parents. If Native learners are to be prepared for the future, then we must take advantage of the lessons of the past, workings of the present day, and preparation of tomorrow's culturally responsive teachers.

Teachers in a multicultural society need to hold an attitude of respect for cultural differences, know the cultural resources their students bring to class, and be skilled at tapping students' cultural resources in the teaching–learning process. They must believe that all students are capable of learning and they must implement an enriched curriculum for all students. Finally, they must have a strong sense of professional efficacy (Villegas, 1991).

SUGGESTED LEARNING EXPERIENCES

1. Interview several American Indian adults about their experiences in elementary and secondary schools. Ask where they attended school, what they liked most about their schooling experience, what their favorite teacher was like, and what they wish could have been different. Compare and contrast the data from the interviews with the principles presented by the author of this chapter.
2. This author describes culturally responsive teaching for American Indian students. Explain how the principles he describes can be applied to other ethnic groups and in different situations.

REFERENCES

Aaronsohn, E., Carter, C. J., & Howell, M. (1994). Preparing monocultural teachers for a multicultural world: Attitudes toward inner-city schools. *Equity and Excellence in Education, 28*(1), 5–9.

Adams, D. W. (1995). *Education for extinction: American Indians and the boarding school experience, 1875–1928.* Lawrence: University of Kansas Press.

Blum, R. W., Harmon, B., Harris, L., & Resnick, M. D. (1992). American Indian/Alaska Native youth health. *Journal of American Medical Association, 267*(12), 1637–1644.

Bowers, C. A., & Flinders, D. J. (1990). *Responsive teaching: An ecological approach to classroom patterns of language, culture, and thought.* New York: Teachers College Press, Columbia University.

Brendtro, L. K., Brokenleg, M., & Van Bocken, S. (1990). *Reclaiming youth at risk: Our hope for the future.* Bloomington, IN: National Educational Service.

Brislin, R., & Yoshida, T. (1994). *Intercultural communication training: An introduction.* Thousand Oaks, CA: Sage.

Charleston, G. M. (1994). Toward true Native education: A treaty of 1992. *Journal of American Indian Education, 33*(2), 5–56.

Cole, M., & Griffin, P. (Eds.). (1987). *Contextual factors in education.* Madison: University of Wisconsin, Wisconsin Center for Educational Research. (Eric Document Reproduction Service No. ED 288 947).

Delpit, L. D. (1988). The silenced dialogue: Power and pedagogy in educating other people's children. *Harvard Educational Review, 58*(3), 280–298.

Diaz, S., Moll, L. C., & Mehan, H. (1986). Sociocultural resources in instruction: A context-specific approach. In *Beyond language: Social and cultural factors in schooling language minority students* (pp. 187–230). Los Angeles: Evaluation, Dissemination and Assessment Center, California State University. (Eric Document Reproduction Service No. ED 304–241).

Gallimore, R. (1985, May). *The accommodation of instruction to cultural differences.* Paper presented at the University of California Conference on the Under Achievement of Linguistic Minorities, Lake Tahoe, CA.

Gilliland, H. (1992). *Teaching the Native American.* Dubuque, IA: Kendall/Hunt.

Greenberg, P. (1992). Teaching about Native Americans? Or teaching about people, including Native American? *Young Children, 47*(6), 27–30, 79–81.

Hillabrant, W., Romano, M., Stang, D., & Charleston, G. M. (1992). Native American education at a turning point: Current demographics and trends. In P. Cahape & C. B. Howley (Eds.), *Indian Nations at risk: Listening to the people* [Summaries of papers comissioned by the Indian Nations at Risk Task Force of the U.S. Department of Education]. Charleston, WV: Clearinghouse on Rural Education and Small Schools.

Hilliard, A. (1989). Teachers and cultural styles in a pluralistic society. *NEA Today, 7*(6), 65–69.

Howard, G. R. (1993). Whites in multicultural education: Rethinking our role. *Phi Delta Kappan, 75*(1), 99–104.

Irvine, J. J. (1990). *Black students and school failure: Policies, practices and prescriptions.* Westport, CT: Greenwood Press.

Johnson, J. A., Dupuis, V. L., Musial, D., Hall, G. E., & Gollnick, D. M. (1996). *Introduction to the foundations of American education.* Boston, MA: Allyn & Bacon.

Jordon, C. (1985). Translating culture: From ethnographic information to educational program. *Anthropology and Education Quarterly, 16*(2), 104–123.

King, J. E. (1991). Dysconsciousness racism: Ideology, identity, and the miseducation of teachers. *Journal of Negro Education, 60*(2), 9–27.

Mancall, P. C. (1995). *Deadly medicine: Indians and alcohol in early America.* Ithaca, NY: Cornell University Press.

McIntosh, P. (1989, July/August). White privilege: Unpacking the invisible knapsack. *Peace and Freedom,* 10–12.

Nelson-Barber, S., & Meier, T. (1990). *Multicultural context a key factor in teaching: Academic connections.* Princeton, NJ: The College Entrance Examination Board.

Ogbu, J. U. (1992). Understanding cultural diversity and learning. *Educational Researcher,* *21*(8), 5–14, 24.

Pavel, D. M., Curtin, T. R., Christenson, B., & Rudes, B. A. (1995). *Characteristics of American Indian and Alaska Native education: Results from the 1990–91 schools and staffing survey.* Washington, DC: U.S. Department of Education, Office of Educational Research and Improvement.

Pewewardy, C. D. (1994). Culturally responsible pedagogy in action: An American Indian Magnet School. In E. R. Hollins, J. E. King, & W. C. Haymon (Eds.), *Teaching diverse populations: Formulating a knowledge base* (pp. 72–92). Buffalo: State University of New York Press.

Pewewardy, C. D., & Willower, D. J. (1993). Perceptions of American Indian high school students in public schools. *Equity and Excellence in Education, 26*(1), 52–55.

Pinker, S. (1994). *The language instinct: How the mind creates language.* New York: HarperCollins.

Roop, I. (1993). Native American issues. *Social Work Perspectives, 4*(1), 34–37.

Sleeter, C. E. (1992). *Keepers of the American Dream: A study of development and multicultural education.* Washington, DC: The Falmer Press.

Smith, G. P. (1991, October). *Parameters of the knowledge base for a culturally responsible pedagogy for teacher education.* Paper presented at the annual meeting of the American Association of Colleges of Teacher Education, University of Northern Florida.

Stalvey, L. M. (1989). *The Education of a WASP.* Madison: University of Wisconsin Press.

Szasz, M. C. (1992). Current conditions in American Indian and Alaska Native communities. In P. Cahape & C. B. Howley (Eds.), *Indian Nations at risk: Listening to the people* [Summaries of papers commissioned by the Indian Nations at Risk Task Force of the U.S. Department of Education]. Charleston, WV: Clearinghouse on Rural Education and Small Schools.

Terry, R. W. (1975). *For Whites only.* Grand Rapids, MI: William B. Eerdmans.

Trimble, J. E. (1981). Value differentials and their importance in counseling American Indians. In P. B. Pedersen, J. G. Draguns, W. J. Lonner, & J. E. Trimble (Eds.), *Counseling across cultures* (pp. 203–226). Honolulu: University of Hawaii Press.

Unrau, W. E. (1996). *White man's wicked water: The alcohol trade and prohobition in Indian country, 1802–1892.* Lawrence: University Press of Kansas.

Villegas, A. M. (1991). *Culturally responsive pedagogy for the 1990's and beyond* [Trends and Issues Paper No. 6]. Washington, DC: ERIC Clearinghouse on Teacher Education.

Part III

DRAWING ON THE LANDSCAPE: DEVELOPING A GLOBAL PERSPECTIVE

OVERVIEW

Part I provided us with a picture of a classroom rife with problems resulting from the cultural mismatch between the curriculum and the student body. Our beginning teacher, acknowledging the failures around her and the inadequacy of the preservice training she had received, is forced by necessity to develop her own theoretical framework based on her own emerging pedagogy centered around the needs of her students. Step by step, and with an awareness of the cultural commonalities between her and her students, she forges a curriculum that is culturally based and inclusive of the values and perspectives of the community.

Part II expands this practice by looking into a variety of classrooms, using culturally relevant materials, pedagogical practices, and curricula. Student success begins to be measured according to self-affirmation, identity, and feelings of belonging. Moving away from the dominant cultural values, restrictive and irrelevant curricular programs, and teaching strategies that further alienate students from diverse backgrounds, teachers utilize similar experiential knowledge and cultural understandings to bring about more positive classroom opportunities.

The authors in Part III look at these same issues from a more global perspective. Suggesting changes in curriculum and content design and methods of instruction, the authors of this section provide programmatic changes based on historical evaluation, their understanding of the status quo, and an awareness of transforming educational programs through what have been heretofore exclusionary materials, information, and knowledge. In short, the following authors propose to expand our understanding of rhetoric, composition, literature, social science, music, and theater arts through the diversity of a transcultural world.

This section begins with Villanueva's journey from the streets of Brooklyn to the Pacific Northwest; from his Puerto Rican "ways with words" that do not reflect the "rain in Spain" of the elocutionary movement in this country to a scholar with enormous flexibility in language usage. He makes the point that not all of America's Englishes are accepted. Tracing the work of Labov, Cole, Scribner, and Heath, he explains that even within the same language (English), speakers from different cultures use words differently. Kaplan's concept of "contrastive rhetoric" provides a new way of looking at language and at how people use language as part of their thinking, as part of their experiences.

Villanueva gives us an important history lesson, showing how one's linguistic ancestry (in the case of the Latino-Spanish) is displayed in the way one uses words. He explains why the Latino's languaging patterns have roots with the Sophists of fifth century Athens. To explain, the author takes us through a journey of language and rhetorical history. He describes 700 years of Arab domination and 200 years (going back traditionally, 700 more) of Byzantine domination over Spain. He also discusses 400 years of Spanish domination of the New World. He then looks at the Latino's ways with words, which, he says, have been influenced for nearly 2,000 years by several rhetorical styles. He explains various sentence patterns of various groups such as Ecuadorians, Spanish-speaking New York Puerto Rican college writers, and Mexican students, each using Sophistic characteristics. Even Anglo American students raised among Chicanos in Arizona show characteristics of Sophistic rhetoric.

Villanueva encourages us to become discourse analysts, to attempt to find these patterns of rhetoric in our students' writing and thus avoid penalizing some for a different rhetorical heritage. He speaks of Aristotle, whose rhetoric is that of the academic, contending that it is our responsibility to provide this background for our students. Villanueva provides a number of avenues to approach the writing classroom. First, he gives advice and illustrates a system for dealing with sentence-level errors. Next, he talks about the discourse level, showing how the student's writing and the school's required writing are different, not wrong.

Finally, Villanueva offers an activity that allows students to research their own linguistic origins, giving examples of his own students—some Navajo, Hopi, and Oneida. An awareness of language and how one uses language, he claims, makes contrastive rhetoric both viable and enjoyable for students of color and for all students.

In his chapter on expanding the literary canon for the secondary class-room, Athanases points out that the literature of diverse groups has been traditionally excluded from the English classroom. He presents a realistic look at what exists today in many classes and follows with a framework for planning curricula. He then provides units of study designed for inclusive-ness, emphasizing literature of diverse groups, ending with the construction of an overall plan. Although professional organizations have long called for inclusive literature, teachers often lack time, materials, and support for making changes in their curricular choices. Consequently, the literature used in many classes remains narrowly defined and written predominantly by White men. Due to lack of expertise, use of anthologies, and insecurity in teaching various genres popular among diverse writers (e.g., poetry), and state mandates, little change has been evidenced in recent years.

Athanases believes in transformative curriculum and advocates the use of writings by "authentic" authors. He makes the case that literature written about a particular group is not the same as literature written by someone from that group. For students of color, such literature validates them in the same way literature from the dominant culture has validated students of that culture for a long time. He also stresses that literature within an ethnic minority group should be considered diverse (much the same way all literature is defined). It behooves us to create a balance of readings lest we fall into the trap of stereotyping the various groups we study. The author suggests developing a literature program in which feelings can be expressed and steps to find similarities among peoples are taken. The author recommends using authentic writers, providing a variety of voices within a particular culture, and illustrating thematic and crosscultural units using both short and long works. He offers a number of excellent titles for use with the units in each discussion.

Athanases completes his chapter by creating a literary unit. He encour-ages preservice teachers to consider first their audience, then selection of topic, theme/focus, and key areas for study and resources. He advises them to devise an overall plan, a rationale, and lesson plans which include reader-response instruction and integration of reading, speaking, listening, and writing.

Shropshire's work presents an even more disturbing account of the continued Eurocentric approach to teaching history and the social studies, often limited by the boundaries of the textbook. Discussing the current status of the history curriculum, the author illustrates the discrepancy that exists between the tenets of multicultural teaching and the constraints of the traditional text that, on the one hand, lauds the heritage of our citizens, and on the other, confines information so as to exclude many of our students. Critiquing several current history texts, Shropshire shows the discrepancies that exist between the dominant group and parallel cultures.

Citing an analysis of slavery in history texts, he notes that none of the texts reviewed discussed the origins and consequences of the slave trade then or now. The author states that the ramifications for such misrepresentation have grave repercussions for people of color. If teachers fail to acknowledge this misinformation, they are maintaining the status quo.

Shropshire calls for the multiculturalizing of the history curriculum. Citing the struggles in California and New York as background, she describes the current debate. She warns of the tug-of-war that threatens to maintain the status quo. She raises the question that confronts all of us involved in curriculum transformation: Do we challenge the traditionalists who cling to their notion of a "common culture" (which amounts more or less to the status quo)? Or, do we accept the challenge of changing our curriculum to offer a more honest look at the history of this country? Often our decisions are made by tradition, publishing companies that want their books to sell, budget concerns, and community constraints. The author calls for a more responsible decision-making process.

In her discussion of the establishment of the U.S. history standards, Shropshire describes the importance of critical thinking skills and reasoning that the creators adhered to in their "eras" of chronological development and different cultural perspectives. Reactions were split, and the attacks focused on political correctness and multiculturalism. This chapter ends with a discussion of what to teach in history classes. The importance of involving students in the history-teaching process is central in creating change. The author encourages teachers to challenge textbooks and ask students to evaluate several aspects of the information presented.

Mueller's chapter on multiculturalizing an integrated unit with music as its base professes that a "broad spectrum of cultural diversity should be reflected in the study of music." Culturally responsive curricula should acknowledge music as a vehicle for connecting various disciplines through a strong creative bond. The author offers guidelines to incorporating multicultural concepts/ideas and diversity issues: collaborate with other teachers, select materials from literature and other disciplines, emphasize songs and activities from various cultures, maintain authenticity of materials, select relevant materials, creatively interpret basic ideas within a culture, and utilize expertise of students, parents, and community resources.

Mueller develops a collaborative project that consists of culturally diverse activities. Selected southwest Native American cultures are represented through musical experiences. Collaborative teams are described and many materials are suggested. Multiculturalism as it relates to academic subjects, related arts, music, and community is examined. Included as well is a final presentation of a broader perspective on integrating music and multiculturalism across the curriculum. Within the context of this framework, Mueller includes geography, language arts, foreign language, and literature.

Mathematics is also represented, along with science and social studies/history. Creative and dramatic theater are articulated, including selected Native American stories, imagery activities, activities for movement, dance, physical education, folk dances, sports, and visual arts. The author concludes by telling us that music is an art form and has value not only as a subject, but also as an effective tool to facilitate learning across the curriculum. Diversity in music and other disciplines must be incorporated into school curricula to increase cultural awareness and respect.

The volume ends with Abell's work on the pedagogical process of assisting preservice teachers in learning to recognize and value difference. In this chapter, the author explores the similarities and differences among stages of development of college students, women, and racial minority groups in terms of knowledge and identity. The importance of acknowledging, respecting, and appreciating many perspectives is stressed. Discussing the research on changing patterns of thinking, Abell mentions Perry's model in which European American men are subjects, as well as Belenky, Clinchy, Goldberger, and Tarule's (1986) work on European American women of a variety of ages. She comments on the developmental stages of women ranging from silence to constructed knowledge. Abell ends this review with Margolda's work on gender-related patterns of knowing and reasoning. Noted here is the lack of attention to race and class that the author presents as an important element in preparing preservice teachers. Abell extends the stages identified in *Women's Ways of Knowing* (Belenky et al., 1986) to look at and value difference among her students. She begins by showing how a dualistic perspective allows no distinction of difference. Describing the move from silence to finding one's voice, she expands this concept to include race, class, ethnicity, and sexual orientation of both men and women.

Abell discusses how her students begin to respect one another's views as they integrate personal experience with course content, entering into the dialogical process in order to understand others. The students begin to develop a sense of racial identity, the rich diversity of their past, and use specific patterns of thought with regard to knowledge. Abell demonstrates how identity theory (Black racial identity and White racial identity) can assist teachers in developing strategies to promote the valuing of difference. She proposes a pedagogy that employs personal experiences of self and others to construct knowledge. She encourages "speaking with each other in class, listening and reflecting" to create a critical process in pursuit of cultural identity and mutual respect.

This section challenges you to look at curriculum and instruction on a meta-cognition level. We ask you to consider ways in which you might transcend the status quo and offer new perspectives in your teaching, instructional design, and the way you view your classroom. We are asking you to take risks, to dare to go beyond what has been done before, to allow your students to share in the successes of your teaching.

This volume has taken you from the struggles of a beginning teacher, trained in ways that are inadequate for the classroom and her students, to a broad-based look at transforming our thinking to include and value the perspectives and experiences of everyone. We have looked at materials, we have considered classroom context, we have made suggestions for teaching in a culturally responsive environment. We hope that what you have learned here can be applied to your own teaching and learning.

Chapter 8

Sophistry, Aristotle, Contrastive Rhetoric, and the Student of Color

Victor Villanueva, Jr.
Washington State University

FOCUS QUESTIONS

1. How might an elementary or high school teacher use knowledge of "contrastive rhetoric" to enhance the development of communicative competence, especially in writing, for youngsters from diverse cultural and experiential backgrounds?
2. What are the implications of "different ways with language" for teaching and learning in classrooms beyond the development of communicative competence for students from different cultural and experiential backgrounds?
3. How does this author's historical account of language and rhetoric inform preservice teachers' understanding of cultural differences, similarities, and influences that are directly linked to the politics of preference for a particular rhetorical style?

INTRODUCTION: DIFFERENT PLACES, DIFFERENT DISCOURSES

I know I really have no right to ask, but I must. I must ask you to trust me here. Go along with me, even though the connections, at first, won't be clear, even though I slip from autobiography to linguistics, from the

107

history of the Western language movement to empirical research to a short brush with Aristotle. Trust me—after the winding journey, I promise we'll end up in the classroom.

When you read about the contributors to this volume you will get some information about us. You'll find out about our academic rank (I'm like an army major, maybe, a PhD associate professor with an administrative post or two). You'll learn about our schooling, the things that lend us a certain sanctioned authority. But, even after reading about us, you won't know us. You won't likely know how we came to know the things we know. What you read will tell you that I teach rhetoric and writing, but it won't tell you what that means, really, and it won't tell you how I perceive of such things, or why I think they're important. This information won't tell you. But I will.

I was born and raised, for the first 16 years of my life, in Brooklyn, New York, where I lived in predominately African American and Puerto Rican neighborhoods, Williamsburgh and Bedford-Stuyvesant. The 3 years after were spent in southern California—Compton, North Long Beach, and Huntington Park—crossing from African American to working-class White, to Chicano and other neighborhoods. I spent the following 7 years in the U.S. Army as an enlisted man with a high school equivalency certificate (a GED), during which time I traveled to wartime Vietnam, northern California, peacetime Korea, and the Pacific Northwest. Many travels. And in my travels, I came across different ways with words. Despite the differences, however, I always somehow felt at home in a lot of discourse communities.

I mean, I understand intimately something that comes out of some research conducted by folks like Sylvia Scribner and Michael Cole (1981), Shirley Brice Heath (1983), and William Labov (1972). What these various researchers discovered is that different cultures, even those sharing the same language, reflect different ways with language. Anthropologist Heath (1983) studied, for nearly a decade, the language ways of African American folks in their community, working-class White folks in theirs, and of the mix of races in the relatively urban center of the greater community (areas of the Carolina Piedmonts she names Trackton, Roadville, and Townspeople). All were English-speaking, all she studied possessed reading and writing abilities. But they didn't do the same things with their literacies. Each had different "ways with words." Labov (1972) discovered the formal, rule-governed ways of the English of African Americans and Puerto Ricans of New York City. He called those particular ways Black English Vernacular, an unfortunate term because Labov's Black Vernacular wasn't exactly like that described by Heath (1983). In trying to assert the legitimacy of one community's ways with words, he inadvertently labeled an entire race (including Puerto Ricans, only some of whom were Black, who experienced different cultures and languages at home, in the street, and at school).

There was a plus to Labov's work, however—the recognition that there was more to the language spoken in the New York City ghettoes and many other northern, urban centers, than slang. There was also a negative in his legacy—a too facile analogy between the problems often experienced by those learning a new language and the problems African Americans experienced in discovering the ways of language required by the schools. Meanwhile, Latinos were thrown into the foreign-language bin, along with Asians and American Indians. All of us became foreign-language learners, including those of us who knew no language other than English. Then again, these others of color weren't exactly taught like foreign-language learners. Nor were they taught like the African Americans, who, when it came to writing, weren't really being taught. The intention was there, but the method wasn't.

And just to confuse matters, some of the markers of the nonnative writer could be found among African Americans. The Asian international student would find the English use of the article confusing: when to use the indefinite *a* or *an*, when to use the definite *the*. Black English speakers would use *a* in all indefinite cases—*a analogy*. The Asian international student might forget inflectional endings—*-s* or *-ed*. The Black English speaker would do some of the same in writing. The correlation is clear, some said, even if there were few similarities between the various Asian tongues and Black English Vernacular.

But coincidence would be sufficient, apparently, given that dialects and foreign languages are both instances of difference from the language of prestige, the written dialect (*grapholect*, according to E. D. Hirsch, 1977)—or at least that was the reasoning of some, maybe even many. And there were the theories of Stephen Krashen (1982), who argued that second-language acquisition (L2) went through a similar process to first-language acquisition (L1), so that speaking must precede writing, just like it does in the normal acquisition of the mother tongue. Within the acquisition of L2, writes Krashen, are sedimentations of the prior language. What all this amounted to was "Our Fair Basic Writer," George Bernard Shaw, returning to the classroom, now dressed in Black English Vernacular:

"No, not 'What up,' but 'How do you do?' "
"Not 'Aa-ite,' but 'All right.' "

I'm poking fun. But you can see the problem. Krashen's (1982) theory of language acquisition, applied to speakers of other dialects rather than speakers of other languages, amounts to a scheme that has never worked: Teach students who speak different dialects to speak the standard dialect and the writing will follow. When the writing "falls," then the problem must be that the "inappropriate ways" of the original spoken dialect have interfered with the writing. We are left with just another version of the

eloctionary movement of a century ago, a movement, we know, that
disparaged the ways of speaking of America's people of color who are
monolingual in English or at least proficient in one of America's Englishes.

CONTRASTIVE RHETORIC

At the same time Labov (1972) was pointing out dialect difference as
legitimate, and other folks were doing other things with the teaching of
writing, Robert Kaplan (1966) was developing a way of thinking about
writing instruction for speakers of languages other than English that he
called *contrastive rhetoric.* Simply put, contrastive rhetoric argues that people
from different cultures put arguments together differently: their rhetoric
is different from the rhetoric of English. English, we know, seeks to be
straightforward, linear, and hierarchical (unlike, say, this chapter).
Different cultures might not regard the linear as best, might—not even
consciously—decide on another way to lay out an argument. Kaplan's
theory was not greeted with open arms. He was claiming that different
people think differently, and there really is no way to know about thought.
But thought wasn't really the issue. The issue was what happens in students'
writing. Kaplan had been less interested in creating a theory than he was
in developing a pedagogy for L2 students.
    Kaplan's (1966) work has not yet apparently entered the realm of basic
writing, of teaching writing to students whose primary language happens
to be English. Speakers and writers of English, after all, would reflect the
discourse of English. There must have been other problems, the problems
of coming from an oral culture, said Thomas Farrell (1982) and Walter
Ong (1983), problems that sounded a lot like the notions of L1–L2 interference, leading—again—to the "Rain in Spain" (or "How do you do")
solution. The problems concerned a too-facile definition of culture, a
familiar one in our society, which viewed the languages of cultures as either
sophisticated or lacking. There is simply difference. And that difference,
writes Kaplan (1966), is rhetorical.
    Then, maybe, the problem turns on the word *rhetoric.* When the word
rhetoric comes up in day-to-day conversation, it tends to mean bombast, a
bunch of fancy words, a flair for speaking, a put-up job, a con. Rhetoric
tends to be associated with dishonesty:

*The president's speech last night showed some impressive rhetoric but contained
little that was of substance.*
Let's cut through all the rhetoric and get to the real issues at hand.

Rhetoric is an ancient word. Although it does have plenty to do with
looking at how people are persuaded through language, its domain is all

language use. Kaplan and others like Labov and Heath have opened the door to reconsiderations of how all cultures and all cultures' ways with words (without regard to particular languages) display historically based ways with words.

I'll make clear my meaning here by looking to the Latino, the American whose linguistic ancestry is predominately Spanish, but who may know only English. Although the overwhelming majority of Latinos in the United States are natives, often reaching back over a century to the time Mexican land was ceded to the United States or Puerto Rican land given to the United States at the end of a war, bigotry and political economy have kept the overwhelming majority of Latinos in ghettoes, where new immigrants expose the American Latino to the ways of Spanish and English dialects mix with the dialects of others of color. What happens is that the rhetoric retains its ancestry.

A look to the history of ways with words shows a Spanish rhetoric that is rooted in the rhetoric of the sophists of fifth century B.C.E. Athens, where the language wasn't Spanish or English.

Take a journey with me, then: a whirlwind tour through ancient times, from the Greek golden age to the discovery of America. It won't take long.

SOPHISTRY'S JOURNEY[1]

These are the streets of Ancient Greece. It's the fifth century, B.C.E. There are no wars for the time being. There is peace. There is prosperity. New things are happening: great new drama, sculpture, architecture—and an attempt at democracy—at least the democracy of free Athenian-born men. The most popular entertainer of the times is the orator. And the most popular of these is the sophist, Gorgias, someone whose fame as an orator is unquestioned and extends over a long time. He's the Mick Jagger, the Michael Jackson, the Tito Puente of his time. The orator holds the entertainment status that the musician does now, but he also has a greater potential for making things happen in his world than today's musician. The orator's skills and talents are the skills and talents needed to get things done in government. Rhetoric is the art for entertainment, as well as for law and for government.

The sophists, then, are the most popular among those looking to be entertained, but they not too popular in other important circles. Of the sophists, the most popular are Protagoras and the aforementioned Gorgias. But both are minorities, not native Athenians. They are *mêtics*, one reason,

---

[1]This section and the next have been only slightly altered from the original versions appearing in Villanueva (1993, pp. 79–88). Copyright © 1993 by the National Council of Teachers of English. Reprinted with permission.

perhaps, why they are not well liked among those special circles. *Mêtics*, or aliens, are legislatively second class, not quite enjoying the full benefits of citizenship. Protagoras comes from Abderah, in Northern Greece, and Gorgias from Leontini, in Sicily. Although they are forbidden by law to take more active parts in the politics of Athens, they serve a vital function in maintaining Athenian democracy: They train those likely to take on important roles in Athenian life, using as one of their principal themes, rhetoric in the cause of active participation in domestic, social, and political life.

Protagoras, probably the first of the paid traveling teachers, is something of a problem. His way of seeing things poses a challenge to the dominant ideology in Athens, Ionian natural philosophy, in which things are as they are because they are in the nature of things, meant to be. Protagoras says that "man is the measure of all things." So if man is the measure, then rulers are not specially imbued by nature to rule. If man is the measure, then there can only be a few natural laws, and there can be equally valid truths. Protagoras says that there can be opposing and, in some senses, equally valid arguments to any given case—two sides (at least) to any argument. Not only are there two sides to any argument, but anyone can be taught to present, effectively, either side, or both. Anyone can learn to be a rhetor, not just the select few with natural speaking abilities. Protagoras, and the sophists generally, introduce a humanist ideology: humanity as ultimately responsible and able to be taught the ways in which to take on responsibility.

But a subjective and relativistic ideology causes problems. The aristocracy cannot claim a natural superiority; laws and knowledge cannot claim to be absolute; everything can become subject to challenge. This boy has got to go. Plato takes up the challenge. And he succeeds. Today, the only thing cheaper than "mere rhetoric" is "sheer sophistry."

Democrats of the fifth century also have an argument against the sophists. The democrats complain that the sophists do not offer what they have to everyone. Because sophists charge fees for their services, only the wealthy are able to gain access to the potential inherent in those services. The way to humanism is a commodity.

In their quest to gain customers, the sophists perform public exhibitions of their skills. These are well attended. Because the public demonstrations are intended to gather students, sophistic orators show off their own unique skills, not just the potential powers of rhetoric. Their speeches, then, seem less concerned with content than with displaying artistry.

As already noted, the most popular sophist of the time is Gorgias. Among his demonstrations, one still available to us is the *Encomium of Helen* (Gorgias, 1913), a speech in praise of Helen. Gorgias argues skillfully that despite what the Athenians "know" to be the case, stoic Helen was not guilty of betraying Menelaus, her Attic husband, even if she did go off with the Trojan Paris. Gorgias argues that Helen was either a victim of fate, or a victim of the will of the gods, a victim of love, a victim of forcible abduction, or a victim of language. Gorgias argues that there is a kind of magic to language, making it stronger than individual will. Therefore, it might have been Paris's rhetoric skill that seduced Helen.

For Gorgias, language is an obsession. His demonstration reflects the attention he places on the language. The *Helen* is replete with rhyming words and echoing rhythms, with parallelism and antithetical structures, with parallels that are carefully constructed to contain identical numbers of syllables. This consciousness of demonstrating the rhetorical, stylistic skills of the orator, and this consciousness of the sound of the oration, even over the sense, become the marks of the sophist.

Centuries later. We're in Rome now. Cicero is praetor, something like the president. Cicero is also a gifted lawyer—and a great orator. His ways with language, however, are strange. Cicero is accused of being "Asiatic" in his rhetorical practices. To be Asiatic is to employ the rhetoric of Asia Minor and Greece. Its opposite, the Attic, a reference to Athens, is not at all like the sophists. It is the plain, precise rhetoric of Latin. Cicero's writing and oratory are characterized by amplification, a stylistic device in which a certain point is repeated several times in succession, though using different words. His writing displays sophistic tendencies: parallelism, antithetical structures, and amplification in order to assure a certain sound to the structure.

However, because the sophists were considered morally suspect in working for money, and were surely ideologically and theologically dangerous, they were successfully squelched from Western rhetorical history for centuries. Cicero himself claims not to be Asiatic because the Asiatic is philosophically empty. Yet the Ciceronian style, and its sophistic ways with words, dominates Western oratorical style until the 18th century, when Peter Ramus redefines rhetoric in line with the new modern ways of thinking. Rhetoric is style; ideas are matters of logic, says Ramus. Aristotle's clarity and logic adopted to the rhetorical takes precedence over the Ciceronian (S. Crowley, personal communication, 1973). Then the history is gone as well as the style itself, a reference to the sophists showing up in the writing of Hegel, but really only arising again during the 1970s through the 1990s or so.

Sophistry is apparent in the East, however. By the fourth century C.E. the Roman Empire is virtually destroyed by the German Visigoths. The seat of the empire moves to Constantinople, New Rome, ruled by Constantine. This is the birth of the Byzantine Empire. By 395 C.E. Christianity is adopted as the religion of the empire. Greek is the language, even as the Byzantines refer to themselves as Romans (Arnott, 1973), and the sophistic is the formal use of the language.

Philostratus calls this rebirth of florid rhetoric the Second Sophistic. Like the sophists of old, the second sophists travel the empire giving demonstrations, celebrating the greatness of Greece and its reflection in the greatness of Rome. Maybe as early as the second century C.E., the second sophistic enjoys significant influence, even though Christians were critical of its celebration of pagan mythology and—like the old sophists—of its self-indulgent attention to the speaker's skills and its emphasis on language for its own sake. But by the end of the fourth century, the second sophistic's ways were evident in the Christian patristic homilies and orations of Gregory of Nazianzus, Basil the Great, and his brother Gregory. In 392 C.E. the Byzantine Emperor Theodosius forbids pagan worship. St. John Chrysostom (John Golden-Tongued), patriarch of Constantinople, is regarded as the finest of all Christian orators in Greek, trained by the sophist Libanius (Arnott, 1973; Kennedy, 1980).

Byzantium, and thereby Byzantine rhetoric, remains relatively constant for more than 1,000 years, finally falling to Turkish invaders in 1453. Rome knows no such consistency, even during the Holy Roman Empire, losing to the Visigoths, retaken by Byzantium, falling to the Ostrogoths, taken and retaken for centuries. But more important for what I am presenting here is Byzantium's relations to the Arabs and to Spain. We're in what is modern Turkey now, Constantinople (now Istanbul), the Byzantine Empire.

Byzantium had an uneasy relation with the Arabs—frequent fighting mainly along the long border along the Caucasus and the desert and occasional attempts by Arabs to take Constantinople itself. But the Byzantines and Arabs both face a common threat from the Slavs and the Goths. So, from about 395 to 636 there is an alliance between the Byzantine Empire and an Arab federation, the *foederati*. These Arabs learn enough of Constantinople's Greek ways to act as something like border mediators between Byzantium and the Arab peninsula. There are also the Rhomaic Arabs who take residence in Byzantium (Shahid, 1989). Add Byzantium's possession of Syria and Persia, later taken by the Saracens, Moslem Arabs, and there remains a relatively strong Byzantine influence to Arab rhetoric.

During these early centuries of the Byzantine Empire, the Visigoths move into Spain. There, they share the peninsula with the Suevi, another Germanic people. Northern Africa is taken by yet another group of Germans, the Vandals, who had settled first in southern Spain, sharing that part of the peninsula with another wandering group, the Iranian-speaking Alans. Except for the Ostrogoths in Italy, the Germanic conquerors are content to exploit without regard to converting the native populations. We still speak of vandals as despoilers. The Byzantine Empire, however, has its sense of "Roman-ness," a historical right to rule, now joined with the Christian sense of mission. Byzantium could not allow this blow to the empire's historically proven legacy and to the empire's moral mission. By the mid-sixth century, the Byzantine Empire retakes northern Africa and southern Spain (Jenkins, 1966). A continuity from the old Roman Empire is reestablished in Spain, now more visibly bearing something of the older Greek ways. Eventually, Spain is again taken by the Visigoths, but there is nothing to suggest any attempts by the Germans at removing the Greek ways of New Rome in the ancient colony of Old Rome (Jenkins, 1966).

Mohammed enters the picture in the seventh century. In 622, Mohammed, having moved to Medina, begins to gather a following. It is at this time that the Byzantine Emperor Heraclius is on a campaign to regain Persia for the empire, a campaign which is to succeed 6 years later, establishing the True Cross in Persia, the Orthodox Christianity of the Byzantines. Persia is again part of what Heraclius sees as the Roman Empire, Heraclius himself hailed as the new Scipio, Persians having to take on Christianity, the Hellenistic language of the empire, and Greco-Roman rule generally. But Orthodox Christianity has its problems: nearly 200 years of debate over the nature or natures of Jesus. Officially, Jesus is to be regarded as having two natures, the Father and the Son. The dominant "heresy," known as *monophysite*, is that Jesus had one divine nature. Heraclius tries to bring the factions together, declaring in 639 that whether two natures or one, Jesus was possessed by a single energy or will. The orthodox patriarch of Jerusalem, Sophronius, condemns the idea. Pope Honarium disavows it. Mohammed offers the Arabs, Persia, Syria, and Egypt, poor and once again subject to Greco-Roman rule, an alternative, likely drawn from the Christian, the Jewish, and the Persian creeds that had been implanted in Yemen during Persian rule there: There is but one God, and Mohammed is His prophet. By 628, the same time as Heraclius's retaking of Persia, Mohammed with powerful followers, generals, and caliphs occupies Mecca, only 1,000 miles south of Byzantium, formally expelling Mecca's idols. Four years later, Mohammed dies, but the wheels have been set in motion. By 639 the Saracens are in Syria and taking Egypt. Within a few decades Islam, the "Surrender to God" religion, is established in Persia and most of the southern and eastern parts of the New Roman Empire (Jenkins, 1966).

In 711 the Saracen Tariq ibn-Ziyad, accompanied by northern African Berban volunteers, sails the 9 miles that divide the Pillars of Hercules and takes Spain from the Visigoth Roderic. Within the year Spain is under the control of Moslem Arabs. These are the Moors, likely getting their name in having come from Morocco. The Pillars of Hercules are eventually renamed to Jabal Musa on the African side and Jabal Tariq, Gibraltar, on the Spanish. In 732 the Saracens cross the Pyrenees, but are stopped by the Frankish ruler Charles Martel. In 756 Prince Abd-al-Rahman runs to Spain when Syria overthrows the Saracen capital. The new capital is established at Cordoba. Within 150 years Cordoba is established as the largest city in western Europe, a cultural rival to Baghdad and Constantinople. The *mezquita*, the mosque at Cordoba, remains today, Arabic calligraphy and all, Byzantine mosaics and all. The Spanish have been Byzantine and so have the Arabs. The Arabs remain (although not without conflict, like Charlemagne or the Crusades) until 1492, when Ferdinand and Isabella finally oust the Saracens, the Moors. Later in the same year Isabella commissions Christopher Columbus (Abercrombie, 1988). The Spanish conquerors of the New World bring the Arab and the Byzantine, the sophistic, with them.

Now, I have taken this dizzying route through language and rhetorical history because I believe it is interesting and because a special perspective is gained in understanding the historical. The particular perspective gained here is that the Latino's ways with words could not help but be influenced by the 400 years in which Spain dominated so much of the New World, and that those ways would have been influenced by the 700 years of Arab domination over Spain, and by the 200 years of Byzantium, with its rhetorical heritage going back yet another 700 years. Nearly 2,000 years of certain rhetorical ways, albeit in different languages, are not likely to be overcome in the 100 years and less of English domination, especially when we consider that the rhetorical history of English, although through another route, mainly Cicero, also gave a kind of sophistry special privilege up to the 18th century.

SOPHISTRY AND CONTRASTIVE RHETORIC

This is the history. There is also the research. A study of the writing of Ecuadorians conducted by Lux and Grabe (1991), for instance, found that the Ecuadorians tended to form longer sentences than Anglo-American writers, preferring coordination, sentence parallels, over subordination, displaying an attention toward establishing a rhythm to the coordinate, a tendency to deal in the abstract, and a tendency toward greater reader–writer interaction by way of narrative discourse. Lux and Grabe refer to studies that find similar tendencies among Arab writers.

Sister Olga Santana-Seda's 1974 dissertation found the same tendencies among Spanish-speaking New York Puerto Rican college freshman writers. She also found that these writers tended toward nonsequential sentences, that the logical connections between sentences were not always apparent. María Montaño-Harmon (1991) corroborated Sister Santana-Seda's findings in studying Mexican student writers. She found that the digressions in logic appeared to be conscious. She also found that the Spanish writers had a tendency for amplification (although Montaño-Harmon referred to the tendency as hyperbole): Sentences repeat a point several times, each time using different words, each more ornate than the previous. This is the sophistic tendency found in Cicero.

In a side comment within her study, Montaño-Harmon mentions that 5 of the 50 Anglo-American students she studied showed rhetorical patterns more like the Spanish than the other Anglo-American writers. These five lived in a border town in southern Arizona, grew up among Chicanos, and considered themselves relatively bilingual. She only made note, given the constraints of statistical significance. Taking her side comment further, I surmise that having come in contact with the sophistic, the five found it easy to take on the Spanish ways because those ways also find expression in English, particularly in the writings of older literary figures, like Samuel Johnson. I'm not saying that the Anglo subjects had read folks like Johnson, just that there is a rhetorical history to those ways in English as well, a history a lot older than the Aristotelian ways we think of as "right" in the late 20th century. Historical and empirical research suggest that for Spanish speakers, or those exposed to the ways of the Spanish speaker, the preferred or "natural" rhetorical ways with written discourse are fundamentally sophistic.

ARISTOTLE, THE WRITING CLASSROOM, AND DIFFERENCE

So what does this mean for the classroom? It means we should become discourse analysts, rhetorical critics. We should look to the writing of students of color, even when they are monolingual in English, and see if a pattern emerges over two or three essays. This is a variation of something that was discussed some time back, that student writers display patterns of error that we should be able to discover and to which we should thereby tailor our instruction on grammar and mechanics (Shaughnessy, 1977). That patterning, both for smaller bits (grammar) and for larger bits (discourse), is a time consumer only when analyzing those first two papers. Then, tailored responses follow discovered patterns.

Donald Murray (1978) says "writing is revising" (p. 85). I tell this to my writing students. I let them give vent to their own ways with words in creating early drafts with papers, let them rely on their entire linguistic arsenal, tell them not to worry about "right" and "wrong." There is neither. There is, however, switching codes, adjusting the language to fit the situation. Even those with trouble in Standard English know of switching codes, speaking one way to their "homies," speaking another to their teachers and parents (we would hope). Even those seeming to come from White, middle-class suburbia switch codes. Besides, we can never tell what the linguistic backgrounds of our students might be. (The blonde young woman in the front row speaks in a manner that reminds me of southern California affluence, but her writing tells of her having come from South Africa just a few years ago.) And because I teach in the college classroom, I'm concerned with a kind of written discourse, a code, that most have not been exposed to—the writing of academics.

In the classroom, I speak of conquests and the rhetoric that traveled with the conquerors. I introduce Averröes, the Arab ibn-Rushd, who wrote commentaries on Aristotle, and the class becomes 11th century Toledo (Spain, not Ohio), where Christians, Jews, and Muslims translated Averröes and thereby Aristotle into Latin. You might want to know more than the few words in this paragraph, but little more is needed.

What you would need to know is Aristotle. It is Aristotle's ways with words that comprise the code that students must come to learn. We know it, even subconsciously. We have been book-folks. That's how we came to be teachers. Getting through college is being exposed to the ways with words of academics. We must, to become teachers. But I would argue we need to know just a little more. We need to look at Aristotle himself—his rhetoric, a short work, and his logic—a little longer.

Aristotle's logic stays with us. Aristotle, for instance, gave us our basic principles for defining terms. The ways he laid out for structuring a definition are still seen in dictionaries. And we can intentionally pass on those ways. It is Aristotle who claimed that the definition is basic to persuasive and expository or informational discourse. Have you ever started working on an assignment by looking up a key term in a dictionary? Have you ever begun an essay with "Webster's Dictionary defines . . ."? The impulse comes from your basic, intuitive understanding of Aristotle's principles of definition, principles that you have picked up in your reading because professional writers tend to define important words as they go, even though seldom turning to dictionaries to come to their definitions. They have been exposed to the Aristotelian, the long academic legacy.

From Aristotle we have a particular way of pursuing a line of logic—syllogistic reasoning. We know the syllogism:

All men are mortal beings.
Socrates is a man.
Therefore, Socrates is a mortal being.

Now, I realize that the syllogism is seldom taught, seldom used, even overthrown by modern philosophers like Chaim Perelman or Stephen Toulman, but we do continue to use what Aristotle called the rhetorical version of the syllogism—the *enthymeme* (used, although seldom taught). The enthymeme is a syllogism without one of the premises that lead to the conclusion. It is a rhetorical device that exploits consensus while seeming to employ the distance we associate with logic. The enthymeme exploits the things we take for granted. That really well-known syllogism about Socrates, for example, would come out like this when converted to an enthymeme: Because Socrates is a man, he is a mortal being. We'll just assume that men are mortal beings. That doesn't pose much of a problem.

But what happens with: With all this welfare and Medicare and other aid, we must be turning socialist. Convert that into a syllogism, and two un-spoken premises are possible: either All socialists are recipients of welfare, Medicare, and other care, or All persons on welfare, Medicare, and other aid are socialist. Neither premise pans out as acceptable, I would think. There would be some who would buy one or the other, however. What we have in the enthymeme, then, is an emotional appeal in the guise of logic, insofar as it always takes the form of a causal relation, common forms using *because, consequently, therefore,* and the like. In the red-scare enthymeme just described, there is an assumed *because: Because* there is all this welfare, . . . Our ways with Aristotle's logic are ubiquitous.

When it comes to writing, Aristotle writes in the *Rhetoric* that "the lan-guage of prose is distinct from that of poetry," and that "speeches of the written or literary kind owe more of their effect to their diction than to their thought" (Aristotle, 1984, p. III.i.27,18). Therefore he advises clarity, declares "that a writer must disguise his art and give the impression of speaking naturally and not artificially" (p. III.ii.19), and notes that the metaphor must be used sparingly, to clarify, not to ornament. From Aris-totle's *Rhetoric* comes the basic elements of what will come to be known as the Plain Style, today's preferred discourse of the schools—but not the preferred form of discourse for all cultures, not even for all English-speak-ing cultures. There is a need to be familiar with Aristotle, I would argue. We can turn to those who have explained Aristotle for the classroom, folks like Edward P. J. Corbett (1990). These folks will prepare you for turning the classroom into Averröes's Toledo (to which I have added some Arab artifacts in the classroom, music of Arabia and of Spain, the ready mixes provided by musicians like Otmar Liebert and some later Weather Report, and others, maybe a potluck).

And so I present Aristotle's ways. After some talk on Aristotle's logic and rhetoric—the essential definition, induction and deduction, the syllo-gism, and the enthymeme—we work on the logic and language of a stu-dent's text, suggesting ways for a rhetorical translation. We test those trans-lations by consciously seeking to use cohesive devices: words like *however* or *consequently* at the sentence level, word repetitions between sentences, and transitions among paragraphs. I supply a relatively short list of such devices (see Markels, 1984). We try to find cohesive devices that fit and discuss when none does. Sometimes none should, and it's okay. Often, re-visions, or new ways of seeing what is being attempted, present them-selves. "Tighter," rather than minimally "corrected," papers result.

The idea that ways with words have historical precedents lights students up. They try to discover their ancestry linguistically, rhetorically. They develop a metalinguistic awareness, an understanding of language in large terms. It is metalinguistic awareness that separates effective writers from the less able, says Patrick Hartwell (1980) in an article discounting the dialectic-interference notion (L1 slipping into L2 in writing). Native American students I have taught—Navajo, Hopi, Oneida, and others—have come to realize the different histories of migration among different Indian nations as a possible explanation for their different ways with words in English, for instance. Those who know only English—no longer Swahili or any other African tongue, no longer Native American tongues, no longer Azteca, or Mayan, or Boricua, or Spanish—can nevertheless take pride in having both adopted the language of the majority while maintaining the ways of ancestry and adapting the adopted, thereby establishing an all new way of code-switching. Ways of seeing, worldviews, and rhetorical predispositions are allowed expression. Logic is not reduced to right and wrong, or even propriety; rather, logic is explicitly discussed as yet another convention. Discussion of the historical and the rhetorical becomes one way to encourage a critical consciousness of writing, of writing processes and linguistic difference, without denying the technical training required for academic success.

PUTTING IT ALL TOGETHER

So what does this mean for the classroom? Well, there are two levels of classroom work: in-class instruction and response to student papers. Initially, responding to student papers in the way I'm about to outline is time-consuming, but only when there is a new batch of students. Understanding that different cultures have different ways with words means tailoring responses to address those differences—both at the sentence level and at the discourse level—accounting for the kinds of discoveries made by linguists like Labov and the discourse-level concerns of a Heath and a Kaplan.

At the sentence level, establish a grid that presents the titles of a student's paper along the top of the grid and presents the grammatical concern along the left side (Table 8.1). Alongside the error or other than Standard sentence-level concern, write the number of instances that the concern occurs. The instruction to students: Lower the number from essay to essay. Students inevitably in my experience get into self-competition, not wanting

TABLE 8.1
Grid of Grammatical Concerns in Student's Papers

	Assignment 1 Auto 31	Assignment 2 Culture?	Assignment 3 Reading . . .
Comma-splice	10	7	9 careful!
. . . to be	4	4	2
Noun/pronoun	8	5	1 good work!

to see that number go up; thereby, a Standard grammatical concern is learned. Although you'll see the basic sets of sentence-level differences from the Standard (and some downright errors), for the students to understand how to "translate," the number of items must be kept at a minimum, maybe three items at a time, adding more as the chart shows that a sentence-level concept has been understood (Haswell, 1983).

At the discourse level, what is needed is an analyst's eye. Look to the writing of students of color, even when they're monolingual in English, and see if a pattern emerges over two or three essays. Don't assume *problems* in logic, just *difference*. This means looking at students' papers and drawing arrows where the connections are made, making explicit the differences between the student's writing and the writing required of the schools—and explaining them as differences. Students get it—without having to believe that their customary ways with words are simply wrong.

When it comes to classroom instruction, it's important to emphasize not only that writing is a process but that "writing is revising." In earlier drafts students are allowed to give full vent to their own ways: Write it like you were explaining it to a parent. Next draft: Switch codes. Even those with trouble in Standard English know of switching codes, speaking one way to their "homies," speaking another to their teachers and parents. For those who appear to be White students, there is nevertheless the code of written discourse for the schools—the grapholect.

What's most fun in the classroom, and what elicits surprising results from students, is having the students explore the histories and theories that underly what they are being asked to do. Students take to sophistication if they are believed capable of it. For the histories, students take on an ethnography, interviewing family members and family archives, finding out the way arguments or even sentences are put together in the language of the family's ancestry (because most, the overwhelming majority, are not originally from English-speaking heritages). In every class, there's someone who hasn't access to family, but there is a knowledge of the ancestry. And there's the library. The realization that ways with words have historical precedents lights students up.

Students begin to discover their ancestry linguistically, rhetorically. The histories that students devise are nothing like the history I traced here, but they are interesting to the students and willingly shared among them.

The big deal is that the students become conscious of language—of written discourse—in all ways. As Patrick Hartwell (1980) discovered—as I have discovered—what separates better writers from less able writers is not the dialect that they speak but the degree to which the writers contain and display a metalinguistic awareness, an awareness of language as language. And that makes contrastive rhetoric a viable and enjoyable classroom enterprise for students of color, indeed for all students.

SUGGESTED LEARNING EXPERIENCES

1. Compare and contrast contemporary attitudes toward bilingual education and African American language usage with the historical perspective on political preferences for certain rhetorical styles described in this chapter.

2. Examine the literature describing specific features of the language spoken by a specific group of students at the elementary or secondary level. Develop a module for teaching writing to this particular population based on what you have learned about their language usage. Describe the theoretical basis for your module.

REFERENCES

Abercrombie, T. J. (1988). When the Moors ruled Spain. *National Geographic, 174*(1), 87–119.

Aristotle (1984). *The rhetoric and poetics of Aristotle* (W. R. Roberts, Trans.). New York: Random House.

Arnott, P. (1973). *The Byzantines and their world.* New York: St. Martin's Press.

Corbett, E. P. J. (1990). *Classical rhetoric for the modern student* (3rd ed.). New York: Oxford University Press.

Farrell, T. J. (1983). IQ and Standard English. *College Composition and Communication, 34*, 470–484.

Gorgias, L. (1913, February). *Encomium of Helen* (Vol. 6, p. 484) (L. Van Hook, Trans.).

Hartwell, P. (1980). Dialect interference in writing: A critical view. *Research in the Teaching of English, 14*(2), 101–118.

Haswell, R. H. (1983). Minimal marking. *College English, 45*, 600–604.

Heath, S. B. (1983). *Ways with words: Language, life, and work in communities and classrooms.* New York: Cambridge University Press.

Hirsch, E. D., Jr. (1977). *The philosophy of composition.* Chicago: University of Chicago Press.

Jenkins, R. (1966). *Byzantium: The imperial centuries, A.D. 610–1071.* Toronto: University of Toronto Press.

Kaplan, R. B. (1966). Cultural thought patterns and intercultural education. *Language Learning, 16*, 1–20.

Kennedy, G. A. (1980). *Classical rhetoric and its Christian and secular tradition from ancient to modern times.* Chapel Hill: University of North Carolina Press.

Krashen, S. D. (1982). *Principles and practice in second language acquisition.* Oxford: Pergamon.

Labov, W. (1972). *Language in the inner city: Studies in the Black English vernacular.* Philadelphia: University of Pennsylvania Press.

Lux, P., & Grabe, W. (1991). Multivariate approaches to constrastive rhetoric. *Linguas Modernas, 18*, 133–160.

Markels, R. B. (1984). *A new perspective on cohesion in expository paragraphs.* Carbondale: Southern Illinois University Press.

Montaño-Harmon, M. R. (1991). Discourse features of written Mexican Spanish: Current research in contrastive rhetoric and its implications. *Hispania, 74*, 417–425.

Murray, D. M. (1978). Internal revision: A process of discovery. In C. R. Cooper & L. Odell (Eds.), *Research on composing: Points of departure.* Urbana, IL: National Council of Teachers of English.

Ong, W. J. (1982). *Orality and literacy: The technologizing of the word.* London: Methuen.

Santana-Seda, O. (1974). *A contrastive study in rhetoric: An analysis of the organization of English and Spanish paragraphs written by native speakers of each language.* Unpublished doctoral dissertation, New York University, New York.

Scribner, S., & Cole, M. (1981). *The psychology of literacy.* Cambridge, MA: Harvard University Press.

Shahid, I. (1989). *Byzantium and the Arabs in the fifth century.* Washington, DC: Dumbarton Oaks.

Shaughnessy, M. (1977). *Errors and expectations: A guide for teachers of basic writing.* New York: Oxford University Press.

Villanueva, V., Jr. (1993). *Bootstraps: From an American academic of color.* Urbana, IL: National Council of Teachers of English.

Chapter 9

Including Diverse Perspectives in the History Curriculum

Sonya Y. Shropshire
Florida State University

FOCUS QUESTIONS

1. Who should participate in curriculum decision making and how should final decisions about curriculum content be determined?
2. How should ethnic and culturally diverse perspectives be represented in history textbooks used in the nation's schools?
3. To what extent should curriculum decision makers consider the impact of historical perspective on the psychological and social development of youngsters in school?
4. Under what conditions should biased textbooks be included as appropriate instructional materials?

INTRODUCTION

At a time when more public consideration is being given to instruction of students from ethnically diverse populations, textbook-based curriculum still depicts history from a Eurocentric perspective. This makes it difficult for teachers to effectively construct history lessons from culturally and ethnically diverse perspectives. Teachers need productive strategies that will enable students to critically analyze the past without feeling disenfranchised by the process. This chapter explores the politics and the philosophical assumptions of the current state of the history curriculum, as well as approaches to making improvements.

EXPLICATING THE CURRENT STATE
OF THE HISTORY CURRICULUM

Presently, the primary method for imparting information to students regarding history is the textbook (Arries, 1994; Loewen, 1995a). Using textbooks is convenient and easier than conducting research to find other sources of information. It has been said, however, that schools depend too heavily on textbooks (Komoski, 1985).

Nevertheless, historians maintain that history textbooks are ideally used to teach facts about the past and stories of groups during a particular time period. Others argue the information in textbooks serves purposes that have little to do with the original intent (Commeyras & Alvermann, 1994; Loewen, 1995a; Romanowski, 1996). In essence, there are two kinds of curriculum: explicit and implicit (Hollins, 1996a, 1996b). Explicit curriculum teaches students about important dates and events, and issues regarding important people in the nation's history. Implicit curriculum is "the subliminal transmission of values, practices, and perceptions of the dominant culture that determines acceptable modes of communication, social interaction, ways of thinking and knowing, and ways of distributing power, status, and resources" (Hollins, 1996b, p. 85). From this implicit curriculum, students learn what is expected of them in society.

Loewen (1995b) identifies patriotism and nationalism as values transmitted by history textbooks. History textbooks convey the message that good citizens are proud of their heritage, and that, although many people experienced conflict, the conflicts were effectively and democratically resolved. Loewen points out that this optimistic view is not bad, but it is unrealistic, and may lend to blaming those ethnic groups who have not been successful using European American approaches to life's challenges.

How one perceives the accuracy in textbook information depends on the perspective presented. Traditionally, information in history textbooks has been constructed from the European immigrants' perspective. For example, few books speak unfavorably about Christopher Columbus or his "discovery" of the Americas. He is typically portrayed as an innovative, daring navigator, initially a friend to Native Americans. The fact that he was responsible for enslavement of human beings is either distorted or omitted (Loewen, 1995a). Traditional history textbooks also credit Europeans with discovering the North Pole, the "taming" of the "wild frontier," and other accomplishments (Wolf, 1992).

American history textbooks portray non-European Americans differently. Various researchers have examined the differences in textbooks' depictions of ethnic groups, as well as the implications of the findings on history curriculum in general. Commeyras and Alvermann (1994) conducted a content analysis of three high school world history books. They found the following: "Third World" countries were underrepresented in coverage, there was no mention of certain historical events, European imperialism was emphasized, and the reports of current conditions of "Third World" countries (since 1945) depicted bleak conditions (pp. 270–271).

Arries (1994) analyzed two American history textbooks to examine the role of Chicanos in history. One book in the survey did not include the fact that some defenders of the Alamo were Hispanic. Also, the story of westward expansion of the United States was accomplished in less than a few paragraphs in both textbooks.

In another study, Wolf (1992) examined the portrayal of minorities in U.S. history textbooks between the years of 1945 and 1995. He cited references that concluded that textbooks of the 1950s portrayed the United States primarily as a White society, virtually ignoring any other ethnic groups, except to maintain that slavery was the most defining event in African American history. Chinese Americans were not treated much better. They were portrayed as sources of cheap labor and on the receiving end of exclusion laws. Analysis of textbooks of the 1960s found that the treatment of African Americans was "inadequate and superficial" (p. 293). Mexican Americans were almost omitted from history, and when they were mentioned, it was to describe their "second-class" citizenship and why that was the case (p. 294). Native American historical accounts were similarly treated. Textbooks written between 1970 and 1985 were still found lacking in adequate and accurate information regarding non-White populations. The tendency in this era was also to treat women as parts of movements in American history, not as a unique group with a history of its own. Many of these textbooks are still used today in classrooms.

Gordy and Pritchard (1995) conducted a content analysis on the presentation of slavery in history textbooks. Specifically, three issues were examined: the triangle trade and U.S. voyage, treatment of life conditions under slavery, and Emancipation and Reconstruction. The textbooks surveyed failed to include the origins and consequences of the slave trade; they contained "sanitized" accounts of events (p. 207). All books studied, however, included descriptions of slavery conditions in the colonies. None of them describe the perpetrators of these conditions. The Emancipation Proclamation was mentioned in all of the textbooks in terms of dates and names. No mention was made of the terms of slaves' freedom, how many were actually freed, or other pertinent issues pertaining to Reconstruction.

Tatum (1992) maintains that African Americans are either treated as "invisible or represented in ways that are based on negative stereotypes" (p. 331). African Americans are seen as "victims or martyrs," not truly having a sense of their own unique history as a people.

The inclusion of selective, biased information in textbook curriculum contributes to negative perceptions of people of color. These perceptions may be internalized by people of color themselves. Thus, both majority and minority group members may actively participate in maintaining present institutional structures. According to Romanowski (1996), "Textbooks are influenced by the political, ideological, or moral beliefs of their authors. Usually these beliefs support the status quo or understanding about what is praiseworthy or blameworthy in history" (p. 170). Textbook prefaces or introductions usually exclude any discussion of the use of textbooks as socialization agents. The content of textbooks has a profound impact on students. They learn about their relationship to the world in textbooks. Wolf (1992) points out that "it is a serious matter when textbooks portray minorities as coming from backgrounds of low socio-economic status, poor education, and high crime and ignore their important contributions to American society" (p. 38). Arries (1994) describes the history curriculum as "the assembly line that delivers the raw product, information, that teachers and children use to construct a common vision of the world and society" (p. 38). If critical information is omitted or distorted, children who are not part of that select group may believe they are somehow inferior. That same scenario may allow other children to believe they are superior to those who are portrayed as oppressed. Teachers run the risk of maintaining the status quo that continues to present erroneous explanations of current societal beliefs and behaviors.

MULTICULTURALIZING THE HISTORY CURRICULUM

A multicultural curriculum includes multiple perspectives of history and achievements of different ethnic groups in society (Banks, 1992; Hollins, 1996b). Guidelines for creating a multicultural curriculum posit that a multicultural curriculum should: (a) include the continuous study of the cultures, historical experiences, social realities, and existential conditions of ethnic and cultural groups, including a variety of racial components; (b) conceptualize and describe the United States as a multiracial society; and (c) make maximum use of experiential learning, especially local community resources (National Council for the Social Studies, 1992).

The implementation of these and other guidelines has been challenging. Various attempts have been made to create frameworks and resolutions that would implement multicultural perspectives of history in the schools. The examples of California and Texas' struggles to deal with multicultural education issues provide background knowledge of how ideas incorporating cultural/ethnic diversity in history may or may not be realized, as well as of the sociopolitical influences (Cornbleth & Waugh, 1995).

Confronting Controversial Realities

In 1987, the California State Board of Education unanimously adopted a social studies framework designed by a committee of teachers, principals, and university professors. It called for an innovative approach to history and social studies, and mandated multicultural perspectives in teaching history. Former California Schools superintendent, Bill Honig, commented during a *MacNeil/Lehrer News Hour* interview that the framework was designed to "tell the story of history, use original documents, present alternative viewpoints, and talk about common values that hold us together" (Crystal, 1991). The framework emphasized and encouraged teachers to expand knowledge beyond their classrooms by exposing children to myths and folktales from other countries. It also emphasized the teaching of geography and history: Grades 5, 8, and 11 curriculum concentrated on U.S. history, and Grades 6, 7, and 10 curriculum focused on world history. *E pluribus unum* (out of many, one) was the catch phrase of this framework.

Based on this framework, publishing companies submitted textbooks to the state for possible use in classrooms. The textbooks were judged on criteria predetermined by the California State Curriculum Commission: effective discussion of civic values and democratic principles, cultural diversity, critical thinking, and controversial issues (History-Social Science Curriculum Framework and Criteria Committee, 1988). Two textbooks met the standards of the framework.

Although local school boards were not required to purchase the textbooks, the issue generated a heated debate among school board members and communities across the state. The books were denounced by many ethnic groups whose perspectives the authors claimed to have portrayed in their account of history. Matters became more complicated when those who approved the books, as well as their authors, claimed as a positive that the series made frequent references to people of color.

As a result of the criticisms, the Oakland and Hayward school districts voted to reject textbook usage, deciding to create their own supplementary materials (Olsen, 1991; Reinhold, 1991). These districts had populations with a heavy concentration of people of color. Despite the debate, however, the California State Curriculum Commission voted to recommend textbook adoption by a 10 to 3 vote, with Joyce King being one of the dissenting members (Cornbleth & Waugh, 1995).

In a similar situation in 1987, Thomas Sobol was appointed the commissioner of education in New York. He created a Task Force on Minorities for the purpose of reviewing personnel department practices and the states' curriculum and teaching materials. The task force assessed the level of ethnic diversity-oriented information contained in the materials and surveyed the existing curriculum. Two years later, controversy ensued when the task force released its findings in the report *Curriculum and Inclusion.* A large portion of this report focused on social studies education. Although improvements were noted in terms of information contained in the state's curriculum, the materials were found inadequate. The task force concluded that the instructional materials did not "adequately and accurately reflect the cultural experiences in America" (Task Force on Minorities, 1989, p. 16).

Despite objections from historians who advocated an "Americentric" curriculum, more multicultural programs gained support. Resolutions were created to promote multicultural studies in schools, as well as support the construction of a comprehensive multicultural education program (Cornbleth & Waugh, 1995). Very little substantive action was taken by Sobol's office until almost a year later when a second review committee was created. According to Cornbleth and Waugh (1995), the report *One Nation, Many People: A Declaration of Cultural Independence* "was not a radical document, but it could be seen as undermining the conventional heroes and contributions approach to school history that in effect keeps minorities on the margins . . ." (p. 121).

Throughout the debate over the history curriculum, ethnic minority voices went unheard. Allowing the testimony of ethnic minority experiences and recommendations would have enabled committees to realize the feasibility of proposed programs. It would also have provided helpful critiques of proposed instructional materials for the classroom. The absence of ethnic minority participation may have been a major reason for the failed implementation of these proposals.

Maintaining the Status Quo

There are scholars and historians, known as traditionalists, who maintain that a multicultural history curriculum is divisive to our national identity. They recommend including contributions made by people of different ethnic groups only if they validate a common culture. Historian Arthur Schlesinger (1991) contends that there are aspects of U.S. history that are shameful, but dwelling on those would singularly undermine the concept of *e pluribus unum.* Schlesinger admits that school curriculum is a tool for instilling national pride. If schools begin to include specific information about the nation's controversial beginnings that are as yet still unresolved, how would students feel about the republic?

Schlesinger (1991) does not support the inclusion of unfavorable information about the nation's past, nor does he support the kind of multicultural education he describes as belonging to the "cult of ethnicity" (p. 74). Nevertheless, he views cultural pluralism, the inclusion of people of color's experiences in the framework of American history, as acceptable. There are exceptions, however. For example, Schlesinger feels an Afrocentric viewpoint in history curriculum is racist and fallacious. He maintains that the self-esteem of African American youngsters will be negatively affected when they discover how history has been distorted. These views are supported by other professors like Diane Ravitch (1990), who contends, "it is dubious to assert that programs to bolster racial pride will raise children's self-esteem or academic performance" (p. 46).

Do we have a common culture, even though ethnic groups' experiences, struggles, and concerns have been dissimilar? Or is the term *common culture* more a concept designed to socialize and homogenize ethnically diverse populations toward being good citizens who adhere to democratic ideals? Arries (1994) defines *common culture* as "that which was common to white, Protestant, small town Americans" (p. 37). This common culture perspective is reflected in value transmission in the implicit curriculum. Bina (1991) claims, "Citizenship means commitment to family, community, and country. If schools are expected to be agents of social change, character, excellence, and citizenship must be regenerated lest the democratic ethos itself is threatened" (p. 13). Thus, curriculum decision making is a process that has potential impact on the future of the nation.

Rethinking and Redesigning the Curriculum

Committees. As seen in California, individuals first design a framework that specifies what information will be presented in classrooms. With this criteria in mind, publishers submit textbooks adhering to the framework. Those with expertise in the given area form a review committee (Bushweller, 1995). The review committee makes its recommendations, and public hearings are conducted. The California State Curriculum Commission decides whether to approve or disapprove the text. There are, however, other factors that influence the decision-making process. California, Texas, and 19 other states have adoption boards for textbook curriculum that influence the decisions of states that do not have adoption boards (Loewen, 1995a). Therefore, factors like the relevance of the textbooks' content to different populations and the ability of many states to influence their own textbook choices are minimized.

For those who let textbooks guide or become their history curriculum, decision making is often a matter of dollars and cents. What is taught in schools usually comes down to cost expenditures and what has been approved by textbook adoption boards, not necessarily quality of product and accuracy of knowledge (Bushweller, 1995; Loewen, 1995a, 1995b).

Budgeting. Purchasing costs are paid by the districts that adopt the approved textbooks (Smollar, 1991). If local districts vote against using the approved textbooks, the decision could be costly for them (Bushweller, 1995).

A factor seemingly lost in this process is often the curriculum content itself. Cost and availability influence curriculum, not content suitability for all populations, especially ethnically diverse populations. Teachers use materials with content that is not necessarily relevant for their students from ethnically diverse populations.

The reliance on textbook adoption boards to choose curricula can be problematic. In many cases, they are responsible for choosing curricula for other states. This process does not allow for meeting the needs of the states and the local communities contained within them. Allowing states to guide their own choice of history curricula may help schools provide relevant information for the populations they serve.

Response to Community. In *Transforming Curriculum for a Culturally Diverse Society*, Hollins (1996b) provides a different approach for curriculum decision making. According to Hollins (1996b):

> curriculum is defined as all of the learning, routines, and interactions that occur among all participants as a function of schooling, whether planned or not, which inform and shape responses to the environment within and outside of school. (p. 1)

Based on this definition, Hollins suggests that curriculum decision making should involve thoughtful analysis of the impetus or reason for curriculum change or development, include representative participation by all groups to be impacted, involve systematic inquiry into school practices and their effect on all groups within the particular community to be served, and result in informed practice based on the application of data from systematic inquiry to transforming curriculum for a culturally diverse society. Relying primarily on textbook approved by the state or school district may not be adequate to engage the process of decision making Hollins describes. The approach to curriculum decision making Hollins recommends was not followed by those groups attempting to establish national history standards.

ESTABLISHING NATIONAL HISTORY STANDARDS

In 1992, the National Endowment for the Humanities and the U.S. Department of Education jointly funded the National Center for History in the Schools (NCHS) to develop national history standards. According to Nash and Dunn (1995), the NCHS goal was to "provide American youth with a comprehensive, challenging, and thought-provoking education that is equal to other industrialized countries" (p. 5). NCHS specified 15 criteria to guide the development of the history standards for Grades kindergarten through 12. It was with this criteria that the NCHS developed its standards. In general, the 15 criteria emphasized critical thinking skills and reasoning, rather than memorization often used to learn historical names and dates.

The NCHS incorporated the 15 standards into its 10 "eras" designed to chronologically examine U.S. history. NCHS (1994) defines *eras* as "periods into which the written histories of the United States or the world are divided" (p. 4). The teachers are expected to construct exercises designed to foster critical thinking skills for each era, as well as an understanding of issues surrounding certain historical occurrences. Each of these eras is accompanied by at least two standards and different criteria held for historical thinking. There are five standards. Standard 1 emphasizes chronological thinking, where the students "distinguish between past, present, and future time" (p. 18). Standard 2 emphasizes historical comprehension, where the students "reconstruct the literal meaning of an historical passage" (p. 18). Standard 3 stresses historical analysis and interpretation, in which there are 10 criteria for student learning. One of these criteria is to "consider multiple perspectives" (p. 19). Standard 4, with four criteria, stresses historical research capabilities; one of these criteria is to "obtain historical data" (p. 19). Standard 5 emphasizes historical issues analysis and decision making, and contains six criteria. One of these is to "identify issues and problems in the past" (p. 19). (See Table 9.1 for identification and description of the 10 eras.)

The NCHS attempted to create history standards that represented different cultural perspectives. Release of the standards brought immediate reactions. According to Natale (1995), the debate could be divided into three camps: (a) those who felt the standards are a disappointment, with too much concern placed on political correctness; (b) those who approved of the attempt to include ethnic diversity into accounts of history; and (c) those who admitted that even though the standards are flawed, they give teachers ways to evaluate their lesson plans (p. 19). Following are reviews of reactions from two of the camps.

Negative Reactions. Critics of the standards claimed that with the inclusion of these different perspectives, students would not learn the "facts" about what made the United States the country it has become: the significant influence of its presidents and the accomplishment of its inventors (Gorton, 1995; Leo, 1995). Lynne Cheney felt that the national standards did not feature enough presidents and other influential men (Dellios, 1996). Stern (1994) stated that "students taught by these standards alone

TABLE 9.1
Summary of Era Concepts

Title of Era	Description of Era
Era 1: Three Worlds Meet (Beginnings to 1620)	Examines the "historical convergence of European, African, and Native American people, beginning in the late 15th century."
Era 2: Colonization and Settlement (1585–1763)	Examines three themes during this time period: the intermingling of Native Americans, Europeans, and Africans; the development of political and religious institutions and values; and the economic development of the colonies through agriculture and commerce.
Era 3: Revolution and the New Nation (1754–1820s)	Examines the extent of revolution in the Revolutionary War.
Era 4: Expansion and Reform (1801–1861)	Examines the territorial expansion between 1800 and 1861, the economic development of the expanding American republic, and the extension, restriction, and reorganization of the political democracy after 1800.
Era 5: Civil War and Reconstruction (1850–1877)	Examines the debate over the power of the federal government versus state rights, the complexities of the Civil War, and the success and failures of Reconstruction (p. 121).
Era 6: The Development of the Industrial United States (1870–1900)	Examines the economic transformation, expansion of big business, and development of large scale agriculture and national labor unions. This era also examines immigration and urbanization and conflicts that accompanied them.
Era 7: The Emergence of Modern America (1890–1930)	Examines issues central to Progressive Era, the Harlem Renaissance, plus resurgence of the Ku Klux Klan. Also examines tensions among different religious denominations.
Era 8: The Great Depression and World War II (1929–1945)	Examines the Great Depression and World War II. Examines the onset and effects of both.
Era 9: Postwar United States (1945 to early 1970s)	Examines nuances of the Cold War and changes in the 1950s and 1960s.
Era 10: Contemporary United States (1965 to late 1990s)	Examines the role the United States plays in global politics, as well as major social and cultural changes of most recent decades.

are likely to develop a smug, superior, and self-righteous attitude toward people and conflicts of the past" (p. 69).

Positive Reactions. There were individuals and organizations who endorsed the standards. The Organization of History Teachers (OHT) Focus Group in U.S. History applauded the standards (Bell, 1994). Bicouvaris (1994) concluded that the standards presented historical information in ways that rejected one-sidedness.

TEACHING DIVERSE POPULATIONS' HISTORY

Knowledge of society's political and philosophical assumptions regarding history is important when deciding what to teach in history classes. Realizing that history curriculum is often the tool for transmitting cultural values is paramount, as is the fact that students are products of a unique cultural and historical heritage often omitted from history textbooks. Curriculum can be transformed into lessons that will help students feel empowered by what they have learned. To do this, the teacher must take into consideration that the students are of differing ethnic/cultural backgrounds, and integrate that knowledge into the history curriculum.

When using history textbooks, it is important to recognize the presence of the traditional European American ethnocentric perspective. It is not always necessary to discard such textbooks. They can be used as a tool to help students understand differing perspectives and accounts of history by contrasting them with other perspectives and accounts. Teachers can facilitate informed discussions among their students about how different ethnic groups may have perceived certain events in history. As Commeyras and Alvermann (1994) suggest, students can select a history book chapter and critically examine it to discuss why some historical events are described more in length than others. Teachers and students can then rewrite the chapter to include other perspectives, more ethnically/culturally inclusive, of historical events. They also suggest finding supplementary materials by conducting library searches to provide other interpretations of specific events. Commeyras and Alvermann (1994), as well as Hollins (1996a), point to local resources for learning history. For example, contacting local community members who may have more intimate knowledge of historical occurrences will enable students to critically analyze other interpretations of the events.

Actively involving students in the history-teaching process is also an effective vehicle for changing how history is viewed. Loewen (1995a) suggests that it is ideal for teachers to challenge information espoused in textbooks. There are specific questions students can answer to begin thinking critically about different accounts of history:

1. Why was the work written; who was its intended audience?
2. Whose viewpoint is being presented? Whose is left out?
3. Is the historical account believable? Do some of its assertions contradict others?
4. Is the historical account backed up by other sources?
5. After reading the words or being presented with the image, how is one supposed to feel about the America that has been presented? (Loewen, 1995a, p. 311)

As Loewen points out, teachers do not have to possess all of the knowledge that has been traditionally omitted from textbooks. Teachers act as facilitators to help students discover answers and critically discuss some of the issues and philosophical assumptions supporting a particular account of history. Students should understand that historians represent accounts of historical events as they perceive them. Thus, historical accounts represent one perspective of an event or situation. The particular historical account cannot be separated from the historians' perspective which is framed by a particular cultural and experiential background.

CONCLUSION AND RECOMMENDATIONS

This chapter examined the politics and philosophical assumptions that have guided the current state of history curriculum. One of the conclusions reached in this chapter is that the history curriculum in its present form has very little to do with the creation of innovative teaching methods and information relevant to varying ethnic/cultural populations. History curriculum is currently about the transmission of Eurocentric cultural values, maintenance of the status quo, and the effectiveness of saving money, time, and energy by using assembly-line history textbooks as curriculum.

Acknowledging the complexities involved in the current state of history curriculum does not mean, however, that the process is immune to change. Caution students against relying on history textbooks as the primary source of information, and make sure that there are supplementary materials available to examine different perspectives regarding historical events. Involve other faculty and administrators in the decision of what to include as curriculum materials. Understand the reasons for implementing new or different history curriculum. Know the children's ethnic/cultural heritage in the classroom, and realize that the instructional manual being used may not include diverse perspectives of historical occurrences. This allows teachers to prepare lessons that are relevant and inclusive of the students' heritage. Understanding these issues will help teachers empower their students of ethnically diverse populations, rather than encouraging feelings of victimization by particular historical accounts.

SUGGESTED LEARNING EXPERIENCES

1. Review several social studies textbooks at the same grade level to identify the particular perspective presented (conservative, liberal, distorted or biased, groups omitted or misrepresented).

2. There are several instances of state-adopted textbooks including those in California and Texas. Request information about the procedure and criteria used in the textbook adoption process. Discuss the adequacy of the criteria used in the selection process for ensuring high quality textbooks with a minimum of bias. Explain the extent to which members of different ethnic minority groups are included in the textbook adoption process.

REFERENCES

Arries, J. (1994). Decoding the social studies production of Chicano history. *Equity and Excellence in Education, 27*(1), 37–44.

Banks, J. A. (1992). Multicultural education: For freedom's sake. *Educational Leadership, 49*(4), 32–36.

Bell, E. (1994). *Response to the proposed United States history standards from Reconstruction to the present.* Paper prepared by the U.S. History Focus Committee, Chicago, IL.

Bicouvaris, M. V. (1994). Setting national standards for history: A teacher's view. *Journal of Education, 176*(3), 51–60.

Bina, C. A. (1991). *The bonfire of the buffalo commons: A multicultural view from the mid-continent.* Paper presented at the Regional Equity Consultation Meeting of the Midcontinental Regional Education Laboratory, Aurora, CO.

Bushweller, K. (1995). Open and shut: How you select a new textbook depends in large part on where you live. *The American School Board Journal, 182*(1), 27–28.

Commeyras, M., & Alvermann, D. E. (1994). Messages that high school world history textbooks convey: Challenges for multicultural literacy. *The Social Studies, 85*(6), 268–274.

Cornbleth, C., & Waugh, D. (1995). *The great speckled bird: Multicultural politics and education policymaking.* New York: St. Martin's Press.

Crystal, L. (Executive Producer). (1991, November 28). *The MacNeil/Lehrer news hour.* New York and Washington, DC: Public Broadcasting Service.

Dellios, H. (1996, April 3). Conservatives won't give national history standards a passing grade. *Chicago Tribune,* pp. 110, 112.

Gordon, S. (1995, January 18). Senate Rep. 1025, No. 10, 104th Congress, 1st Session.

Gordy, L. L., & Pritchard, A. M. (1995). Redirecting our voyage through history: A content analysis of social studies textbooks. *Urban Education, 30*(2), 195–218.

History-Social Science Curriculum Framework and Criteria Committee. (1988). *History social science framework.* Sacramento: California State Department of Education.

Hollins, E. R. (1996a). *Culture in school learning: Revealing the deep meaning.* Mahwah, NJ: Lawrence Erlbaum Associates.

Hollins, E. R. (1996b). *Transforming curriculum for a culturally diverse society.* Mahwah, NJ: Lawrence Erlbaum Associates.

Komoski, K. P. (1985). Instructional materials will not improve until we change the system. *Educational Leadership, 42*(7), 31–37.

Leo, J. (1995, February 6). History standards are bunk. *U.S. News & World Report, 118*(5), p. 23.

Loewen, J. (1995a). By the book: Who's to blame for the sorry state of history textbooks? *The American School Board Journal, 182*(1), 24–27.

Loewen, J. (1995b). *Lies my teacher told me.* New York: New Press.

Nash, G. B., & Dunn, R. E. (1995). National history standards: Controversy and commentary. *Social Studies Review, 35*(2), 4–12.

Natale, J. A. (1995). Bone of contention. *The American School Board Journal, 182*(1), 18–23.

National Center for History in the Schools. (1994). *National standards for United States history: Exploring the American experience.* Los Angeles: University of California.

National Council for the Social Studies. (1992). Curriculum guidelines for multicultural education. *Social Education, 56*(5), 274–294.

Olsen, L. (1991). Whose culture is this? Whose curriculum will it be? In K. Kam (Ed.), *California perspectives: An anthology for the California tomorrow education for a diverse society project* (2nd ed., pp. 3–13). San Francisco: California Tomorrow.

Ravitch, D. (1990). Diversity and democracy: Multicultural education in America. *American Educator, 14*(1), 16–20, 46–48.

Reinhold, R. (1991, September 29). Class struggle, cowgirls, and the bantu immigration: In its controversial new textbooks, California is rewriting history. *The New York Times Magazine,* pp. 26–29, 47–52.

Romanowski, M. H. (1996). Problems of bias in history textbooks. *Social Education, 60*(3), 170–173.

Schlesinger, A. M. (1991). *The disuniting of America: Reflections on a multicultural society.* New York: Norton.

Smollar, D. (1991, May 1). School board votes yes on controversial texts. *Los Angeles Times,* p. B2.

Stern, S. (1994). Beyond the rhetoric: An historian's view of the national standards for United States history. *Journal of Education, 176*(3), 61–71.

Task Force on Minorities (1989). *A curriculum of inclusion.* Albany: New York State Education Department.

Tatum, B. D. (1992). African American identity development, academic achievement, and missing history. *Social Education, 56*(6), 331.

Wolf, A. (1992). Minorities in U.S. history textbooks, 1945–1985. *The Clearing House, 65*(5), 191–197.

Chapter 10

Building Cultural Diversity Into the Literature Curriculum

Steven Z. Athanases
University of California at Davis

FOCUS QUESTIONS

1. How do the process and principles of unit construction proposed by this author apply to other content areas?
2. How can a unit of instruction be designed to draw on the cultural and experiential backgrounds of all youngsters in a culturally diverse classroom setting?
3. What guidelines can be used for selecting authentic literature for specific cultural groups?

INTRODUCTION

Reviews of multicultural education have identified and described various forms of multicultural education that serve a range of purposes for students. Of these forms, the one that Banks (1993) calls *content integration* provides teachers of English and language arts with direction for transforming their literature curricula. This model holds that the infusion of ethnic and cultural content into the curriculum (for literature, in the form of texts by and about people of a range of ethnicities) validates the experiences of all students, with particular attention to students of color whose histories and stories have been overwhelmingly excluded from classroom study. In addition, such inclusiveness strengthens the knowledge base of all students by providing a view of U.S. history and literature that more accurately reflects the range of experiences of all people in the population. A more inclusive curriculum can embrace diversity as defined by a range of factors including race, ethnicity, class, nation of origin, religion, gender, and sexual orientation. Whereas diversity based on any of these factors deserves attention in school curricula, this chapter focuses primarily on ways to diversify literature curricula in terms of race and ethnicity.

Given this backdrop, what is the current status of multicultural literature in school curricula? What factors have served as impediments to teachers' engaging in content integration to make traditional literature programs more inclusive? What principles can help teachers select literary works that more equitably represent the range of cultures that comprise the American fabric? Given the constraints of time, resources, and sometimes mandated curricula, how can teachers realistically and efficiently build diversity into their literature curricula? What planning principles and unit designs can support the efforts of preservice and in-service teachers toward these ends? These are the questions this chapter addresses in a number of ways.

After briefly reviewing the status of multicultural literature in schools, the chapter provides the following. First, a four-part framework identifies principles of multiculturalism that can guide planning decisions. Second, four unit structures for inclusiveness are discussed, each illustrated with highlights from literature units designed by primarily preservice teachers for use in their classes.

MULTICULTURAL LITERATURE IN THE CLASSROOM

Calls for Inclusive Curricula

In recent years, at nearly all levels of the teaching profession, guidelines have called for greater multicultural emphasis in the teaching of literature. Frameworks and brochures encourage greater representation of women and people of color as both the authors and subjects of materials students read. More inclusive curricula, according to these recommendations, would help insure that all students learn through imaginative texts about the pluralistic nature of the United States, about the contributions of all groups to American letters, and about the history of racism and oppression that have generally marginalized people of color in this country.

The Task Force on Racism and Bias in the Teaching of English (1986) for the National Council of Teachers of English, for example, recommended the selection of materials by authors of color in more than token representation, works that present authors of color in more nonstereotypical, balanced, accurate, and realistic ways. The report from the English Coalition Conference (Lloyd-Jones & Lunsford, 1989), a gathering of a diverse group of educators at all levels, as well as linguists, literary theorists, and researchers on minority literature, offered statements related to more inclusive curricula for all levels of schooling. According to the report, elementary students should have

> many opportunities, through reading literature from various cultural groups and interacting orally with a variety of people, to be able and willing to see the world from the perspectives of others. They will not only have a sense of the richness and distinctiveness of the life of particular groups, but also a sense of common humanity. (pp. 4–5)

According to the report, high school students should read literature by women and men representing many racial, ethnic, and cultural groups, because literature "makes real the cultures we inherit, as well as those of people different from us" (p. 20). In various states, as well, departments of education and associations for teachers of English and language arts have included recommendations for more inclusive literature curricula.

The Status of Multicultural Literature in Schools

At the elementary level, the basal reader dominated literacy instruction for many years, but more frequently now it shares space with children's literature books. However, because teachers have lacked the time, materials, and leadership support to help guide their selections of books, many have relied heavily on their own often lifelong familiarity with particular books to guide their choices for use in class. Walmsley and Walp (1989) argue that although a canon of most frequently taught children's books had not yet evolved at the elementary level as it had in the upper grades, classics by European American authors, such as *Charlotte's Web* (White, 1952) and *Little House on the Prairie* (Wilder, 1953), still dominated teachers' selections.

According to a set of national studies conducted in middle schools and high schools in the United States around 1990, despite calls for attention to diversity by all of the major language arts associations, and despite social phenomena of the past decades including the Civil Rights Movement and the Women's Movement, the literature curriculum had remained narrow, composed predominantly of works by European American men. Works by women comprised only 16% of reading teachers asked students to do, and works by authors of color less than 7% (Applebee, 1992). In a study of book-length works required at 488 urban, suburban, and rural high schools, for example, Applebee (1989) found only 2% of these works were written by authors of color, and on the list of the top 50 most commonly taught authors, only 2 authors of color, Lorraine Hansberry and Richard Wright, appeared. These figures revealed very little change since an early 1960s national study was conducted of book-length works taught in schools, and the canon of most frequently taught titles likewise had changed little (Applebee, 1989).

When the scope broadened to include works in literary genres typically shorter than book length (short stories, poetry, nonfiction essays), the figures were similar. A study of works of all genres taught over a 5-day period in 650 junior and senior high schools revealed 7% of works by authors of color, but much of this increase over the 2% of book-length works by authors of color was due almost entirely to the inclusion of the poetry of a single writer, Langston Hughes (Applebee, 1990).

Impediments to Diversifying Literature Curricula

The persistent lack of inclusion of works by women and authors of color in middle and secondary school curricula, despite calls for change by all of the major professional organizations for teachers, appears attributable to various factors. First, teachers have claimed a lack of familiarity with works by authors of color and a lack of time to search for and read a range of new works from which to select appropriate titles (Applebee, 1991). Second, teachers tend to rely heavily on literature anthologies, and although some new publications have made strides in addressing diversity, the most popular anthologies have typically limited their selections by women and authors of color to sections at the back of these books devoted to categories such as modern poetry (Apple, 1992; Applebee, 1991; Pace, 1992). Such placement often precludes the introduction of these authors to students, because many teachers work their way sequentially through anthologies and, given time constraints and the sheer volume of works included in these collections, seldom complete the sequence with their students. "In light of these realities," Pace notes, "I suspect many classes may not get to the modern age; thus most minority writers may never be read or discussed in class" (p. 35). Moreover, confining the bulk of inclusive selections to the genre of poetry insures their exclusion from many curricula. Poll any group of English teachers in the United States, and the teaching of poetry emerges as one of the most troublesome and therefore neglected features of their curricula, due to a high level of insecurity regarding academic preparation in poetry and to the challenge of working on this often formidable genre with students.

Meanwhile, longer fiction selections in these anthologies tended to remain narrow, authored almost entirely by European American men, and the images of women and people of color in the anthologized works remained stereotypical: The women in the short fiction are physically weak, "voiceless victims of negative experiences with men" (Pace, 1992, pp. 35–36) and the people of color are victims of oppression. Few if any images emerged of strong women, positive experiences in minority cultures, or dissent and anger by women or people of color to balance the tales of victimization.

A third factor that works against more inclusive curricula is the set of recommendations and mandates that direct curriculum planning. State departments of education, for example, institutionalize canonical works by specifying, and in some cases requiring, that particular texts be taught to all students statewide at particular grade levels. At a national level, when the Educational Testing Service published its *Advanced Placement Course Description for English* in 1987, for example, it specified that these courses should concentrate on works of "recognized literary merit worthy of scrutiny because their richness of thought and language challenges the reader" (p. 36). Lake (1988) notes that the list of specified texts included few by women or ethnic minorities, and the exclusion of women from various genres (drama, political thought, and critical work) minimized the roles women have played in American thought and letters.

Through their selections of literary works, the editors of anthologies, the teachers in the schools Applebee studied, the Educational Testing Service and some state departments of instruction have provided what Smith (1983) calls "culturally certified endorsements" (p. 23). Each of these acts has brought particular texts into the orbit of attention. Other acts of endorsement—reprints, purchases, citations, recitations, quotations, critiques, articles, awards, reviews, syllabi, reading lists—contribute, some more articulately than others, to what Smith calls the economic value of a text. For students in schools, the result is a portrait of history, of lives, of what schools value.

A fourth factor that has contributed to the near exclusion of literary works by women and people of color in schools centers on the personal characteristics of teachers. Even if we imagine teachers using anthologies inclusive of a variety of works by women and people of color and works that represent all groups beyond merely stereotypical ways, even if we imagine school districts providing teachers with appropriate supplementary resources and release time to read and examine contemporary works with which they are not familiar, we still must consider the reluctance many teachers feel about engaging in terrain possibly unfamiliar and capable of stirring turmoil in class.

To what degree do teachers themselves value the voices of women and people of color in the literary canon? To what degree might the inclusion of such voices in curricula force some teachers to confront their own prejudices, their discomfort with cultural difference? To what degree do teachers subscribe to the notion of universality as a key criterion of literary merit and therefore exclude works too "particular" or seemingly narrow in focus? What are the genders, the cultural heritage of the teachers, their students? To what degree do these factors affect teachers' literary selections? Some European American teachers who are thoughtful about issues of diversity have reported discomfort in trying to do justice to texts that tell stories of oppression they have not themselves known. Also, European American teachers and teachers of color, particularly those working in urban multiethnic settings, often report fear of working with literature that exposes controversial topics, particularly when issues raised include racism, sexism, and other forms of oppression. Clearly, a range of factors account for the rarity of more inclusive literature curricula in schools.

The Need for Guiding Principles

Even if teachers are committed to more inclusive curricula and have available to them some appropriate resources, how might they approach the selection and treatment of such texts? Within the world of literature, teachers can work to sensitize students to difference, cultivate cultural pride, nurture an appreciation of similarities and differences across the lines that divide, teach tolerance, and foster the challenging of inequality and social injustice. But with what texts, in what organizational structures, and with what instructional approaches can teachers accomplish these goals? Recent work has gone a long way toward providing teachers with suggestions of titles and annotated bibliographies for more inclusive curricula (e.g., Athanases, Christiano, & Drexler, 1992; Duff & Tongchinsub, 1990; Harris, 1992; Sasse, 1988; Yokota, 1993), as well as criteria for selection of multicultural literary works (Bishop, 1992; Sasse, 1988; Stotsky, 1992; Yokota, 1993). There remains, however, a need for material to assist teachers in building diversity into their curricula and in planning appropriate instruction to accompany such works, objectives teachers consistently cite at professional conferences and workshops. (See, however, Miller & McCaskill, 1993, and Rogers & Soter, 1997, two recent contributions to this work.) The following portions of this chapter provide teachers with assistance in addressing these concerns, with ways to work toward cultural inclusiveness in the context of teachers' constraints.

**A FRAMEWORK FOR TRANSFORMING
THE LITERATURE CURRICULUM**

One of the goals of content integration in literature study is a transformative curriculum, one in which diversity becomes the given, when infusion of works by women and people of color happens consistently and naturally, not in contrived and merely additive ways. Whether you are in a position to transform a curriculum in this way or you are constrained by narrow lists of required and/or available core works and constrained further by having little opportunity to effect curricular change at the department or school level, a framework can guide selection of literary works to either shape or supplement the curriculum, as well as provide some approaches for dealing with these texts. A review of works on multiculturalism and teaching multicultural literature reveals four recurring themes that shape such a framework: authentic portrayals, variations within cultures, sociological perspectives, and the search for common ground.

Diversity Through Authentic Portrayals

At the heart of the framework rests a goal of cultivating understanding and respect for difference through the study of works that represent the range of cultural groups in the United States. Whereas works by European American authors that feature people of color can play important educational functions (e.g., Harper Lee's, 1960, *To Kill a Mockingbird*, which depicts discrimination against African Americans in Alabama in the 1930s), the inclusion of works by authors of color gives vital voice to members of historically silenced groups (Bishop, 1992; Sasse, 1988) as "distinctive members of the plurality, appearing before one another with their own perspectives on the common, their own stories entering the culture's story, altering it as it moves through time" (Greene, 1993, p. 18).

The notion of cultural authenticity, although slippery and complex, is essential here. Cultural accuracy can be discerned through "a richness of cultural details, authentic dialogue and relationships, in-depth treatment of cultural issues, and the inclusion of members of 'minority groups' for a purpose" (Yokota, 1993, pp. 159–160). Grossly stereotyped characterizations have appeared in many children's books about Latino, Asian American, and Native American experience written by outsiders (Lass-Woodfin, 1978; Nieto, 1982; Reimer, 1992; Yokota, 1993). Sims (1982) likewise documented how children's literature has had a history of few African American characters and that even as these numbers have increased, old stereotypes have frequently given way to new ones, in part because these characters have appeared in books written by European American authors for European American audiences. One of the key false notes in many of these works is the depiction of people of color working hard to assimilate into the dominant culture, without regard for socialization into the subculture and for maintenance of strong distinctions between the majority and minority cultures.

In one study illustrative of this issue, Trousdale (1990) analyzed four prize-winning children's books about African American experience and found that the three books written by European American authors presented worlds in which racism and inhumanity are tolerated or endorsed (one even suggesting that slavery was beneficial to Africans) and in which there exists among African Americans a theology of submission to oppression, a culturally inaccurate depiction of experience. Only in *Roll of Thunder, Hear My Cry* (Taylor, 1976), one of four prize-winning titles written by an African American author, do readers learn of the cruelty of racial injustice experienced by African Americans and only in this book, argues Trousdale, do African American children find positive African American characters to emulate.

For students of color, more inclusive curricula composed of culturally authentic portrayals of experience can engender a sense of validation about one's culture, history, family, and importance. Inclusion and exclusion of texts representing groups can have a powerful impact: "Texts are really messages to and about the future. As part of a curriculum, they participate in no less than the organized knowledge of society. They participate in creating what a society has recognized as legitimate and truthful" (Apple, 1992, p. 5). Students can feel legitimized and even proud when texts representing their worlds are authentically and critically examined in class. When students identify with characters and texts, they reflect on personal concerns, including family nostalgia and loss; adolescent challenges; and culture, gender, and sexual identity formation (Athanases, 1998). The attention to diversity serves all students, however, for "none of us can afford to remain ignorant of the heritage and culture of any part of our population" (Simonson & Walker, 1988, p. xi).

Variation Within Cultures

In the study of literature, diverse cultures are often grouped under cultural conglomerates (Reimer, 1992), blurring, for example, Puerto Rican and Mexican experiences, as well as Asian experiences as diverse as Japanese, Vietnamese, and Pakistani. In addition, members of any given ethnic group, of course, represent a range of individuals and cultures determined by many factors: geography, historical period, gender, sexual orientation, degree of assimilation into the dominant culture, the point of the family's entry into the United States, socioeconomic status, personal values, and individual personality. Advocates of more inclusive curricula remind us of the value of selecting literature that represents as much of this variety within groups as possible (Bishop, 1992; Sasse, 1988) so that individuals in literary works, and by extension in classrooms, do not always have to be viewed as representative of or symbols of their cultures. To reduce the rich variety within any group is to perform a disservice that may in fact contribute to too much categorizing, classifying, pigeonholing, stereotyping (Gibson, 1984). Although culture plays a role in shaping identity, "We do not *know* the person in the front row of our classroom . . . or the one drinking next to us at the bar by her/his culture or ethnic affiliation" (Greene, 1993, p. 16).

Contemporary authors who explore issues of culture repeatedly address the complex nature of culture in the Americas, talking of the complexity and even absurdity of notions such as ethnic purity and cultural identity in lands so culturally mixed (e.g., Anzaldua, 1988; Cliff, 1988; Fuentes, 1988; Gomez-Peña, 1988). Gomez-Peña, for example, describes the "hybrid realities" of many people like himself who live at the borderland between the United States and Mexico:

> At the border they call me "chilango" or "mexiquillo"; in Mexico City it's "pocho" or "norteno"; and in Europe it's "sudaca." The Anglos call me "Hispanic" or "Latino," and the Germans have, on more than one occasion, confused me with Turks or Italians. My wife is Anglo-Italian, but speaks Spanish with an Argentine accent, and together we walk amid the rubble of the Tower of Babel of our American post-modernity. (p. 128)

Cliff (1988) likewise reminds us that the lines that divide are complex, that one's sense of cultural otherness can shift quickly, causing what Gomez-Peña calls "colliding visions within coalition" (p. 130). Depending on circumstances, Cliff can feel "other" defined by any number of factors defining her cultural identities: race, country of origin (Jamaica), color (light-skinned black), gender, level of education, socioeconomic status, and sexual orientation. "The whole business is very complicated," she says; "we/they/I connect and disconnect—change place" (p. 81). These hybrid realities, the variations within groups, the shifting coalitions marked by various cultural indicators—all of these call for a realistic treatment of culture as complex (Suzuki, 1984).

Realistic treatment of the lives of people of color in the United States must include stories of oppression. However, students need the balance of stories containing positive experiences for members of these groups (Bishop, 1992; Greene, 1993; Pace, 1992), works that move beyond depictions of victimization. In her analysis of literature anthologies, Pace asks, "What message do we send to students when we present them with an American story in which most of the active, powerful characters come only from one race, only from one gender?" (p. 38). The varied representation of cultural groups can prevent the perpetuation of simplistic depictions of groups that either stereotype its members or present them merely in terms of oppression and victimization (Greene, 1993).

Sociological Perspectives

An effective program in multicultural education must address societal and historical forces that have shaped experiences women and authors of color frequently write about. Allen (1988) argues that "the root of oppression is loss of memory" (p. 18), that we must uncover lost stories of Native Americans and other oppressed groups to understand the truth of what has often been denied in the American story students learn in school. Likewise, curricula must address racism and include analysis of institutional structures that cause social ills (Gibson, 1984; Hilliard, 1974), as well as the history of atrocities perpetrated on people of color in the United States, including the slave trade, destruction of Native American cultures, and the internment of Japanese during World War II, horrors the United States has failed to come to terms with (Mura, 1988). Programs of multicultural education, in celebration of diversity, have often failed to address the societal forces that have caused the victimization depicted in much literature by and about people of color.

In classrooms with students from ethnic minority groups, when discussions of literature by and about people of color deal with issues of oppression, anger will likely surface. Mura (1988) argues:

> As should be obvious to anyone, those who are oppressed cannot change their situation, cannot own themselves, unless they finally own their rage at their condition and those who have caused it. . . . One does not overcome or stand above this rage: one first goes through it, and then leaves it behind. (pp. 148–149)

When students of color have the opportunity in class to confront issues of racism, tempers can flare. A framework for the teaching of multicultural literature, particularly in urban multiethnic schools, includes the construction of a forum in which such anger can be expressed.

Search for Common Ground

Although ethnic histories in the United States are distinct, multicultural education in literature should enable students to examine the collective history of oppression in the United States, allowing them to see the bonds across oppressed groups. Multiculturalism for a member of a racial minority group "is not simply tolerance, but an essential key to survival" (Mura, 1988, p. 141). Mura argues that although the bond of rage people of color feel can grow intoxicating, at times perpetuating a myth of sainthood for those victimized by European Americans, the bond is based in truth and warrants recognition.

One of the conceptual failings of much of multicultural education, according to the review by Gibson (1984), is its lack of attention to the similarities of people across groups, a lack of examination of what people share across cultures. This lack of attention results in merely a focus on difference that perpetuates patriarchal, condescending, racist notions about groups. Greene (1993) argues that much of this failing originates in "defining ourselves against some unknown, some darkness, some 'otherness' we chose to thrust away, to master, not to understand" (p. 15), rather than opening ourselves to authentic personal encounters that help us move beyond categorizing, distancing, and allowing ourselves to be made "other." Such needed encounters, she argues, can be real or imagined, the latter being those that literature creates, providing English and language arts teachers with a clear argument for the teaching of more inclusive literature-based curricula.

A FIRST STEP: FOUR UNIT STRUCTURES
FOR INCLUSIVENESS

One way to begin building diversity into the literature curriculum, particularly for the preservice teacher who seldom has voice in the shaping of a yearlong or semester-long curriculum, is to focus on a unit of instruction that embodies elements of the larger curriculum they hope to someday help shape. The assignment calls for the construction of a 3- to 5-week literature unit shaped by principles of multicultural education and by principles of effective literature instruction. Because of the investigative nature of the assignment (the search for appropriate literary works) and the sharing of unit designs at the end, the assignment expands the pool of works by authors of color to which a group will have been exposed before holding full-time positions with the constraints of time, specified curricula, and limited resources. In addition, the assignment offers a variety of unit structures that help build diversity into curricula no matter what constraints are faced at a school site. This variety can help provide new teachers with a repertoire of strategies for continually constructing more inclusive curricula. The following four unit structures are examples to guide your thinking.

Adding Cultural Authenticity

In this first unit structure, when students read a work by a European American author that deals with experiences of people of color, they will also read works that address the experiences from various perspectives of members of the group "under study." One example from high school curriculum might be Harper Lee's (1960) *To Kill a Mockingbird*, one of the most frequently required literary works nationally. A unit built around this book, which examines discrimination against African Americans in 1930s Alabama, would include works by African American authors that address related experiences. Authors of the Harlem Renaissance provide a wealth of material to enable students to hear African American voices of the 1920s and 1930s. These authors present themes of racial protest that show African Americans in more empowered states than the *Mockingbird* character of Tom Robinson who has been victimized by racism and falsely convicted of the rape of a European American woman. Students can further see how Harlem Renaissance authors explored other themes at the time, including racial affirmation, love, daily urban living, and variations on African American music, particularly blues and jazz.

Depicting Variation Within Cultures

This unit structure begins with the work of a member of a particular ethnic group, a core text that teachers might very likely have available to teach. The structure then extends the unit thematically with works by other members of the same ethnic group. In this way, students hear how a variety of voices from a single ethnic group address a theme. An example of a unit for middle school students using this structure may have as its core work *Anne Frank: Diary of a Young Girl* (Frank, 1978), supported by other short works by Jewish authors. A children's book, *The Children We Remember* (Abells, 1986), can be used to open the unit with background information on children and the Holocaust. Works by Elie Wiesel (excerpts from *Night*, 1960, and *One Generation After*, 1970) further explore experiences of anti-Semitism and the Holocaust, and the collection *I Never Saw Another Butterfly* (Volavkova, 1962) provides the children's perspective (linked well to Anne Frank's story) through children's poetry and drawings from Terezin Concentration Camp in Czechoslovakia where nearly 15,000 children were killed.

Extending Core Works Thematically and Cross-Culturally

This third unit structure extends themes cross-culturally, so that a unit in this category might begin with *Anne Frank* and themes of racial and religious fear and hatred in Nazi Germany, and then use these understandings as a framework for examining the American internment of Japanese and Japanese Americans through works such as *Farewell to Manzanaar* (Houston, 1983), Mitsuye Yamada's *Camp Notes and Other Poems* (1986), and poems by Janice Mirikitani (*Shedding Silence*, 1987). The unit asks questions such as these: How is Anne's statement that she believes that people are basically "good at heart" consistent with the Germans' killing of 6 million Jewish people? How could several nations turn their backs on the plight of the Jews? And how could these same nations fail to stop Hitler from carrying out his slaughter? Similarly, what does the internment of thousands of Japanese and Japanese Americans during the same war say about Americans and about a world at war?

A Cross-Cultural Thematic Unit of Short Works

This structure results in a unit that can be inserted within any curriculum, no matter how rigid. The teacher links short stories, essays, and poetry around a theme, such as the tensions in families between cultural traditions and the pull in school to assimilate into the dominant culture.

Although this unit structure allows an enormous amount of freedom, it also can create a great deal of frustration for the unit planners. How should choices of texts and themes be selected from among so many? Three principles can be used to guide choices: cultural balance, thematic cohesiveness, and thematic relevance to the interests of teenagers. The unit includes a range of cultural voices.

An example of a theme for such a unit might be "negotiating two or more cultural worlds." A core work for this theme might be "A Measure of Freedom," where Jade Snow Wong (1972) attempts to work out a compromise between the traditional Chinese values important to her parents and the "modern American" values she encounters in the larger society beyond her home. She is interested in integrating the two—winning "*a measure* of freedom" for herself rather than complete freedom.

The unit could include Daniel Inouye (1972) to demonstrate an intense desire to be assimilated into mainstream American culture and pain caused by the lack of acceptance from European Americans. In "One Sunday in December," Inouye describes the comfortable identity he had established as an American, the painful shattering of that identity due to the Japanese bombing of Pearl Harbor, and the subsequent unwillingness of European Americans to accept Japanese Americans as "true" Americans.

In "Teenage Zombie," Amina Susan Ali (1983) writes about the conflict between two sisters—one of whom accepts her Puerto Rican heritage and one of whom denies it in her attempt to be accepted by her American friends. Millie even goes so far as to reject her neighborhood church in favor of the American one a few blocks away and becomes angry with her sister for speaking Spanish ("What's the matter? Can't you speak English? What's wrong with you?").

In "Kiswana Browne" from *The Women of Brewster Place* (Naylor, 1982), there is an interesting reversal of the traditional conflict between a family with "old" values and the young adult who chafes at having a family with such outmoded ways. In this story, Kiswana is seeking independence from her family and is in conflict with them because she believes they are too assimilated and have given up their African American heritage. She has even changed her name from Melanie to Kiswana in her attempt to "re-cover" some of her cultural heritage. The name change brings up the interesting ideas of what's in a name, what makes us members of certain cultures, what makes us who we are. Near the end of the story, mother and daughter argue with each other over these very issues.

The contrasting approaches taken by the characters selected for this unit provide students not only with multicultural perspectives but with rich and engaging material for comparison and contrast, one of the literacy tasks central to academic writing.

CONCLUSION

Although less information has been documented regarding the existence of a literary canon in the elementary grades in U.S. schools, literature taught at the middle school and high school levels continues, despite widespread calls for more inclusive curricula, to be composed predominantly of works written by European American men. Change has been slow due to various factors, including teachers' lack of familiarity with literary works by people of color (particularly more contemporary titles), inadequate literature anthologies, lack of supplementary resources, curricular constraints, insufficient planning time, and the personal characteristics of teachers, such as fear of dealing with controversial issues often raised in works by authors of color.

While we work at or wait for substantive school reform to address some of these impediments to curricular change, this chapter provides direction within the realities of school life. First, a four-part framework has identified principles of multiculturalism that can guide planning decisions. Second, four unit structures for inclusiveness have been discussed and illustrated. The design and teaching of such units makes a contribution to diversifying the literature curriculum in schools. Even small changes in the curriculum that increase inclusiveness make a significant difference in the responses to literature of students, especially those of color.

SUGGESTED LEARNING EXPERIENCES

1. Examine the standards for teaching English/language arts prepared by the National Council of Teachers of English to determine the extent to which they are consistent with those recommended by this author.
2. Examine several school district curriculum guides for English/language arts to determine the extent to which they are consistent with the standards recommended by this author. Explain any discrepancies and make suggestions for improvement.

ACKNOWLEDGMENTS

Research on the background and framework for this chapter was funded, in part, by a Spencer Dissertation-Year Fellowship from the Woodrow Wilson Foundation and by a grant-in-aid from the National Council of Teachers of English. Portions of the chapter appear in a different form in *Diverse Learners, Diverse Texts: Tenth Graders Exploring Literature, Culture, and Identity* (Athanases, 1993).

My thanks to Steve Hawkins, Colleen Kerrigan, and Renee Patton, former students from the Stanford Teacher Education Program, whose unit materials are used as illustration in this chapter.

REFERENCES

Abells, C. B. (1986). *The children we remember.* New York: Greenwillow Books.

Ali, A. S. (1983). Teenage zombie. In A. Gomez, C. Moraga, & M. Romo-Carmona (Eds.), *Cuentos: Stories by Latinas* (pp. 82–87). New York: Kitchen Table, Women of Color Press.

Allen, P. G. (1988). Who is your mother? Red roots of white feminism. In R. Simonson & S. Walker (Eds.), *The graywolf annual five: Multi-cultural literacy* (pp. 13–27). St. Paul: Graywolf Press. (Original work published 1986)

Anzaldua, G. (1988). Tlilli, tlapalli: The path of the red and black ink. In R. Simonson & S. Walker (Eds.), *The graywolf annual five: Multi-cultural literacy* (pp. 29–40). St. Paul: Graywolf Press. (Original work published 1987)

Apple, M. W. (1992). The text and cultural politics. *Educational Researcher, 21*(7), 4–11, 19.

Applebee, A. N. (1989). *A study of book-length works taught in high school English courses* (Rep. 1.2). Albany, NY: Center for the Learning and Teaching of Literature.

Applebee, A. N. (1990). *Literature instruction in American schools* (Rep. 1.4). Albany, NY: Center for the Learning and Teaching of Literature.

Applebee, A. N. (1991). *A study of high school literature anthologies* (Rep. 1.5). Albany, NY: Center for the Learning and Teaching of Literature.

Applebee, A. N. (1992). Stability and change in the high school canon. *English Journal, 81*(5), 27–32.

Athanases, S. Z. (1993). Discourse about literature and diversity: A study of two urban tenth grade classes. *Dissertation Abstracts International, 54*, 05–A. (University Microfilms No. AAD93-26420).

Athanases, S. Z. (1998). Diverse learners, diverse texts: Exploring identity and difference through literary encounters. *Journal of Literacy Research, 30*(2), 273–296.

Athanases, S. Z., Christiano, D., & Drexler, S. (1992). Family gumbo: Urban students respond to contemporary poets of color. *English Journal, 81*(5), 45–54.

Banks, J. A. (1993). Multicultural education: Characteristics and goals. In J. A. Banks & C. A. McGee Banks (Eds.), *Multicultural education: Issues and perspectives* (pp. 3–28). Boston: Allyn & Bacon.

Bishop, R. S. (1992). Multicultural literature for children: Making informed choices. In V. J. Harris (Ed.), *Teaching multicultural literature in grades K–8* (pp. 37–53). Norwood, PA: Christopher-Gordon.

Cliff, M. (1988). If I could write this in fire, I would write this in fire. In R. Simonson & S. Walker (Eds.), *The graywolf annual five: Multi-cultural literacy* (pp. 63–81). St. Paul: Graywolf Press. (Original work published 1985)

Duff, O. B., & Tongchinsub, H. J. (1990). Expanding the secondary literature curriculum: Annotated bibliographies of American Indian, Asian American, and Hispanic American literature. *English Education, 22*(4), 220–240.

Educational Testing Service. (1987). *Advanced placement course description for English.* New York: College Entrance Examination Board.

Frank, A. (1978). *Anne Frank: The diary of a young girl.* New York: Random House.

Fuentes, C. (1988). How I started to write. In R. Simonson & S. Walker (Eds.), *The graywolf annual five: Multi-cultural literacy* (pp. 83–111). St. Paul: Graywolf Press.

Gibson, M. A. (1984). Approaches to multicultural education in the United States: Some concepts and assumptions. *Anthropology and Education, 15*, 94–119.

Gomez-Peña, G. (1988). Documented/Undocumented. In I. R. Simonson & S. Walker (Eds.), *The graywolf annual five: Multi-cultural literacy* (pp. 127–134). St. Paul: Graywolf Press.

Greene, M. (1993). The passions of pluralism: Multiculturalism and the expanding community. *Educational Researcher, 22*(1), 13–18.

Harris, V. J. (Ed.). (1992). *Teaching multicultural literature in grades K–8.* Norwood, PA: Christopher-Gordon.

Hilliard, A. G. (1974). Restructuring teacher education for multicultural imperatives. In W. A. Hunter (Ed.), *Multicultural education through competency-based teacher education* (pp. 38–52). Washington, DC: American Association of Colleges for Teacher Education.

Houston, J. W. (1983). *Farewell to Manzanaar.* New York: Bantam.

Inouye, D. (1972). One Sunday in December. In K. Hsu & H. Palubinskas (Eds.), *Asian-American authors* (pp. 100–107). New York: Houghton Mifflin.

Lake, P. (1988). Sexual stereotyping and the English curriculum. *English Journal, 77*(6), 35–38.

Lass-Woodfin, M. G. (1978). *Books on American Indians and Eskimos.* Chicago: American Library Association.

Lee, H. (1960). *To kill a mockingbird.* New York: Popular Library.

Lloyd-Jones, R., & Lunsford, A. A. (Eds.). (1989). *The English coalition conference: Democracy through language.* Urbana, IL: National Council of Teachers of English.

Miller, S. M., & McCaskill, B. (Eds.). (1993). *Multicultural literature and literacies: Making space for difference.* Albany: State University of New York Press.

Mirikitani, J. (1987). *Shedding silence: Poetry and prose.* Berkeley, CA: Celestial Arts Publishing.

Mura, D. (1988). Strangers in the village. In R. Simonson & S. Walker (Eds.), *The graywolf annual five: Multi-cultural literacy* (pp. 135–153). St. Paul: Graywolf Press.

Naylor, G. (1982). Kiswana Browne. In *The women of Brewster Place* (pp. 75–88). New York: Viking Press.

Nieto, S. (1982). Children's literature on Puerto Rican themes—Part I: The messages of fiction. *Interracial Books for Children Bulletin, 14*, 6–9.

Pace, B. G. (1992). The textbook canon: Genre, gender, and race in U.S. literature anthologies. *English Journal, 81*(5), 33–38.

Reimer, K. M. (1992). Multiethnic literature: Holding fast to dreams. *Language Arts, 69*(1), 14–21.

Rogers, T., & Soter, A. O. (Eds.). (1997). *Reading across cultures: Teaching literature in a diverse society.* New York: Teachers College Press.

Sasse, M. H. (1988). Literature in a multiethnic culture. In B. F. Nelms (Ed.), *Literature in the classroom* (pp. 167–178). Urbana, IL: National Council of Teachers of English.

Simonson, R., & Walker, S. (Eds.). (1988). *The graywolf annual five: Multi-cultural literacy.* St. Paul: Graywolf Press. (Original work published 1986)

Sims, R. (1982). *Shadow and substance.* Urbana, IL: National Council of Teachers of English.

Smith, B. H. (1983). Contingencies of value. *Critical Inquiry, 10*, 1–35.

Stotsky, S. (1992, April). *Alternative conceptualizations of multicultural literature programs.* Paper presented at the annual meeting of the American Educational Research Association, San Francisco.

Suzuki, B. (1984). Curriculum in transformation for multicultural education. *Education and Urban Society, 16,* 294–322.

Task Force on Racism and Bias in the Teaching of English. (1986). *Expanding opportunities: Academic success for culturally and linguistically diverse students.* Urbana, IL: National Council of Teachers of English.

Taylor, M. (1976). *Roll of thunder, hear my cry.* New York: Bantam.

Trousdale, A. M. (1990). A submission theology for Black Americans: Religion and social action in prize-winning children's books about the Black experience in America. *Research in the Teaching of English, 24*(2), 117–140.

Volavkova, H. (Ed.). (1962). *I never saw another butterfly: Children's drawings and poems from Terezin Concentration Camp.* New York: McGraw-Hill.

Walmsley, S. A., & Walp, T. P. (1989). *Teaching literature in elementary school* (Rep. 1.3). Albany, NY: Center for the Learning and Teaching of Literature.

White, E. B. (1952). *Charlotte's web.* New York: Harper & Row.

Wiesel, E. (1960). *Night.* New York: Bantam Books.

Wiesel, E. (1970). *One generation after.* New York: Random House.

Wilder, L. I. (1953). *Little house on the prairie.* New York: Harper & Row.

Wong, J. S. (1972). A measure of freedom. In K. Hsu & H. Palubinskas (Eds.), *Asian-American authors* (pp. 24–36). New York: Houghton-Mifflin.

Yamada, M. (1986). *Camp notes and other poems.* Berkeley, CA: Shameless Hussy Press.

Yokota, J. (1993). Issues in selecting multicultural children's literature. *Language Arts, 70*(3), 156–167.

Chapter 11

Celebrating Our Differences Through Multicultural Activities: The Collaboration and Integration of Music Across the Disciplines

Alicia Mueller
Washington State University

FOCUS QUESTIONS

1. What preliminary preparation might be helpful to a group of teachers planning an integrated unit such as that designed by this author?

2. If you were planning an integrated unit on a particular cultural group, how would you decide which aspects of culture to include and whether the perspective represented is authentic?

3. What challenges might you anticipate in implementing an integrated unit?

INTRODUCTION

The U.S. population draws on hundreds of different cultures for its artistic expression. Although the majority of the U.S. people have their roots in European cultures, a growing percentage of the population today comes from different minority ethnic groups. Projected population figures show that by the middle of the 21st century, the majority of the U.S. population will no longer be European. The United States will be a truly pluralistic society. According to the Music Educators National Conference (1994b) report on national standards in music education:

> ... music studied should reflect the multimusical diversity of America's pluralistic culture. It should include ... music from outside the art music tra-

dition, music from the various cultures and ethnic groups that comprise American society, and authentic examples from the various musical cultures of the world. Many communities and many schools themselves are already smaller versions of the global village. (pp. 3–4)

As we move to the 21st century, the multicultural heritage existing in our U.S. schools and communities should be viewed as the opportunity to expand our knowledge, skills, awareness, and values of this "multimusical diversity."

A broad spectrum of cultural diversity should be reflected in the study of music in the United States. Teachers must be culturally responsive to the needs of their children, focusing on students' active participation in singing, movement, listening, and instrumental play. Acquiring a working/teaching knowledge of multicultural music materials, methods, and experiences that can be integrated within the context of the public school classroom will prepare teachers to teach students from all ethnic cultures in the 21st century.

Many educators have become concerned with building a school curriculum that encompasses the complete learning experiences of a student with all of his or her needs and capabilities. Students should be stimulated and challenged to use their imagination and intellect, which, in turn, should spark their creative and analytical powers. Encouraging students to interpret their world, as they see it, will produce results that are not only satisfying to the students but that are also meaningful to others. The world these students interpret is not limited to the school environment; it consists of everything they encounter in their lifelong learning experiences, including creative writing, dance/movement/physical education, drama/theater, foreign language, geography, history, language arts, literature, mathematics, music, science, social studies, and the visual arts. The students' world also includes their families, friends, neighborhoods, daily life experiences, and travel experiences.

A school's curricular learning experiences should not be presented to students as isolated entities throughout the school day; rather, these learning experiences should be grouped into larger units or collaboratives. Many educators believe a curriculum that covers all learning experiences operates most effectively if it incorporates the academic disciplines into a framework of collaborative units or projects. Collaborative units consist of the integration of interdisciplinary courses; teachers from different subject areas plan, implement, and evaluate the units. Music can be a vehicle for connecting these units together with a strong creative bond; music can even be part of the core of an integrated collaborative. Music education benefits from collaborative units because it becomes an important part of the total curriculum by relating continually to curriculum subjects that are relevant to a rapidly changing world, thus providing a more accurate and descriptive cultural experience.

Understandably, large-scale collaborative units may not be feasible in many elementary and middle/junior high school curricula; however, schools should strive to incorporate areas of study into collaborative projects, even if only two subject areas are combined. With careful planning, a music teacher, serving as a resource to the classroom teachers, can integrate multicultural music into one or more subject areas and thus enable classroom teachers to implement the collaboration with minimal extra preparation, resulting in effective learning for students.

The following are guidelines for using music to incorporate multicultural concepts/ideas and diversity issues into an existing school curriculum:

1. Collaborate with other teachers in other subject areas to provide comprehensive multicultural experiences for the students.
2. Select materials from literature and other disciplines that can be incorporated with music.
3. Emphasize the utilization of good quality songs and activities from the cultures studied, as well as instructional materials, resources, recordings, and instruments.
4. Maintain authenticity of the materials/resources by using, when available, traditional instruments with the activities.
5. Select materials and resources that are both relevant to musical elements or concepts being studied and developmentally- and age-appropriate.
6. Incorporate creative interpretation and improvisation to emphasize basic ideas and creativity within a culture.
7. Collaborate with and draw on the expertise of students, parents, and available community resources.

A STUDY OF SELECTED SOUTHWEST NATIVE AMERICAN CULTURES

Objectives

This comprehensive unit of study consists of a selection of culturally diverse activities from a collaborative project, emphasizing the integration of music with academic subjects and related arts areas. I focus on the use of a multicultural context as a way to practically connect and integrate music with other related arts and academic subjects. I show how selected southwest Native American cultures can be represented through practical music experiences, including singing, chanting, movement, dance, listening, and instrumental play. Activities provided can be modified for various grade levels ranging from kindergarten through eighth grade, although age and developmental appropriateness should be kept in mind. Attention has been given to aural, visual, and kinesthetic learning styles of children.

Collaborative Teamwork

The collaborative team consists of all teachers involved with the collaborative unit. Many schools already employ various types of team teaching. Examples of teaching teams include: (a) teachers of a particular grade level; (b) teachers of special areas such as music, physical education, and visual arts; (c) particular teachers of primary, intermediate, and/or upper grade levels; and (d) special area teachers combined with particular grade-level teachers, for example, the librarian, reading resource teacher, music teacher, and fourth-grade teachers. Methods of organizing a collaborative team include the following: (a) discussing a collaborative unit idea with the principal, who can be instrumental in setting up an initial meeting of teachers; (b) working with existing school teams; and (c) initiating and leading a meeting with any interested teachers.

Each teacher in this cooperative group must participate in every stage of planning, from the overall goals and objectives formulated and the materials and resources required to the teaching processes and strategies and methods of evaluation. Following the initial planning stage, each teacher determines his or her own agenda for participation in the collaborative project. The project can culminate in a presentation to other classes, the school, and the parents.

The collaborative team may consist of two or more of the following: classroom teachers, music teacher, art teacher, drama/theatre teacher, physical education/movement/dance teacher, librarian, other special area teachers (e.g., special education, reading resource), and community resources (e.g., Native American parents, experts).

Collaborative Unit Organization

The following segment consists of two sections, each with suggested learning experiences to be incorporated within the context of the collaborative unit. These sections include a collaboration of academic subjects and a collaboration of related arts areas. A more in-depth coverage of teaching processes and strategies, such as specific songs, listening examples, dances, and creative movement experiences, is provided in the section about related arts areas.

Academic Content Structure

The subject areas listed here lend themselves to inclusion in a collaborative unit on the culture of selected southwest Native Americans. Only general activities are provided, which can serve as a guide for a more specific curriculum. The teachers of the collaborative team should develop more detailed lesson plans utilizing these ideas. Additionally, the special area teachers, such as the special education and reading resource teachers, can focus on enhancing individual awareness of the special learners (e.g., guide students in language arts and creative dramatic activities to aid in their understanding of a Native American folktale), and the librarian can supplement the activities with enrichment in the academic subjects.

1. Geography experiences: Locate selected southwest Native American tribes on a map. Study the geographical characteristics of these locations.

2. Language arts experiences (see also the Movement Experiences on pp. 163–167, this volume)

   a. Creative writing: Create original stories, poems, or dialogue that portray life and culture of selected southwest Native American cultures. Focus on expressive speech and vocal sounds when performing. Explore various musical dynamics, textures, and tempi when telling a story. Learn sign language for Indian songs and stories.

   b. Foreign language: Examine vocables and words in selected songs of these cultures. A general characteristic of Native American music is its use of vocables, which are generally nontranslatable sounds or syllables. Often the authentic text is translatable and may relay a message or tell a story.

   c. Literature: Examine, compare, and learn authentic texts of Native American literature. Read stories, folktales, myths, and poems of these cultures (e.g., the "coyote tales" of the southwest Native Americans).

3. Math experiences: Integrate the meter of various music and movement/dance activities with fundamental math concepts (i.e., counting, addition, subtraction, multiplication, and division). For example, if the meter of a song, such as "I Walk in Beauty" (Burton, 1993), is in 4, create a four-count body percussion to do while listening, singing, or dancing to the music.

4. Science experiences: Explore various aspects of animals, fish, plants, trees, and weather elements related to ways of life of selected southwest Native American cultures.

5. Social studies/history experiences: Examine the people, cultures, customs, and celebrations of selected Native American tribes. Compare/contrast characteristics of southwest Native American cultures. Discuss traditional and contemporary lifestyles of Native Americans. Read current newspapers and magazines to explore the current issues relating to southwest Native Americans (e.g., land, economy).

Visual and Performing Arts Content Structure

Creative Dramatics/Drama/Theater Experiences

Creative drama is a means of self-expression, especially for young children. It is a form of artistic communication that can be either an individual or a group activity. Imagination and creativity are the main ingredients needed for the activity; therefore, it is the least difficult of the arts to implement. In creative drama the child participates in an experience within set parameters and explores the world of imagination. The child creates a finished product through experimentation.

Creative drama is different from drama, which usually has a preexisting text and more clearly defined parameters. In drama, a child's imagination enters the set world of the text, or whatever parameters are used, and creates the finished product.

Theater experiences offer great potential for learning and are especially helpful in the area of multicultural learning experiences. When a student role-plays the part of a certain character, he or she experiences the everyday actions and feelings of that character. If this is a character from a different culture, the student is "walking in that person's shoes" and living his life.

The text of the *Antelope Woman* (Lacapa, 1992), selected for this collaborative unit activity, lends itself to a dramatic interpretation of the concept of respect for everything in life, especially family, friends, and community. The Antelope Woman story is an Apache folktale about a man who comes to a village "speaking of reverence for all things great and small." A woman from the village follows him as he leaves and watches as he disappears through four sacred hoops. He reappears from the fourth hoop as an antelope. The woman follows the antelope man, learns his ways, and becomes the antelope woman. The couple marries and the woman gives birth to twins. After which, the couple and their children return to the woman's village to share this knowledge. They are rejected by the people in the village. The context of the story can be understood by a child, and there are possibilities for pantomiming the story, through both concrete and abstract interpretations. This dramatic activity can include an entire classroom.

Group Imagery Activities. These activities act as preparation for creative movement and drama activities.

- Discuss and brainstorm about favorite topics of interest. This will vary according to grade level.
- Portray selected animals, or create ways to act out a favorite outdoor activity, such as playing a sports activity with friends or camping/hiking

with family. Allow students the opportunity to explore various ways of creating these activities by encouraging part- and whole-body movements, and working individually, with partners, and in small groups.

- Discuss and brainstorm about more abstract topics, as they relate to the preceding activities, such as the feelings and emotions that may be experienced.
- Portray "becoming" these more abstract ideas, allowing students time to explore them through part- and whole-body movements, and working individually, in partners, and in small groups.

Creative Drama Activities.

- Read the *Antelope Woman* story and ask students to listen for the main ideas, concrete or abstract interpretations of the story's context.
- Brainstorm and identify some of the story's main ideas or characters.
- Discuss and examine characteristics of these ideas or characters. Compare and contrast their particular characteristics.
- Discuss various ways of reading and performing the text, utilizing choral speaking: unison (speaking together), antiphonal (alternating text between two groups), solo (speaking alone), and line-around (speaking specific lines of text as individuals or groups) (McCaslin, 1990).
- Assign students and student groups main ideas or characters to describe or represent through dramatic interpretation.
- Give individuals or cooperative groups time to designate, create, and practice movements depicting their assigned ideas or characters. Provide guidance as necessary, especially for the more abstract ideas to be depicted.
- Encourage students to use movement ideas from the group imagery activities and to add movement qualities personifying and describing their ideas and characters.
- Instruct students to listen for their ideas or characters as the story is read/performed, and portray them accordingly.
- Perform the *Antelope Woman* in context with the collaborative unit.

Movement/Dance/Physical Education Experiences

Movement is a natural or inherent response in children and therefore another means of self-expression and artistic communication. Findlay states that children's "joy in movement serves as an ever-present incentive for learning and practice" (Findlay, 1971, p. 58). The phenomena of movement exist within everyday life activities. As a part of nature, movement may be viewed as a reaction to sound, although largely unconscious, perceived by the senses. Stinson (1990) states that "awareness of movement is made possible by the kinesthetic sense. . . . This sense tells us what our body is doing" (p. 2).

Many children can express physically what an adult states in words. There is also a certain pleasure that children derive from moving and exploring creative movement. Most children enjoy moving their bodies and exploring different ways of traveling through space. In a multicultural context, where language may be a problem, children can rely on body language to communicate their ideas. The pleasure that children find in creative movement leads to dance and athletics.

Dance is less spontaneous than creative movement. The child moves within more limited parameters in the dance world. One of these set parameters is rhythm, where body moves must be set into groupings of beats.

The physical movement used in dance is similar to movement used in athletics. The main difference is the lack of a definite rhythmic pattern in most athletic activities. Therefore, dance and movement are activities usually covered in physical education classes. Folk dances from different cultures can be enrichment multicultural activities for any physical education class.

Included here are creative movements, dances, and related activities from selected southwest Native American tribes. They have been chosen as part of the collaborative unit and coordinate well with the *Antelope Woman*.

Creative Movement Activities. These activities consist of locomotor and nonlocomotor movements to explore space (ideas integrated with those of *Music for Children*, 1977).

- Socialization, Part I (finding a comfort level)
  * Have students walk freely around the room at their own paces, making eye contact, smiling, and looking at others' faces.
  * Have students shake hands and chat with different people as the walking continues.
  * Have students get out of the circle formation and explore different directions, different ways to walk, and different locomotor movements.
  * Instruct each student to find a partner to walk with who seems to be walking at his or her pace.
  * After allowing partners to walk at ease, encourage them to try to walk more at their partners' paces.
  * Remind partners, periodically, to explore different directions and locomotor movements.

* Instruct students to establish a common beat to walk to with their partners, then with the class.
- Socialization, Part II (finding a comfort level)
  * Lead class in simultaneous imitation: keep a steady beat, starting with one body part; expand steady beat to two, then three body parts.
  * Establish a three-beat pattern for imitation.
  * Have students face partners and experiment with three-beat patterns, using different body parts; reinforce that this is to be done with no talking.
  * Ask students to settle on a pattern they like.
  * Start a pattern for the class to imitate.
  * Give three long beats on the drum, and direct students to find a new partner and repeat the activity.
  * Give specific instructions before students move to new partners (backward, running, skipping, turning).
- Pathways on the ground—spatial patterns
  * Have students begin walking, filling up all the spaces of the room.
  * Pick up the beat of the class on a hand drum.
  * Instruct students to respond to new tempos by trying out various locomotor movements, nonlocomotor movements, and combinations of both types of movements.
  * Remind students, periodically, to fill up the empty spaces.
  * Have students explore different types of locomotor movements in free/shared and personal/self spaces.
  * Have students explore different types of nonlocomotor movements in personal/self spaces.
  * Explore new types of shared space by suggesting the following: direction changes, circular paths, and straight paths.
- Word exploration
  * Have students find a personal space. Give a series of verbs. Ask students to put each word into their whole body and do what the verbs tell them to do. Use such words as: jump, drop, rise, spin, bend, scurry, prance, soar, flow, fly, freeze, relax.
  * Give a series of verbs with adverbs. Ask students to show these with movement. Some examples are stomp loudly, stop suddenly, walk lazily, jump quickly, scurry frighteningly, prance lightly, freeze suddenly, reach longingly, stop partially, skip happily, and look around hopefully.
  * Have students create their own verb and adverb combinations.

* Give a series of nouns with adjectives. Have students move, finding a quality and a shape to show the qualities of the noun. Uses such words as shining sunlight, darkening clouds, twittering birds, fleeting deer.
* Have students create their own noun-with-adjective combinations.
* Incorporate movements from the preceding creative movement activities within the Creative Dramatics/Drama/Theater Experiences of the collaborative unit.
• Round dance song activities (Burton, 1993)
  * Introduce song/dance by listening to the Pueblo Round Dance (Burton, 1993) and discussing its context as it relates to the universal use of round dances among modern tribes. Inform students that Native Americans attach a deep significance to the circular formation of round dances: "moving clockwise in a circle is believed to be moving in harmony with the forces of creation; living 'within the circle' refers to maintaining harmony with the universe and all nature" (Burton, 1993, p. 61). Lead students in one version of a round dance: move clockwise with joined hands and step sideways to the beat.
  * Add authentic Native American drums and rattles to emphasize the beat and its dotted rhythms.
  * Following the dance, discuss its form (Burton, 1993).
  * Introduce another round dance song by listening to the Apache/Navaho song, "I Walk in Beauty" (Burton, 1993).
  * Teach song by rote, having students imitate phrases and sections.
  * Add authentic Native American drums and rattles to emphasize the beat.
  * Add the previously learned version of the round dance to the singing and instrumental play.
  * Perform the round dance songs in context with the collaborative unit.
• Folk dance activities—*Cuero Mohelam* (a Yaqui Pascola dance; Burton, 1993)
  * Listen to the music of a Yaqui Pascola Dance, and discuss its cultural context, style, and form (Burton, 1993).
  * Lead students in a circle dance to the music of this excerpt. Have students move to the beats, utilizing a variety of 16-count locomotor movement patterns selected by the leader. During the short interludes bounce in place. Suggested 16-count patterns include the following (ideas integrated with those of Weikart, 1989):
  1. 16 steps forward, moving clockwise; 16 steps forward, moving counterclockwise.

2. Eight heel-toe combinations in place (each two beats); repeat.
3. Facing middle of circle, eight steps forward, then eight steps backward; repeat.
   * Perform dance to the music of this Yaqui Pascola Dance, in context with the collaborative unit.
 • Suggestion for additional activities—various traditional sports of these cultures

Music Experiences—Listening, Instrumental Play

Music is a powerful stimulus for creative thinking. Recordings of music are an effective means of establishing mood and may be used to arouse the imagination of a child. Music from a specific culture can tell a story to a young child that words cannot. Music from the Native Americans can be added to this collaborative unit to create the mood of the people from this culture. For older children the actual sounds that are heard in the music can be a topic of discussion. This can lead to the discussion of sounds (timbres or tone colors) of instruments, especially the traditional instruments, such as the flute music of the "Pueblo Sunrise Song" (Burton, 1993) in the Guided Listening Activity I presented here.

Music that comes from existing cultures can have a different sound from that of the same society from generations past. A comparison of contemporary music with traditional or ethnic music from a given culture can broaden the scope of a music listening activity. ". . . Then There Was Wood" (Burton, 1993) is a Native American contemporary fusion piece, consisting of a blend of traditional Native American music elements with jazz, rock, and urban contemporary music elements. The stylistic differences of the "Pueblo Sunrise Song" and ". . . Then There Was Wood" can be discussed. Both have been selected for incorporation with the collaborative unit.

 • Guided Listening Activity I
   * Listen to the Native American flute music of the "Pueblo Sunrise Song" (Burton, 1993) and discuss its cultural context and style.
   * Add this excerpt to the creative drama context of the collaborative unit.
 • Guided Listening Activity II
   * Listen to the Native American contemporary fusion excerpt, ". . . Then There Was Wood" (Burton, 1993), and discuss its cultural context and style.
   * Add this excerpt to the context of the collaborative unit.

Music Experiences: Songs, Chants, Instrumental Play

Individual participation in the music-making process is a natural incli-
nation for young children. Even the smallest child uses singing as a means
of communication and a vehicle of self-expression. Many folk songs from
the cultures of the world are fairly singable melodies. The rhythms can be
easily understood and translated into basic patterns that can be performed
by imitation or have beat patterns that can be used as a basis for original
rhythm accompaniments. The singing of folk songs from a variety of cultures with traditional instrument accompaniments adds another level of
experience to a music activity.

Because most Native American songs have been passed down aurally
through generations, the mere existence of songs in print may take away
their authenticity. Like folk music, Native American music is spontaneous,
reflective of expressive interpretations. According to Curtis (1968), "[Native
American] music is a trinity. It is composed of three elements—rhythm,
melody, and harmony. . . . Song becomes the cry of the heart and the
transfiguration of the spoken word" (pp. xxv–xxvi).

The Native American songs chosen for the following activities can be
incorporated within the collaborative unit of the *Antelope Woman.* The songs'
contexts relate to the concept of respect for family, friends, community, and
life in general, all issues implied throughout the *Antelope Woman.* "I Walk in
Beauty" (Burton, 1993) is an Apache/Navaho song based on the concept of
"seeking universal harmony," and is "commonly sung at pow-wows in many
languages and versions" (Burton, 1993, p. 51). "Corn-Grinding Song" is a
traditional Zuni song about "the main sustenance of the Pueblo people"
(Curtis, 1968, p. 429). The text of "Now I Walk in Beauty" (Libana, 1990) is
from the Hopi Indians, and it speaks of the beauty of Mother Earth. The
three songs, "Ancient Mother," "The Earth Is Our Mother," and "Mowtay"
(Libana, 1986), celebrate the beautiful Mother Earth and cultural heritage.
"The Earth Is Our Mother" and "Mowtay" contain additional harmony lines
that allow for growth in musical intensity.

- "I Walk in Beauty" (Burton, 1993)
  * Round dance song activity (see p. 166).
- "Corn-Grinding Song" (Curtis, 1968)
  * Teach this traditional Zuni song by rote (have students imitate
    phrases and sections) and by note reading, with a focus on the
    recurring melodic and rhythmic notations.
  * Discuss the meaning behind the song, as it relates to the importance
    of corn to this Pueblo tribe and the Zuni women who grind the
    corn. Inform the students that during this time "the youths some-
    times sing, or play the flute and drum, while the maidens ply the

stones, and when the grinding is done the maidens dance" (Curtis, 1968, p. 430).

  * Create a way to perform the text in chant form (e.g., choral speaking—unison, antiphonal, cumulative [one group beginning, joined by another, then another]), solo (McCaslin, 1990).
  * Add creative dramatic movements simulating the grinding of corn.
  * Add authentic Native American drums and rattles to emphasize the beat.
  * Incorporate this song activity within the context of the collaborative unit.
• "Now I Walk in Beauty" (Libana, 1990)
  * Teach this traditional song by rote.
  * Discuss the strength of meaning expressed in this spiritual and beautiful text; draw attention to its reminder "to be always aware of our Mother Earth's astonishing beauty" (Libana, 1990, p. 31).
  * Divide students into groups and sing in a round.
  * Incorporate this song within the context of the collaborative unit.
• "Ancient Mother," "The Earth Is Our Mother," "Mowtay" (Libana, 1986)
  * Teach these traditional Native American songs by rote and by note reading.
  * Teach the harmony lines of music to "The Earth Is Our Mother" and "Mowtay."
  * Discuss the meanings behind the songs, as they relate to the *Antelope Woman*.
  * Add authentic Native American drums and rattles to emphasize the beat and subdivisions of the beat of each of these songs.
  * Allow these songs to build in power with the addition of harmony lines, instruments, and repetition.
  * Incorporate these songs within the context of the collaborative unit.

Visual Arts Experiences

The visual arts convey ideas that also spark the imagination. They can serve as a strong means for communicating ideas of a given culture. A story or pantomime can be created from a single picture. Pictures can be especially helpful in the introductory stages of a discussion about a particular culture. Children can express their own ideas about a given culture in their individually created works of art.

Another way cultural understanding of Native Americans can be acquired is by studying their crafts. Many of these crafts contribute to daily living, such as eating, communication, or protection. Children can better understand these cultures not only by examining their crafts but also by making simple crafts themselves.

Specific art experiences are listed below that can be included in the collaborative unit based on the *Antelope Woman*. They should be included to broaden the understanding of the southwestern tribes of the Native American.

- Collect pictures representing the main ideas, concepts, and characters of the story. Draw pictures of these story characteristics.
- In preparation for the creative drama activities for the story, design and create costumes for the characters.
- Select, introduce, and examine artwork, photographs, and pictures of various media from selected southwest Native American tribes.
- Engage students in creating arts and crafts using some of this media (e.g., make percussion instruments such as drums and rattles and participate in basketry and pottery activities).

CONCLUSION

The previously described collaborative project serves as a guideline for learning experiences for any comprehensive unit of study. Additional activities can be organized and established between the collaborative team and community resource people: For example, knowledge about traditional ways of Native American life can be acquired from tribe members, experts in Native American ways of life, and school parents of Native American students. This project can culminate in a final presentation for the school and parents of the team teachers' and students' collaborative unit activities.

Children in today's multicultural U.S. society are surrounded with music from many cultures. Music plays a valuable role in "creating cultures and building civilizations" (Music Educators National Conference, 1994a, p. 8), as well as providing global and universal connections to the other related arts and academic disciplines. Future teachers need assistance and training in developing the knowledge base necessary to foster an integrated structure in their curriculum. This will enable their future students to develop some sense about how knowledge in one area relates to what is studied and learned in another, thereby deepening their respect and appreciation for their own and others' ways of everyday life.

Music exists as an art form, a way of learning, a means of self-expression, a therapeutic resource, and a social activity. Therefore, music has value not only as a subject in itself—taught for its intrinsic value—but it is also effective as a tool to illuminate and facilitate other subject areas. It can fill many needs, ranging from expressive and aesthetic to emotional, psychological, and social, of today's students. This art form functions as a great connector "among and across the arts and other disciplines" (Music Educators National Conference, 1994a, p. 10), thereby playing a strong role in collaboratives used in education today and contributing to all students' learning experiences. Consequently, music provides a vital role in today's schools.

The diverse ethnic backgrounds making up our U.S. society must be recognized and appreciated. Incorporating and integrating multicultural music resources and culturally diverse ideas into existing school curricula should complement and enhance the programs so they not only enrich but also increase cultural awareness and respect for our increasingly pluralistic society.

SUGGESTED LEARNING EXPERIENCES

1. This author uses music as a vehicle for interrelating content and infusing multiculturalism across the curriculum. Select a different topic and content area and explain or illustrate how it might be used to interrelate content and infuse multiculturalism across the curriculum.

2. Discuss the benefits of this author's approach to curriculum design using a developmental learning theory perspective.

TEACHER'S RESOURCE

American Indian Studies Center. (1984). *Sharing a heritage*. Los Angeles: The Regents of the University of California.

Anderson, W. M. (1991). *Teaching music with a multicultural approach*. Reston, VA: Music Educators National Conference.

Anderson, W. M., & Campbell, P. S. (Eds.). (1989). *Multicultural perspectives in music education*. Reston, VA: Music Educators National Conference.

Anderson, W. M., & Lawrence. J. E. (1998). *Integrating music into the elementary classroom* (4th ed.). Belmont, CA: Wadsworth.

Baylor, B. (1975). *The desert is theirs*. New York: Charles Scribner's Sons, Macmillan.

Bergethon, B., Boardman, E., & Montgomery, J. (1997). *Musical growth in the elementary school* (6th ed.). Fort Worth, TX: Harcourt Brace College Publishers.

Bierhorst, J. (1979). *A cry from the earth: Music of the North American Indians*. New York: Four Winds Press.

Bierhorst, J. (1994). *On the road of stars: Native American night poems and sleep charms*. New York: Macmillan.

Blackwood, A. (1991). *Music of the world*. New York: Facts on File, Ltd.

Blumenfeld, L. (Ed.). (1993). *Voices of forgotten worlds: Traditional music of indigenous people*. Roslyn, NY: Ellipsis Arts.

Bruchac, J. (1992). *Native American animal stories*. Golden, CO: Fulcrum.

Campbell, P. S. (1991). *Lessons from the world: A cross-cultural guide to music teaching and learning*. New York: Schirmer Books.

Campbell, P. S., McCullough-Brabson, E., & Tucker, J. C. (1994). *Roots & branches: A legacy of multicultural music for children*. Danbury, CT: World Music Press.

Chace, G. E. (1977). *Wonders of the pronghorn*. New York: Dodd Mead.

Cohen, C. L. (1988). *The mud pony: A traditional skidi Pawnee tale*. New York: Scholastic.

Collaer, P. (1973). *Music of the Americas: An illustrated music ethnology of the Eskimo and American Indian peoples*. London: Curzon Press Ltd.

The College Music Society. *Music in the undergraduate curriculum: A reassessment* (CMS Report No. 7). (1989). Boulder, CO: Author.

The College Music Society. *Racial and ethnic eirections in American music* (CMS Report No. 3). (1982). Boulder, CO: Author.

Cresci, M. M. (1989). *Creative dramatics for children*. Glenview, IL: Scott, Foresman.

Curtis, N. (1950). *The Indians' book: Songs and legends of the American Indians*. New York: Dover Publications.

Davidson, M. C. (1994). *The music of Paul Winter. Earth: Voices of a planet*. Miami, FL: CPP/Belwin.

DePaola, T. (1988). *The legend of the Indian paintbrush*. New York: Scholastic.

DeSpain, P. (1993). *Thirty-three multicultural tales to tell*. Little Rock, AR: August House.

Erion, C., & Monssen, L. (1982). *Tales to tell tales to play: 4 folk tales retold and arranged for music and movement*. New York: Schott Music Corporation.

Fox, M. (1997). *Whoever you are*. San Diego, CA: Harcourt Brace.

Frisbie, C. J. (Ed.). (1980). *Southwestern Indian ritual drama*. Albuquerque: University of New Mexico Press.

Gates, F. (1982). *North American Indian masks: Craft and legend*. New York: Walker & Co.

George, L. A. (1987). *Teaching the music of six different cultures: Revised and updated*. Danbury, CT: World Music Press.

Hamm, R. P. (Ed.). (1982). *Music for children: Fence posts and other poems*. New York: Schott Music Corporation.

Heth, C. (Ed.). (1993). *Native American dance: Ceremonies and social traditions*. Washington, DC: National Museum of the American Indian Smithsonian Institution with Starwood Publishing.

Hirschi, R. (1992). *Seya's song*. Seattle, WA: Sasquatch Books.

Howard, C. (Coord.). (1971). *Authentic Indian dances and folklore*. Deal, NJ: Kimbo Educational.

Hunt, W. B. (1973). *The complete how-to book of Indiancraft*. New York: Macmillan.

Joosse, B. M. (1991). *Mama, do you love me?* New York: Scholastic.

Josephy, A. M., Jr. (1994). *500 nations: An illustrated history of North American Indians*. New York: Knopf.

Katz, J. (Ed.). (1988). *Arts & education handbook: A guide to productive collaborations*. Washington, DC: National Assembly of State Arts Agencies.

Kurath, G. P., & Garcia, A. (1970). *Music and dance of the Tewa Pueblos*. Santa Fe: Museum of New Mexico Press.

Laubin, R. G. (1977). *Indian dances of North America: Their importance to Indian life*. Norman: University of Oklahoma Press.

Leach, R., & Palmer, R. (Eds.). (1978). *Folk music in school*. New York: Cambridge University Press.

Mason, B. S. (1974). *How to make drums, tomtoms and rattles: Primitive percussion instruments for modern use*. New York: Dover.

May, E. (Ed.). (1980). *Musics of many cultures*. Los Angeles: University of California Press.

McAllester, D. P. (1967). *Indian music in the Southwest*. Colorado Springs, CO: The Taylor Museum of the Colorado Springs Fine Arts Center.

McCarthy, T. (1993). *Multicultural fables and fairy tales: Stories and activities to promote literacy and cultural awareness.* New York: Scholastic.
McCarthy, T. (1994). *Multicultural myths and legends: 17 stories with activities to build cultural awareness.* New York: Scholastic.
McDermott, G. (1997). *Musicians of the sun.* New York: Simon & Schuster Books for Young Readers.
McDermott, G. (1993). *Raven: A trickster tale from the Pacific Northwest.* San Diego, CA: Harcourt Brace.
McGrath, J. (Coord.). (1972). *Dance with Indian children.* Washington, DC: Center for the Arts of Indian America.
McGrath, J. (Coord.). (1974). *My music reaches the sky: Native American musical instruments.* Washington, DC: Center for the Arts of Indian America.
McRae, S. (1990). *Sing 'round the world: International folksongs.* Memphis, TN: Memphis Musicraft Publications.
McRae, S. (1995). *Sing 'round the world* (Vol. 2). Lakeland, TN: Memphis Musicraft Publications.
Medearis, A. S. (1991). *Dancing with the Indians.* New York: Scholastic.
Nettl, B., Bohlman, P., Capwell, C., Wong, I. K. F., & Turino, T. (1992). *Excursions in world music.* Englewood Cliffs, NJ: Prentice-Hall.
Newman, G. (1995). *Teaching children music* (4th ed.). Dubuque, IA: Brown & Benchmark.
Olsen, A. (1991). *Songs for one world: Folksongs of the world arranged for Orff instruments.* Vancouver, WA: Alice Olsen.
Reader's Digest fascinating world of animals. (1971). Pleasantville, NY: The Reader's Digest Association, Inc.
Rozmajzl, M., & Boyer-White, R. (1996). *Music fundamentals, methods, and materials for the elementary classroom teacher* (2nd ed.). White Plains, NY: Longman.
Sneve, V. Driving Hawk. (1989). *Dancing teepees: Poems of American Indian youth.* New York: Holiday House.
Titon, J. T. (Ed.). (1992). *Worlds of music: An introduction to the music of the world's peoples* (2nd ed.). New York: Schirmer Books.
Underhill, R. M. (1968). *Singing for power: The song magic of the Papago Indians of southern Arizona.* Berkeley: University of California Press.
Wiewandt, T. (1990). *The hidden life of the desert.* New York: Crown Publishers.
Willoughby, D. (1996). *The world of music* (3rd ed.). Dubuque, IA: Brown & Benchmark.
Woodcock, G. (1977). *Peoples of the coast: The Indians of the Pacific Northwest.* Bloomington: Indiana University Press.

REFERENCES

Burton, B. (1993). *Moving within the circle: Contemporary Native American music and dance* [CD, cassette, slides]. Danbury, CT: World Music Press.
Curtis, N. (Ed. & Recorder). (1968). *The Indians' book: Songs and legends of the American Indians.* New York: Dover.
Findlay, E. (1971). *Rhythm and movement: Applications of Dalcroze eurhythmics.* Princeton, NJ: Summy-Birchard Music.
Lacapa, M. (1992). *Antelope woman: An Apache folktale.* Flagstaff, AZ: Northland.
Libana (Compilers). (1990). *Fire within: Magical and contemplative rounds and songs from around the world* [CD, cassette]. Durham, NC: Ladyslipper.
McCaslin, N. (1990). *Creative drama in the classroom* (5th ed.). White Plains, NY: Longman.
Music Educators National Conference. (1994a). *National standards for arts education: What every young American should know and be able to do in the arts.* Reston, VA: Author.

Music Educators National Conference. (1994b). *The school music program: A new vision.* Reston, VA: Author.

Regner, H. (Coord.). (1977). *Music for children: Orff-Schulwerk American edition volume 2—Primary.* New York: Schott Music Corporation.

Robbins, S. (Artistic Director), & Libana (Compilers). (1986). *A circle is cast: Rounds, chants and songs for celebration and ritual* [CD, cassette]. Cambridge, MA: Author.

Robbins, S. (Artistic Director), & Libana (Compilers). (1990). *Fire within: Magical and contemplative rounds and songs from around the world* [CD, cassette]. Durham, NC: Ladyslipper.

Stinson, S. (1990). *Dance for young children: Finding the magic in movement.* Reston, VA: The American Alliance for Health, Physical Education, Recreation, and Dance.

Weikart, P. S. (1989). *Teaching music & dance: A sequential approach to rhythmic movement* (3rd ed.) [CD, cassette, record, videotape]. Ypsilanti, MI: The High/Scope Press.

Chapter 12

Recognizing and Valuing Difference: Process Considerations

Phyllis Killam Abell
University of New Hampshire

FOCUS QUESTIONS

1. In what ways might we compare and contrast theories and research on the ways college students structure knowledge, women's ways of knowing, and stages of racial identity? How are these theories related to understanding and valuing difference?

2. How might understanding ways of structuring knowledge, gender related ways of knowing, and racial identity support preservice teachers' preparation for teaching in a culturally diverse society?

INTRODUCTION

> Difference is that raw and powerful connection from which our personal power is forged.
>
> —Audre Lorde (1984)

The increasing changes in demographic patterns within the school-aged population and converse changes in the cultural experiences of teacher education students require that careful consideration is given to recognizing and valuing difference in preservice teacher preparation programs. The inclusion of diverse ethnic and racial groups in course content and practicum experiences is essential. However, the value is limited if the educational context in which learning occurs is hierarchical and noncollaborative, thus duplicating the dominant–subordinate social structures and reinforcing the polarization of prejudice.

In 1972, Banks and Grambs (Martin, 1991) said it was

> no longer defensible to send beginning teachers into school . . . to make the same mistakes that generations of teachers made before. . . . The total institution must be staffed by persons aware of how differences are valued, how those differences have been internalized by the individual student, and how the school can reinforce creative differences without demeaning any. (p. 297)

This statement is still valid today. Designing a pedagogical process for preservice teachers, beginning with students recognizing and valuing differences among themselves, is a first step toward preparing students to avoid the mistakes of the past. Instead of denying difference or holding a world view that denigrates difference, it is to be acknowledged, described, valued, and celebrated. Unfortunately, most students come to college with a construction of knowledge that reflects the western middle-class male heterosexual intellectual tradition, which represents the hegemony in the current educational system.

This chapter describes a pedagogical process that can be used in every class, regardless of the content focus. It can help change attitudes toward those who are different from one's self. Creating class experiences that incorporate student perspectives and that are collaborative redefines power relationships between students and teacher and among students. This process socially reconstructs the experience of difference and the prior knowledge associated with it. This chapter begins with a description of the patterns of thinking students bring to college and the transformation that occurs there. Next, how the process of positively valuing difference contributes to a new understanding of intellectual development is followed by a discussion of the congruence between the epistemology of difference, a study of European American college women's intellectual development, and racial identity development theory. Finally, the author proposes the inclusion of student experience in the class process in ways that examine cultural identity and foster mutual respect.

COLLEGE STUDENTS' CHANGING PATTERNS OF THINKING

Changes in students' structuring of knowledge during college years was first noted by Perry (1970), who interviewed young middle-class college-age European American men at a single institution. He characterized student thinking as an ongoing process of change and development, noting how knowledge is perceived and the worldview alters. Perry (1981) describes four major patterns of student thinking. The first is *dualism* where knowledge is divided into two opposing dimensions: good or bad, right or wrong, success or failure, win or lose. Right answers are present, known only by authorities such as professors and textbooks, and memorized by students. The second pattern of thinking is *multiplicity*, where students acknowledge the diversity of opinion and values in areas where the correct answers are not known. Thus each person has a right to his or her opinion; no one is wrong. It is not possible to judge among these varied opinions. The third pattern of thinking is *relativism*, which extends the diversity of opinion to include qualitative aspects and is dependent on a particular context. There are definite sources of knowledge and evidence to be presented, systems and patterns to be used for analysis and comparison. Now one can make a judgment about accepting or rejecting an opinion, values, and ideas. Toward the end of college *commitment* often emerges. Decisions are made by the young men related to various aspects of their lives (career, personal relationships, and values) that join beliefs and values with action. Commitments are made for the future. Perry describes major changes that occur over 4 years, charting how male college students think about knowledge and how they see the world.

Belenky, Clinchy, Goldberger, and Tarule (1986) broadened the inquiry by speaking with women from ages 16 to 65 who participated in nine formal and informal educational settings. Interviewing mostly European American women from varied class backgrounds, these scholars describe five quasi-developmental perspectives that women use across the life span. *Quasi-developmental* refers to inferences made from a subsample of this study and other longitudinal studies that a developmental progression is present. Using voice as a metaphor for the ability to speak up, speak out, and say what you want to say, these researchers identify an initial perspective of *silence*. Women using this perspective had no voice of their own and could not hear or understand the words of others. They learned from concrete experiences and had no sense of ideas, lived in isolation, and responded to authorities such as parents' or husband's use of power through action and abusive words. Women with this worldview were not found in college.

The second perspective noted by Belenky et al. (1986) is *received knowledge*, where the voice is still silent, but the women listen, receive, and remember the words of authorities. Although they see themselves as thinking, the women speak the words of others and authorities who direct their action. Truth and knowledge, where there is only one right answer, come from others. The dichotomy of either/or, Black/White is present, and discrete facts are important.

The next most dramatic and important developmental change occurs with the emergence of one's voice. Belenky et al. call this stage *subjective knowledge.* Knowledge becomes grounded in one's own experience, one's own opinion, not the ideas and truths of authorities. Women describe speaking from their "infallible gut"; ideas are right if they feel right. There is the awareness that each person's experience creates truth, and that there are as many truths as people. Next, the sense of voice changes from a concentration on speaking one's own thoughts to now include listening carefully to others.

In *procedural knowledge* the gender-related procedures of reason, abstraction, and rationality are used as well as procedures employing feelings and empathy with others. Women tend to use feelings and empathy as a connected mode of knowing. Men tend to use the procedure employing rationality, or a separate mode of knowing. Women use empathy to understand the experience and ideas of others. Truth becomes qualified, not always apparent, and things are not always as they seem.

Constructed knowledge is the fifth perspective where through a process of a two-way dialogue, there is an integration of feelings and subjectivity with reason and rationality. The construction of knowledge now is determined by frame of reference and context; different perspectives reveal different aspects of truth. European American women throughout the life span engage in these changing patterns of thinking as they give voice to their thoughts, feelings, and ideas.

M. Baxter Margolda (1992) traces the 4-year journey of intellectual development for a sample of mostly European American middle-class men and women college students. In this study, a progression of four gender-related patterns of knowing and reasoning were identified. It was found that although each gender prefers one particular mode of thinking, often both modes are used by both women and men. The first pattern is *absolute,* where knowledge is certain, objective, rational, logical, and taught by authority figures. Like the previous study, young European American women's voices are silent. In a *receiving* pattern, women listen to professors and share notes with peers, seeing the peers as a source of support. They see themselves and peers as having no knowledge. On the other hand, young European American men focus on a *mastery* pattern, where they imitate the voice of authorities and view peers as valuable in testing achievement. Individual autonomy is important.

Margolda (1992) calls a second pattern *transitional.* Now some knowledge is uncertain. There are multiple points of view, yet absolute knowledge exists in some areas. The class process focuses on understanding the course materials through discussion and hands-on activities. In an *interpersonal* pattern, young women hear each other's views, speak their own views, and resolve the emerging uncertainty by personal judgment. In contrast, young men continue the logical, rational emphasis of the prior pattern using an *impersonal* voice. They want to be challenged by the professor and to debate with both peers and the professor.

In the *independent* pattern, knowledge is mostly uncertain. There are a range of views revealed in the differences of opinion of various authorities, and the focus is on creating one's own perspective in a process of thinking through the issues. Now peers become a legitimate source of knowledge. The gender-related differences appear when young women use an *interindividual* pattern and young men use an *individual* pattern. For women, thinking for oneself and engaging the views of others occurs in a mutual process between peers and instructor. Knowledge contains discrepancies that are due to bias or interpretation. Young men focus on their own independent thoughts and struggle to listen carefully to other voices. Their ideas remain dominant. *Contextual* patterns of knowing and reasoning were used by a few of the undergraduates and no gender-related patterns were described. Knowledge is seen as contextual and judged on the basis of evidence. Students exchange and compare perspectives, integrating and applying the knowledge within the context.

Although these three studies consist mainly of middle-class European American women and men, they accurately describe the dominant patterns of thought used by college students that reflect the present educational structures and processes. The omission of perspectives of minority women and men results in the neglect of substantial portions of the student population. This ignores what Collins (1991) calls a *self-defined standpoint*, which would include the "the interlocking structures of race, class and gender domination" (p. 370). The standpoints or epistemologies (Gordon, 1990) constructed from African American social, economic, historical, and political experiences are omitted, as are the standpoints of Native American tribes, experiences of the multiple contexts of Hispanic Americans, and the various perspectives of Asian Americans. However, the construct of recognizing and valuing difference and the epistemological studies from a European American perspective are valuable. Although each study describes somewhat different patterns of thought, there is congruence among them in charting a developmental progression of thinking as constructed by the dominant culture in a multicultural society, creating a hegemonic structure.

Because both the educational system and the majority of present and future preservice teachers will be European American women who will use these patterns of thinking, my pedagogical model (Abell 1989, 1992) is based on *Women's Ways of Knowing* (Belenky et al., 1986), and my research on the recognition and valuing of difference. This approach provides a method for constructing an inclusive process that teaches students to value the lives and epistemologies of each other and of excluded groups. The model proposes restructuring the pedagogical process to include recognizing and valuing difference, which facilitates increasingly complex thinking, transforms the negative attitudes about others, fosters an appreciation for the ideas and perspectives of others and an understanding of the context of peoples' lives. These processes are essential for preparing students to begin to understand the complexity of our cultural life, thus answering Banks and Grumble's entreaty.

STUDENTS' PATTERNS OF THINKING ABOUT DIFFERENCE

Beginning college students' thinking patterns reflect prior educational experiences that are rooted in the dualist, hierarchical thinking and practices of the dominant, European American culture. In this construction of knowledge described by Perry (1970), Belenky et al. (1986), and Margolda (1992), students use dualistic, polar-opposite thinking. All studies describe many first-year college students as constructing knowledge in an absolute way; there is clearly a right and wrong way of thinking. Authorities possess truth, and students memorize the information and reproduce it on multiple-choice and short-answer tests. The function of the professor as the authority is to communicate the knowledge, answer questions, and ensure that the students understand the knowledge. In the initial perspective, my research on difference resembles these studies.

Dualism

According to my research, the first perspective, dualism, is similar to the previous studies, but encompasses other meanings. Denying difference, European American students see everyone as the same. Denigration of difference occurs along with this denial. Here "difference is construed through a set of binary oppositions that leaves no room for an authentic difference, set outside the established system" (Feral, 1980). It is these patterns of thought that foster the racism, sexism, and homophobia characteristic of much of U.S. society. A young European American student's reflection notes this dualist heritage:

> In my earlier teen years, the sense of difference I had between myself and others was comparable to saying, "Everything I do is right: and anyone who does anything different from that, is weird." Only in the past couple of years have I finally begun to accept what others do and believe in as normal and OK. I am learning that there are viable reasons why each person is different, and that differences are good not bad.

In high school this student saw anyone who was different from herself as not OK. This exhibits thinking from an either/or, I'm OK/you're not OK perspective. Her statement also reveals her movement from a negative to a positive view of difference, part of the developmental process of valuing difference. Other studies describe a process of losing, keeping, or reclaiming one's voice, a process vital to women's intellectual development.

Other Studies

A longitudinal study by Brown and Gilligan (1992) illuminates the process of how European American adolescents in a traditional educational process push aside and then deny childhood knowledge and the clear voice of childhood that expressed their feelings. As young girls seek to become perfect women, they lose their voice and focus on being nice and caring for others. Conversely, an African American adolescent, attending an upper middle-class private school, maintained strong ties with her open, honest mother and succeeded in retaining her voice. Another student at the same school, a working-class adolescent, acutely aware of the difference between herself and her classmates, also resisted, articulating a different perspective. Both lived in two worlds, the European American middle-class school, where peers did not communicate their true feelings, and the family and cultural context of a different reality.

Hancock (1989), interviewing European American women, chronicles adults who reclaim their power through reflecting on the strength and voice from early childhood. In Belenky et al. (1986), half of the 135 women, the majority of whom were students in nontraditional colleges or family service agencies, used what the authors called a subject call a subjectivist pattern of thinking. They grew beyond the dualist and absolute constructions of knowledge labeled as received knowing, where others define and determine their worldview; they rejected male authority and focused on their own opinions and ideas. These subjectivist women chose acting on behalf of self instead of acting on the previous denial of self that gave authority to an external source. These women also rejected a patriarchical educational system that did not validate their lives and found affirmation in less traditional educational settings.

In the traditional college educational process subjectivist knowledge is not valued, yet alternative educational settings allow the beginning of a voice of one's own to emerge. How is it possible to construct an educational process in a traditional college setting that provides a milieu fostering an authentic voice of one's own? How is it possible to provide a way for the multiple voices of both men and women from varied races, classes, ethnicities, and sexual orientations to be heard?

Recognizing Difference

Fostering voices of their own goes hand in hand with honoring student experiences. When asked how she learned best, an adult student in one of my classes confidently replied, "I know what I experience." Speaking from experience is subjectivist thinking. As subjectivist students develop a voice of their own and listen to others, the recognition that others are different occurs and the many differing perspectives of others are acknowledged (Abell, 1991, 1992).

Using an approach that honors student experiences, voices, and perspectives, the initial, dualist perspective of denigration and denial of difference gradually is abandoned. In the second perspective the recognition that others are different from the self occurs. Different people hold differing views and lifestyles; each person has equal rights, and no person is better than another. Part of this view includes not having a right to judge another person and respecting others who are different. It is here that the voices of different cultural contexts begin to be heard. A student writes:

> Even before this course I still had particular stereotypes and close-minded opinions that kept me from accepting others as essentially no different from myself . . . I can confidently say that what I have learned here is gradually helping me, along with the new "eye-opening" experiences that keep presenting themselves in my life, to understand people better and be more willing to accept them. . . . I am learning to see issues differently, and consider the other sides of issues. Perhaps I am the one who is wrong.

By integrating her own personal experiences with the course content, this student's perspective changes and she begins to value others' perspectives, although she at times resists acknowledging difference. Acknowledging other perspectives fosters respect.

Valuing Difference in Traditional Education

Respecting others through keeping an open mind and being willing to listen to others occurs as the third perspective creates an initial appreciation of difference. Students struggle and try not to make assumptions about others, thus letting go of stereotypes based on lingering dualism. They write about accepting others for who they are and what they believe. They keep an open mind about others, and a new respect for others who are seen as different emerges. A process of reflecting on the effects of difference on the self becomes apparent. Thus the differing experiences of gender, race, ethnicity, and class are increasingly understood and appreciated (Abell, 1992). A student writes this about herself:

> I think that since I have been at college I have become more open minded to people who are different from myself, but this change has been happening over the past year and a half. I have met a lot of different people since I have been here at school and I have learned that each individual person is different and that they have different views. I feel I am a very open minded

person and I can get along with a variety of people. As long as the person respects who I am I can respect them and their views.

In traditional educational settings undergraduate students tend to be limited to learning to use procedural knowledge (Belenky et al., 1986). The connected mode uses empathy to understand the experiences and perspectives of others. The separate mode uses abstract, rational thinking and the conceptual frameworks that each discipline employs to organize and analyze information. Here doubting the other and debating differing points of view is a way to know. Those who used separate knowing attended traditional colleges and tended neither to reflect on nor consider their own experiences a valid source of knowing.

As female undergraduate students become procedural knowers, they tend to use the gender-related connected mode more easily in some aspects of their lives than male students do. However, many of these women had developed ways of knowing from previous educational experiences that were based primarily in the rational, objective modes of the separate knower. The diempathic and dialogical processes begin at birth, intertwine in various ways throughout life, and inform all aspects of the developmental process (Abell, 1991). These two processes are gender-related. Women tend to use the diempathic process more often than the dialogical. For men, whose socialization often negates the expression of feelings, the dialogical process is the primary mode. European American women extend the diempathic process to understand others and value difference.

Empathy and Understanding the Multiple Contexts of Lives

A fourth perspective includes being able to see others in their own context, to appreciate difference now by using empathy to understand the multiple contexts of other's lives. Diempathic processors are similar to connected knowers who rely on the "conviction that the most trustworthy knowledge comes from personal experience rather than the pronouncement of authorities" (Belenky et al., 1986, p. 113). To appreciate difference one uses one's own experiences and empathy as a bridge. The individual can now understand the experiences and views of others, and therefore can believe and ultimately value the thinking of others. Students write about being able to understand where others are coming from and the struggles they are going through. They listen, empathize, and have compassion for those who are different from themselves. A student thinks back about her continued change:

I have always generally been open minded about people who are different from me. Everyone is different. However, I never realized how those who are a different ethnicity, gender, age or social class feel or what life is like from their perspective.

Being able to hear what life is like in a different context extends understanding. Along with empathizing with others, the students learn to appreciate the causes of difference. Thus understanding deepens.

Reading about personal experiences from course materials and listening to classmates' perspectives mitigates and alters the negative aspects of a wholly rational, abstract separate mode of knowing, where knowledge comes from sources removed from the personal places of women and men from varied cultural contexts in an increasingly unvalidated place. The distance between their own experiences and the ideas generated by mostly European American men leaves them uncomfortable and in the position of merely memorizing and recounting what is in the textbook or from the professor. The life experiences, the ideas, thoughts, and concepts constructed in their own life experience, are thus denied. Moraga (1983) writes about her experience of listening to a prominent poet from her own culture:

> Sitting in that auditorium chair was the first time I had realized to the core of me that for years I had disowned the language I knew best—ignored the words and rhythms that were the closest to me. . . . The reading forced me to remember that I knew things from my roots. (p. 31)

Here Moraga acknowledges the centrality of her own life experience and the culture of her childhood. One's sense of racial identity is an important aspect of personal identity and self-acceptance.

RACIAL IDENTITY AND PATTERNS OF THINKING: A COMPARISON

As each person brings patterns of thought about knowledge and the nature of truth to a college experience, so too does each person bring a sense of racial identity that grows out of the American experience. Students bring to each course, each educational experience, a rich diversity from their past; each student is in a particular place in her or his sense of racial identity and is using specific patterns of thought with regard to knowledge and truth. Examining Black racial identity theory as one example of a subordinate experience, White racial identity theory as the experience of dominance, and the patterns of thinking used by European American college students about difference enhances our understanding of the congruence between these approaches and informs teaching strategies to foster the valuing of difference by all students.

Black Racial Identity

Cross' (1991) extensive work in Black racial identity is the orientation used to describe five stages in identity development: *pre-encounter, encounter, immersion–emersion, internalization,* and *internalization–commitment.* At Stage 1, the pre-encounter stage, there is a pre-existing identity, shaped by early experiences, that uses the Eurocentric cultural perspective. There is a preference for the dominant notions of beauty, art, music, and content and themes in literature. Also prescribed by the dominant culture is the blaming of victims. According to Cross (1991), the dominant culture emphasizes a one-way accommodation that stresses assimilation and integration, where "blacks will learn to fit in, while whites are asked to simply stop discriminating. . . . The onus is on blacks to prepare themselves in a fashion that will lead to acceptance by whites" (p. 196). Racism is seen as only a superficial problem. This stage is reflected in Gordon's (1992) statement, "I took for granted my sameness with the dominant society." She did not remain in that stage, however: "somewhere along the way of life I learned a different lesson" (pp. 19–20). Her perspective has been altered.

Stage 2, encounter, occurs through a transforming racial experience or through a series of small experiences that result in altering the person's worldview and sense of identity. A single event like the death of Martin Luther King, Jr., can trigger this change. A range of emotions such as guilt, anger, and general anxiety may prompt this movement to the encounter stage, which is characterized by two steps: experiencing an encounter and then personalizing it. By personalizing I mean allowing the meaning and effect of the actual experience to transform a person's life.

Cross' (1991) Stage 3 involves a major transformative process, which has two aspects: immersion and emersion. In making the decision to change, the person begins to "demolish the old perspective and simultaneously tries to construct what will become his or her new frame of reference" (p. 202). Initially immersing him- or herself in the Black experience, this powerful uprooting creates a new dichotomy where "all that is white becomes evil, oppressive, inferior, and inhuman, and all things Black are declared superior, even in a biogenetic sense" (p. 202). At this time, the person participates and often conforms to the requirements of certain Black organizations. The transition is energized by the strong emotions of rage at White people and White culture and of guilt about being "tricked" into believing the previous ideas, and the development of a sense of pride. "Black is beautiful" informs this new identity. The second aspect of this stage, emersion, occurs as the intense emotions diminish, the racist, dualist perspective of either–or recedes, and the simplistic ideology is called into question. Although a reactionary hatred can occur, Cross (1991) notes that "people who move out of oppressive situations regain control of [their] emotions and intellect" (p. 207), suggesting a reorganization occurring through the diempathic and dialogical process of development referred to earlier. Here the life of Malcom X is an example. Following his experiences in Mecca, he describes a change to a less rigid sense of Blackness. A person's sense of Blackness at this stage is less global and absolute, and becomes more complex, textured, and substantive, allowing a movement to the next stage.

In Stage 4, *internalization*, the person works through the previous major transition and the new identity is actually internalized. The conflicts produced by stage three are resolved and one's personality and cognitive style stabilize. With the achievement of an inner peace, feeling and acting on a confidence in one's personal standards of Blackness occurs. Acknowledging anger at racist institutions and reflecting on and analyzing various aspects of life can lead to long-term commitment to and acceptance by the Black community.

This internalized identity performs three functions:

> (1) to defend and protect the person from psychological insults that stem from having to live in a racist society, (2) to provide a sense of belonging and social anchorage and (3) to provide a foundation or point of departure for carrying out transactions with people, cultures, and situations beyond the world of Blackness. (Cross, 1991, p. 210).

An example of this internalized identity is Gordon's (1990) statement that "reclaiming one's culture (cultural history and knowledge) is an essential aspect of an authentic being" (p. 97).

In Stage 5, internalization–commitment, a long-term commitment is made to translating the individual's stable construction of a sense of Blackness into specific actions in various areas of his or her life. Cross (1991) also mentions Parham's (1989) observation that an individual may repeat the cycle in previously unexplored areas. African American students in class may be at any of these stages in their development of racial identity. The European American students also may be at any stage of the following progression in their acknowledgment of racial identity.

White Racial Identity

In U.S. culture, the dominant values often are taken for granted and assumed as normal, but an examination of how European Americans come to understand themselves in a racial context holds important keys to altering the pedagogical process and constructing an altered sense of self in a multicultural society and a different understanding of truth and knowledge. Described by Pugh and Donleavy (1988), Jackson's (1974) and Hardiman's (1978) theory about White racial identity is congruent with Black racial identity theory and provides insight into European American women's educational journeys.

Jackson and Hardiman state that "the identity of a white person in America is strongly influenced by racism and oppression in the American society . . . and that the process of developing a positive or non-racist identity follows a definable sequence of thoughts, feelings and actions" (p. 13). They describe five stages of consciousness that are roughly analogous to the stages of Black racial identity previously described by Cross. Briefly, I compare the Black and White stages of racial identity, and note their congruence with the recognition and valuing of difference and with the perspectives and ways of knowing described by Belenky et al. (1986). The comparison of these congruent perspectives provides a rationale for the class process.

For Whites to develop a healthy White identity in a multicultural country such as the United States, they must let go of and change the racist aspects of the culture and must accept their own Whiteness apart from the perception of themselves as superior. As one of my students explained, the teaching and learning process fosters this awareness. The first stage of White racial identity theory, *active acceptance*, is characterized by the acceptance of Black stereotypes and the belief that Blacks are inferior due to biological and genetic traits. The belief in White superiority causes White thinking and expressions to be viewed positively and Black perspectives to be viewed negatively. This dualist conception is similar to the pre-encounter stage of Black racial identity, where the dominant Eurocentric ideology is accepted and Black perspectives and culture are not valued. In a similar way epistemologically, difference is represented by the perspective of dualism, where difference is both denied and seen as negative. Received knowledge (Belenky et al., 1986) is certain and unambiguous; knowledge originates outside the self, where experts are the source. Margolda (1992) names this beginning stage *absolute knowing*, used by 68% of first-year students and 46% of sophomores.

Stage 1 and Stage 2 merge to form *passive acceptance* (Helms, 1990), in which the person passively or unconsciously supports the assumption that "white is right," but states that Black people should have equal rights in society. This upholds the political statement granted by the constitution, but fails to look beyond this to ascertain the effects of this inequity. Like Blacks at Cross' pre-encounter stage of Black racial identity theory, Whites at this stage of White racial identity expect that Blacks should incorporate White behavior patterns and values and in this way integrate into the dominant society. The second perspective of valuing difference is characterized by the recognition that difference exists and that each person has equal rights, but also is characterized by lack of judgment of and inquiry into the circumstances of difference. This perspective allows for the denial of racial issues or problems and the denial of the existence of another reality.

Katz and Ivey (in Helms, 1990) note that "Whites who deny their racial group membership, consequently deny the values, attitudes and other characteristics associated with their race/cultural group and fail to develop an awareness or understanding of their cultural heritage as White Americans" (pp. 104–105). When this awareness does occur movement to the next stage follows.

Stage 3, *resistance*, informs a sense of White identity, which, like in the encounter stage of Black identity development, occurs when a person has a consciousness raising experience or a series of experiences and is thus jolted out of the previous stage. The person questions the values and beliefs of the dominant culture, actively resisting these beliefs, and viewing suspiciously all the values inherent in major institutions such as education, economics, and laws. It is at this stage that the person recognizes his or her own internalized racist beliefs. Cross (1991) states, "Such a person may resist through demonstration or by dropping out in refusing to support the American way" (p. 14). The dynamics of this stage are similar not only to both the encounter stage and immersion aspect of the next stage of Black racial identity, but also to the subjectivist stage of women's thought, where the women reject the dominant educational setting and focus on the beginning development of their own voices. However, as European American women they benefit in many ways from participating in this hegemony. These European American women often "drop out" because the traditional institutions do not validate their growing sense of self. They see clearly the contradictions in the institutions and how this harms a part of the population, even as they acknowledge their own collusion with this process. All these stages are characterized by the rejection of the dominant ideology through behavior and the expression of emotion that energizes and fosters movement forward.

In a course where the pedagogical process includes student discussion, a respect for and appreciation of difference, an exploration of students' cultural heritage, the third perspective begins to emerge. At the end of a course on race, culture, and power, a student wrote:

> At the beginning of this course my views on the race and power differences in this country were pretty concrete. However after listening to lecture and my classmates' opinions on this subject I began to open my eyes a little

more. Probably the most important lesson I learned about other people is to listen and respect their opinions.

In Stage 4, *redefinition,* the person begins the process of redefining the self in nonracist terms. This often causes an identity crisis when the person realizes that racism is a foundation of U.S. culture and that he or she does not know "what it means to be white apart from the goodness or badness of Blacks and other minorities" (p. 14). Here the person works with other Whites to create a sense of self that does not depend on the perceived deficiencies of minorities and to eliminate racism in the society as a whole. McIntosh (1989) describes this time in her life: "As a white person, I realized I had been taught about racism as something that puts others at a disadvantage, but had been taught not to see one of its corollary aspects, white privilege, which puts me at an advantage" (p. 1). Beginning to understand this advantage opened up new activities for her. Although the nature of the activities are different for Blacks in the immersion–emersion stage and Whites in the redefinition stage, in both the process of personal and societal transformation takes place.

Students begin to appreciate difference by empathizing with different others in the fourth perspective. Students are able to understand the struggles others have gone through in the varied cultural contexts of their lives (Abell, 1994). This opens the door to awareness of differing race, ethnic, and class contexts. Like the women (Belenky et al., 1986) using the connected knowing to listen and hear others and the separate knowing to analyze the rational and abstract, the procedures for reflection and growth become established as the ability to understand the experiences of others different from themselves increases. For Blacks the diempathic process of the connected mode predominates in the immersion stage, whereas the dialogical process of the separate mode is emphasized in the emersion stage.

In Stage 5, *internalization,* being White becomes part of the person's identity. At this point, the individual acknowledges difference, validates differences of race and gender, and finds ways to act on these beliefs and values in her or his life. As in the internalization stage of Black racial identity, there forms in a racist society a stable White identity that values not only its own identity, but also the identity of others who are different.

The journeys described here of Black racial identity, White racial identity, and the patterns of thought used in varied educational settings by European American women across the life span reveal a congruence that speaks loudly to the necessity for recognizing and valuing difference and understanding the diverse contexts of people's lives in the educational process. Each student makes a developmental journey in her or his sense of racial identity and particular patterns of thought. The result is college students who bring multiple perspectives that are used to reflect on and speak about course readings.

CONSTRUCTION OF KNOWLEDGE AND PERSONAL EXPERIENCE

Human beings learn from other human beings. What is relevant here is how these communications are structured, because this influences how knowledge is constructed within the individual. Students and faculty come to each course experience from varied racial and ethnic backgrounds, social classes, and sexual orientations. Each comes with his or her own constructions of knowledge based on a life experience from a specific family, community, and school. Each comes with a certain receptiveness to value difference. The teaching and learning process provides the way for difference to be acknowledged, valued, respected, and celebrated. Providing a gender-sensitive, culturally relevant pedagogical process (Abell, 1992) means bringing into the class dialogue voices of the students themselves, speaking and listening to each other as they reflect on the course content.

Personal experience, that reservoir of thinking and feeling in the diempathic and dialogical process, is an important aspect of the teaching and learning process. Personal experience encompasses all areas of human functioning, including the well of prior relationships. I propose a pedagogy that includes personal experience as well as the abstractions of other people's experience, which is used by the rational procedure of separate knowing.

The emphasis on experience echoes the words of Dewey (1938), who said "education must be based on experience—which is always the actual life experience of some individual" (p. 113). Dewey did not recognize the contributions from diverse cultural contexts, of the influence of race, gender, class, and ethnicity, but his acknowledgment of the importance of experience accentuates what each person brings to educational experiences in our current society. Experience is not only the actual participation in an event; it is also the effect on one's judgment and feelings of interactions with people's ideas and feelings. This process creates an experiential history that continually organizes and joins thinking, behavior, and feelings. This is similar to the two aspects of Cross' encounter stage where an event is experienced and then personalized.

Psychologists have known for a long time that the past of the individual was significant in determining the present, but according to Reigel (1976), they "have failed to recognize that most objectified performances and products are experientially empty for the individual" (p. 237), and that the individual attaches little importance to "his or her performance and behavior unless they are understood within the context of the experienced past" (p. 237). This carries a strong message for a pedagogical model that not only acknowledges the past of the students, but also asks students to reflect on their experiences and how these experiences connect with the course content.

As personal experience, thinking, ideas, and feelings are connected with the course content, different perspectives students hold are validated, and a critical process is created that fosters respect (Abell, 1988a). A student describes the effects of this process:

> In general I think this class was useful for everyone in that it allowed us to look at issues from different perspectives. By exploring others different viewpoints, we may grow to respect the differences that exist between everyone.

Speaking with each other in class, listening and reflecting on these perspectives, creates a different critical process than that used by the separate knower who, in an almost warlike stance, takes a position and defends it. This latter process is the traditional academic method, which combines dualism and objectivity with a separation of the subject/object from the knower. The connected knower, on the other hand, uses empathy to listen carefully and seeks to understand the other. In this way the process of recognizing difference between self and other not only clarifies one's own beliefs and values but also creates understanding and respect for the presence of another perspective.

Friere (1985) supports the view that educators must work with the experiences that students bring to the educational process. He writes that bringing experience into the classroom legitimates these experiences and provides a way for learners to display a distinctive presence and voice. In this way, theory is constructed from the contexts of lived lives and by the persons participating in this process, which also provides the opportunity for a critique of this experience in a larger context and informs action to be taken. Nieto (1992) defines this critical pedagogy as multicultural education.

After reflecting on the stories of the college women and men she interviewed, Margolda (1992) identifies three principles that guide the educational process: "validating the student as a knower, . . . situating learning in the students own experience, . . . [and] defining learning as jointly constructed meaning" (p. 270). She also notes that her principles stand in marked contrast to the traditional assumptions in education of individualistic learning, student subordination, and objectification of knowledge. An educational process grounded in students' personal experiences is one in which knowledge is constructed by all the participants, both faculty and students. It is a process that acknowledges difference. Pugh and Donleavy (1988) posit that "Difference is not to be overlooked and invalidated. It is to be authenticated and valued. Difference then becomes a way of enriching our individual perspectives, through mutual validation of culture or ethnic diversity" (p. 11). A class process that encourages the exploration of cultural identity affirms difference and creates respect.

CLASS PROCESS: CULTURAL IDENTITY AND MUTUAL RESPECT

In this approach to college education, the faculty member is a facilitator of students' thinking, not the expert passing on knowledge. Faculty use their expertise to design the course with consideration for the following three interrelated aspects of multicultural course planning: (a) create a class process that fosters relationships of mutual respect, (b) determine the effects of cultural identity on both the content and the process, and (c) make decisions about course content.

Class Process

A nonhierarchical and collaborative class process that fosters independent student thinking and speaking is important. The construct of recognizing and valuing difference and the patterns of thought described in *Women's Ways of Knowing* (Belenky et al., 1986) provide important keys to such a class process. Opportunities for students to create their own perspectives and to engage in critical thinking are present through requirements that include writing their own perspectives and then speaking and listening to each other in dyads and small groups. In this way individuals are heard, confidence is built, and varied perspectives are heard. Through discussions of issues raised in the course and through connecting students' current and past experiences with the formal course content, students continually construct new understanding. Such a class fosters an increasing awareness and appreciation of differing cultural contexts and a climate of mutual respect. This active class process is in dynamic interaction with the cultural composition and cultural identity of participants.

Cultural Identity

Including race, ethnicity, class, gender, and sexual orientation in the term multicultural, a critical analysis of the cultural identity of three groups involved in and affected by the teaching/learning process provides a foundation to make decisions about certain aspects of the course content and informs the class process. The first group is the community and schools in which the education students are likely to be teaching. For what cultural context are these students being prepared? In what kind of a community are they likely to be teaching? What is the school culture like there? The second group is the students. What do the students bring to the class discourse in these five subareas? What is the ethnic/racial heritage of the students? For European American students this analysis is particularly important, because they tend to be unaware of their often very mixed ethnic and racial heritage and how their ancestors contributed to and were part of the social and historical heritage of the country. Creating knowledge about each student's cultural heritage through course requirements fosters appreciation for differences among students and the multiple contexts of family lives.

European American students often resist being taught about race and relationships. Tatum (1992) experiences three sources of resistance, which she says are important to be aware of and talk about with students. First, she notes that "race is considered a taboo topic for discussion, especially in racially mixed settings." Second, Tatum adds, "many students, regardless of racial-group membership, have been socialized to think of the United States as a just society." Third, she says that "many students, particularly White students, initially deny any personal prejudice, recognizing the impact of racism on other people's lives, but failing to acknowledge its impact on their own" (p. 5). These resistances complicate the dynamics of the course where students (and faculty) are in varying stages of awareness of their own racial identity, where students use diverse perspectives of reasoning and knowing, and where they come from differing economic backgrounds and family patterns of interaction. Rather than tabulae rasae, students are of diverse and complex backgrounds, requiring insight and wisdom of faculty. This diversity is a mirror of the kinds of situations these students themselves will encounter. Creating a process that affirms and values difference as class members come to know each other acts to mitigate the resistance.

The third group is faculty. What is the cultural identity and knowledge faculty bring to the course in each of the five subareas of multicultural? Similar issues are faced by European American faculty as well as by students. How do these issues influence both the course content and the teaching process? An assessment (Abell, 1993) of all three dimensions (i.e., future school or community, students, and faculty) is necessary. Following this assessment, decisions can be made about which readings will complement, extend, and/or validate faculty's and the students' own experiences and meet the students' needs as future teachers. How each group effects the other group needs to be determined. For example, if the professor was born and brought up in Texas, of working-class Mexican American parents, and is married, then he or she brings a gendered, probably heterosexual, working-class experience of Mexican American identity and cultural knowledge to the course, contributing a possible appreciation of cooperation and collaborative process rather than the competitive emphasis of the dominant Anglo culture (Martinez, cited in Williams, 1988). Identifying her own and her students' cultural context, as well as the future communities students will be teaching in, completes the analysis and provides a basis for determining the course readings and cultural emphases.

This example highlights an important difference in cultural values from the dominant pedagogical process, which is characterized by competition (Kohn, 1986) and therefore inequality. Sapon-Shevin and Schniedewind (1992) suggest that classrooms typically are framed by competition, characterized by artificially created scarce resources that structure indicators of comparative achievement and worth. The school environment provides one area of life where oppression is learned.

Another example of the effect of cultural identity is a European American professor teaching Native American students. Christensen (1992) describes five competencies of the extensive Native American oral tradition—the first competency, language, encompasses the values of the culture. It forms and expresses these beliefs and values. The second competency refers to a teaching process where the circle represents a connection to all living things, for example, people, animals, mountains, and the ocean. A third competency reveals a sense of independence and personal sovereignty, where respect is "accorded to each person such that any form of interference is forbidden, regardless of the folly, irresponsibility or ignorance of the other person" (p. 10). This belief is in distinct contrast to the European American value of the responsibility of each person to give advice and be the brother's keeper. The fourth competency, indirect communication, is a way of speaking in which a question, praise, or a quest for knowledge is "wrapped in subtlety and shrouded in a mantle of humbleness, where mutually recognized sovereignty is foremost in any interaction" (p. 11). The last of the five competencies is respect for tribal elders, which means that no one interrupts an elder, everyone acknowledges and serves elders first in a social gathering, and all consult elders when it comes to the education of children in the tribe. For the educational experience to be positive for American Indian students raised in a Native American community these competencies must be used in the class process. Training students who are not Indian to teach American Indian children requires training them to use these values as part of a multicultural education.

Course Content

All of these aspects help faculty choose the various racial/ethnic groups for course readings. Information about gender, social class, and sexual orientation of the three groups informs what readings will be most valuable and pertinent for any one class; this is an important analysis to conduct in designing a culturally relevant course. A class process that examines cultural identity of students, faculty, and future school and community encourages European American students to value the differing contexts of people's lives.

SUMMARY

Acknowledging difference commences a process of self-definition and recognition of the worth and individuality of others, which empowers both self and others. Moving from absolute conceptions of knowledge, characterized by polar-opposite thought where power rests in authorities, to developing one's own voice and perspective, as well as valuing the perspectives of others, involves a continual process of constructing knowledge as students come to comprehend the varied context of others' lives. Becoming aware of one's racial and ethnic identity brings forth many and varied emotions, but has positive effects for understanding one's participation in the inequality of U.S. society. An active class process that situates learning in students' experiences as they connect with the course content allows them to recognize, positively value, and respect difference.

SUGGESTED LEARNING EXPERIENCES

1. Explain what you believe to be the most powerful barriers to recognizing and valuing differences.
2. Explain the extent to which teachers' attitudes about difference might inhibit or facilitate learning for youngsters from different cultural and experiential backgrounds?

REFERENCES

Abell, P. (1988, July). *Discussion, diversity and a critical process.* Contributed papers, improving university teaching. Umea, Sweden.

Abell, P. (1989). *Gender and student learning: The importance of reflection.* Contributed papers, improving university teaching. Vancouver, Canada.

Abell, P. (1991). *Recognizing and valuing difference: Gender considerations in the college educational process.* Paper presented at the sixth annual conference of Research on Adult Development, Boston, MA.

Abell, P. (1992). A culturally responsive, gender-sensitive pedagogical model: The college teaching/learning process. In C. Grant (Ed.), *Multicultural education for the twenty-first century* (pp. 114–134). Morristown, NJ: Silver Burdett Ginn, Inc.

Abell, P. (1993, February). *Constructing a culturally relevant class process: Indices to use.* Paper presented at the meeting of the National Association for Multicultural Education, Los Angeles, CA.

Belenky, M., Clinchy, B., Goldberger, N., & Tarule, J. (1986). *Women's ways of knowing.* New York: Basic Books.

Brown, L., & Gilligan, C. (1992). *Meeting at the crossroads.* Cambridge, MA: Harvard University Press.

Collins, P. (1991). On our own terms: Self-defined standpoints and curriculum transformation. *NWSA Journal, 3*(3), 367–381.

Christensen, R. (1992, October). *Teaching is a circle.* Paper presented at the Research on Women and Education Conference, Pennsylvania State Unversity, Pittsburgh.

Cross, W. E., Jr. (1991). *Shades of black.* Philadelphia: Temple University Press.

Dewey, J. (1938). *Experience and education.* New York: Macmillan.

Feral, J. (1980). The powers of difference. In H. Eisenstein & A. Jardine (Eds.), *The future of difference* (p. 89). Boston, MA: G. K. Hall.

Friere, J. (1985). *The politics of education.* South Hadley, MA: Bergin & Garvey.

Gordon, B. (1990). The necessity of African-American epistemology for educational theory and practice. *Journal of Education, 172*(3), 88–106.

Gordon, B. (1992). The marginalized discourse of minority intellectual thought in traditional writings on teaching. In C. Grant (Ed.), *Research and multicultural education.* London: Falmer Press.

Hancock, E. (1989). *The girl within.* New York: Ballentine Books.

Helms, J. (1990). *Black and white racial identity.* New York: Greenwood Press.

Jackson, B., III. (1974). *White identity development.* Unpublished manuscript, University of Massachusetts, Amherst. (Revised by R. Hardiman 1978).

Kohn, A. (1986). *No contest: The case against competition.* Boston, MA: Houghton Mifflin.

Margolda, M. B. (1992). *Knowing and reasoning in college: Gender-related patterns in students' intellectual development.* San Francisco: Jossey-Bass.

Martin, R. (1991). The power to empower: Multicultural education for student-teachers. In C. Sleeter (Ed.), *Empowerment through multicultural education* (pp. 287–297). Albany: State University of New York Press.

McIntosh, P. (1988). *White privilege and male privilege: A personal account of coming to see correspondences through work in women's studies* (Working Paper No. 189). Wellesley, MA: Center for Research on Women.

McIntosh, P. (1989, July/August). White privilege: Unpacking the invisible knapsack. *Peace and Freedom,* 10–12.

Moraga, C. (1983). *This bridge called my back.* New York: Kitchen Table.

Nieto, S. (1992). *Affirming diversity: The socioplitical context of multicultural education.* New York: Longman.

Parham, T. (1989). Cycles of psychological nigrescence. *Counseling Psychologist, 17*(3), 250–257.

Perry, W. S., Jr. (1970). *Scheme of intellectual and ethical development.* New York: Holt, Rinehart & Winston.

Perry, W. S., Jr. (1981). Cognitive and ethical growth: The making of meaning. In A. Chickering and associates (Eds.), *The modern American college* (pp. 76–116). San Francisco: Jossey-Bass.

Pugh, C., & Donleavy, M. (1988). Collaboration through validation of difference: An interracial model for change. In H. Williams (Ed.), *Empowerment through difference.* Peoria, IL: Glencoe.

Reigel, K. (1976). *Psychology of development and history.* New York: Plenum Press.

Sapon-Shevin, M., & Schniedewind, N. (1992). If cooperative learning is the answer, what are the questions. *Journal of Education, 172*(2), 11–37.

Tatum, B. (1992). Talking about race, learning about racism: The application of racial identity development theory in the classroom. *Harvard Educational Review, 62*(1), 1–24.

Williams, H. B. (1988). *Empowerment through difference.* Peoria, IL: Glencoe.

Author Index

Subject Index

A

Abd-al-Rahman, 115
Ability, and learning access, 65–66
Absolute knowing, 187
Absolute pattern of thought, 178
Academic writing, rhetorical history of, 117–118
Action research, and reflective practice, 23–25
Active acceptance, 187
African Americans
  as authors, 149–150
  children's literature for
    author's culture and, 145–146
    characteristics of, 51
  in history textbooks, 127
  as involuntary minority, 63
  language of, 109
  mathematics education and, 40–41
  science instruction for, 61–71
  as teachers, 69–70
    experiences of, 3–9
Afrocentric history curriculum, 130–131
Alaska Natives, 85–86. *See also* American Indians; Native Americans
Alcoholism, in American Indian population, 86
American Indians. *See also* Native Americans
  cultural identity of, 88–90
  culturally responsive instruction for, 85–100
    application of, 94–97
  difficulties of, 86
  diversity among, 87–90
  education of, 86–87

  history of, 86
  family structures among, 87–88
  language of, 109
    versus English, 90
  physical characteristics of, 87
  use of term, 85
"Ancient Mother," 168–169
Anger, in literature discussions, 148
Antelope Woman, 162, 168, 170
Arabs
  and development of rhetoric, 114
  writing by, 116
Argument
  difference and, 121
  language and, 116–117
Aristotle, 113, 117–120
Arts
  learning experiences in, 158
  self-identity and, 6
Asian Americans, language of, 109
Asiatic rhetoric, 113
Assessment
  culturally responsive, 6, 97
  teacher preparation on, 95
Audience participatory structure, 7, 66
Authors, culture of, 140–141, 145–146
Automaticity in reflective practice, 16–17
Averroes, 118

B

Basal readers, 49, 141
Basil the Great, 114
Bilingual community, writing instruction in, 77–81
Black English, 108–109
Black racial identity, 185